Statewide Locator Map

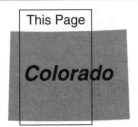

This Page

Colorado

● Easy Trails
■ Moderate Trails
◆ Difficult Trails

*See individual area maps
for more detail.*

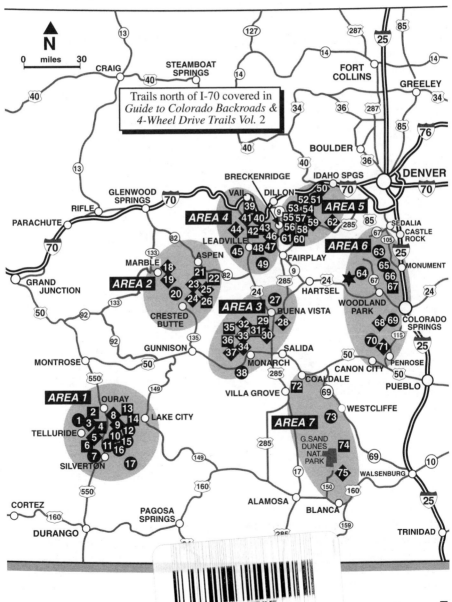

N

0   miles   30

Trails north of I-70 covered in
*Guide to Colorado Backroads &
4-Wheel Drive Trails Vol. 2*

CRAIG   STEAMBOAT SPRINGS   FORT COLLINS   GREELEY

BOULDER

BRECKENRIDGE   IDAHO SPGS   DENVER

GLENWOOD SPRINGS   VAIL   DILLON

RIFLE   *AREA 4*   *AREA 5*

PARACHUTE   SEDALIA   CASTLE ROCK

LEADVILLE   *AREA 6*   MONUMENT

MARBLE   ASPEN   FAIRPLAY

GRAND JUNCTION   *AREA 2*   HARTSEL   WOODLAND PARK   COLORADO SPRINGS

CRESTED BUTTE   *AREA 3*   BUENA VISTA

GUNNISON   SALIDA

MONTROSE   MONARCH   CANON CITY   PENROSE   PUEBLO

VILLA GROVE   COALDALE   WESTCLIFFE

AREA 1   OURAY   LAKE CITY

TELLURIDE   *AREA 7*

SILVERTON   G.SAND DUNES NAT. PARK   WALSENBURG

CORTEZ   PAGOSA SPRINGS   ALAMOSA   BLANCA   TRINIDAD

DURANGO

Trails Listed by Difficulty

● Easy

Trails are grouped into three major categories: easy, moderate and difficult. Within each group, trails at the top of the list are easier than at the bottom. If you drive a trail and find it too easy, try one lower on the list. Conversely, if you find a trail too difficult, try one higher on the list. You may have to skip several trails on the list to find a significant difference.

Easier

More Difficult

Pg.	No./Trail
158	40. Shrine Pass
222	61. Boreas Pass
172	45. Hagerman Pass
242	70. Shelf Road, Phantom Cyn.
234	66. Mt. Herman, Rampart Range
94	20. Paradise Divide
80	16. Eureka Gulch
184	49. Weston Pass
178	47. Mt. Bross, Kite Lake
34	1. Last Dollar Road
230	64. Phantom Creek, Signal Butte
150	38. Marshall Pass, Poncha Ck.
256	73. Hermit Pass
64	11. Red Mtn. Mining Area
228	63. Dakan Rd./Long Hollow Rd.
54	7. Clear Lake
118	27. Fourmile Area
190	51. Saxon Mountain
78	15. Picayne & Placer Gulches
232	65. Balanced Rock Road
240	69. Mt. Baldy
68	12. California Gulch
60	10. Corkscrew Gulch
196	53. Peru Creek
82	17. Stony Pass

Trail Ratings Defined ➡

Trail ratings are very subjective. Conditions change for many reasons, including weather and time of year. An easy trail can quickly become difficult when washed out by a rainstorm or blocked by a fallen rock. You must be the final judge of a trail's condition on the day you drive it. If any part of a trail is difficult, the entire trail is rated difficult. You may be able to drive a significant portion of a trail before reaching the difficult spot. Read each trail description carefully for specific information.

Easy: Gravel, dirt, clay, sand, or mildly rocky road. Gentle grades. Water levels low except during periods of heavy runoff. Full-width single lane or wider with adequate room to pass most of the time. Where shelf conditions exist, road is wide and well-maintained with minor sideways tilt. Four-wheel drive recommended on most trails but some are suitable for two-wheel drive under dry conditions. Clay surface roads, when wet, can significantly increase difficulty.

8

■ Moderate   ◆ Difficult

Pg.	No./Trail	Pg.	No./Trail
126	29. Mt. Princeton	128	30. Mt. Antero, Browns Lake
236	67. Schubarth Road	104	23. Montezuma Basin
218	60. Georgia Pass	40	3. Governor Basin
98	21. Aspen Mtn., Richmond Hill	160	41. Lime Creek, Benson Cabin
102	22. Lincoln Creek Road	88	18. Lead King Basin
254	72. Hayden Pass	146	37. Tomichi Pass
50	6. Ophir Pass, Alta Lakes	90	19. Devil's Punchbowl
70	13. Engineer Pass	56	8. Mineral Creek
156	39. Mill Creek Road	210	57. Radical Hill
166	43. Wearyman Creek	110	25. Taylor Pass
138	35. Tincup Pass, St. Elmo	46	5. Black Bear Pass
74	14. Cinnamon Pass, Wager Gulch	106	24. Pearl Pass
258	74. Medano Pass	216	59. Red Cone
36	2. Yankee Boy Basin	58	9. Poughkeepsie Gulch
180	48. Mosquito Pass	238	68. Eagle Rock
142	36. Hancock Pass, Alpine Tun.	224	62. Slaughterhouse Gulch
202	55. Deer Creek, Saints John	136	34. Pomeroy Lakes
162	42. McCallister Gulch	122	28. Chinaman Gulch
200	54. Santa Fe Peak	132	32. Grizzly Lake
212	58. Webster Pass, Handcart Gulch	176	46. Wheeler Lake
192	52. Argentine Pass, McClellan Mtn.	188	50. Spring Creek
130	31. Baldwin Lakes, Boulder Mtn.	134	33. Iron Chest Mine
112	26. Italian Creek, Reno Divide	168	44. Holy Cross
42	4. Imogene Pass	260	75. Blanca Peak
206	56. North/Middle Fork Swan Riv.	246	71. Independence Trail

Moderate: Rutted dirt or rocky road suitable for most sport utility vehicles. Careful tire placement is often necessary. Four-wheel drive, low range, and high ground clearance required. Standard factory skid plates and tow hooks recommended on many trails. Undercarriage may scrape occasionally. Some grades fairly steep but manageable if dry. Soft sand possible. Sideways tilt will require caution. Narrow shelf roads possible. Backing may be necessary to pass. Water depths passable for stock high-clearance vehicles except during periods of heavy runoff. Mud holes may be present especially in the spring. Rock-stacking may be necessary in some cases. Brush may touch vehicle.

Difficult: Some trails suitable for more aggressive stock vehicles but most trails require vehicle modification. Lifts, differential lockers, aggressive articulation, and/or winches recommended in many cases. Skid plates and tow hooks required. Body damage possible. Grades can be steep with severe ground undulation. Sideways tilt can be extreme. Sand hills very steep with soft downslopes. Deep water crossings possible. Shelf roads extremely narrow; use caution in full-size vehicle. Read trail description carefully. Passing may be difficult with backing required for long distances. Brush may scratch sides of vehicle.

Trails Listed Alphabetically

Author's favorite trails are shown in boldface type.

INTRODUCTION

Cinnamon Pass, Trail #14, moderate. American Basin in background.

Introduction

Much has happened since I published the first edition of this book in 1998. Since then, I've written five more books, one on Moab, Utah, one on Arizona, two on California and a second volume on Colorado. I'm still doing everything myself—the driving, writing, photography and maps. For this book, I redrove every trail and added 25 new ones. And like all my newer books, tracking and mapping were done using GPS.

I continue to marvel at the fantastic places in Colorado you can go in an ordinary four-wheel-drive sport utility vehicle or pickup truck. But remember, before you head out, make sure you are armed with accurate information. It's why I wrote my first book six years ago. I wanted a book that wouldn't get people lost or in over their heads. It had to have lots of photographs, clear directions and easy-to-read maps—a book you could trust to get you home safely with little chance of vehicle damage.

I also wanted the trails to be fun and exciting—not just a collection of long, boring, washboard roads. Take a quick glance through the hundreds of pictures in this book and you'll see what I mean. I try to show everything as it really is, without sugarcoating, and I don't avoid difficult trails. You may not be interested in driving a difficult trail, but you need to know what one looks like so you can avoid it when the time comes. You'd be amazed at how many newcomers think a 4x4 can go anywhere. Many find out the hard way that this is not the case.

If you are an experienced four wheeler with a modified vehicle, you'll be happy to know this book includes some of the best hard-core trails in the state—names like Holy Cross, Chinaman Gulch, Iron Chest, Blanca Peak and Independence. But don't discount the easy and moderate trails. If you haven't driven Paradise Divide, Peru Creek, Argentine Pass or Deer Creek, you're in for a pleasant surprise. Over the years, many hard-core wheelers have thanked me for reminding them how much fun they can have on an interesting scenic trail, especially when the family is aboard.

Apparently, people like my no-nonsense approach. Since I published my first book, it has been selling extremely well. I was able to quit my regular job and write books full time. Happy customers from all over the country call or write to tell me how much fun they've been having.

IMPROVEMENTS TO SECOND EDITION
As you look through this new book, note the many improvements. It has been expanded from 65 to 75 trails with 25 new ones. Some trails have been combined with others, so just a few less-popular trails were eliminated. The number of pictures has more than doubled from 185 to 435. GPS coordinates have been added along with answers to common GPS questions. Almost all trails have been rewritten more succinctly, allowing more room

for reverse directions and history. The appendix has been expanded with more helpful information.

In addition, information about unlicensed vehicles (ATVs and dirt bikes) has been included. All the trails in this book permit unlicensed vehicles, either on the trail itself or on connecting legal side roads.

A special situation involves three trails: Hackett Gulch, Longwater Gulch and Metberry Gulch. At the time of this writing, these trails are closed due to damage from the massive Hayman Fire that occurred in June of 2002. Unofficially known as "The Gulches," these great trails are included in the event they open after this book is printed. Should this happen, they become a bonus beyond the 75 trails mentioned on the cover.

HOW TO USE THIS BOOK

Everything about this book is designed to be simple and easy to use. As you flip through the book, notice how easy it is to find a trail. Type is large and easy to read in a moving vehicle. Directions are written in plain narrative—no tables and few abbreviations. Numerous photos show actual trail conditions, not just scenery. Maps are easy to read, starting with a statewide locator on page 7. Area maps zoom in closer on seven specific areas. Finally, an individual map is provided for each of 75 trails. Besides the general difficulty ratings of easy, moderate and difficult, trails are listed in order of difficulty on pages 8 and 9. Within each category, trails at the top of the list are easier than those at the bottom. Although GPS is not required, waypoints are provided for those who use them. Coordinates are listed in the appendix. Mileages are accurate and rounded to the nearest tenth of a mile. Your mileage will likely vary because of different driving habits and road conditions. Historical information and other activities are included where applicable.

SELECTING THE RIGHT TRAIL FOR YOUR VEHICLE

Today, more people than ever are heading into the backcountry in their 4-wheel-drive vehicles. For your safety and vehicle protection, it is very important that you select a trail matched to your vehicle's capability.

Easy: Suitable for all stock four-wheel-drive sport utility vehicles and pickup trucks with high ground clearance and low-range gearing. (See page 274 for this book's definition of *high clearance*.) Some trails can be driven in two-wheel drive when the road surface is dry. A few trails, under ideal conditions, are suitable for passenger cars.

Moderate: Suitable for most stock sport utility vehicles and pickup trucks with high ground clearance and low-range gearing. (This usually excludes all-wheel-drive vehicles that are low to the ground like an ordinary car.) For the toughest moderate trails, factory skid plates, tow hooks, and all-terrain tires are recommended. These options are available from your dealer or local four-wheel-drive shop.

Difficult: Suitable for some aggressive stock 4WD vehicles with very high ground clearance, excellent articulation, tow hooks, and a full skid plate package. All-terrain tires are a minimum, mud terrains preferred. A winch or differential lockers are recommended for the most difficult trails. Drivers who spend a great deal of time on difficult trails may find it necessary to modify their vehicles with higher ground clearance, oversized tires, and heavy duty accessories. A trail is rated difficult if any spot on the trail is difficult. You may be able to enjoy much of a trail before running into the difficult portion. Difficulty is based on different factors that may or may not affect your vehicle. Read each trail description carefully.

ATVS AND DIRT BIKES

All trails in this book allow unlicensed vehicles either on the main road itself or on marked side roads. **Trails with restrictions are identified with an asterisk on Page 6.** The asterisk may also mean the trail is extremely difficult for ATVs and dirt bikes or it is just not a very good place to ride. Read each trail description carefully for details.

Since I wrote my first book, people have been asking me which trails allow ATVs and dirt bikes. Recently, I've started riding an ATV and realize why people want to know. Most of the roads in my books are really fun for ATVs and dirt bikes. But it's not always easy to determine where you are allowed to ride.

Let me first distinguish between licensed and unlicensed vehicles. ATVs are not licensed in Colorado and must display an OHV sticker.* Motorcycles may or may not be licensed. Dirt bikes without lights and other highway equipment require an OHV sticker. Dual-purpose motorcycles are equipped for highway use and require a license plate similar to a car. They are allowed on OHV trails plus anywhere cars go.

Unlicensed vehicles are generally not allowed on paved roads in Colorado. In addition, many county roads restrict their use. County roads are usually posted, but not always. Generally, if the road is wide and graded with fast moving traffic, unlicensed vehicles are prohibited. In some counties, narrow backroads are marked as county roads. If they allow unlicensed vehicles, the driver may be required to carry a driver's license and proof of liability insurance.

Most narrow forest roads in Colorado allow unlicensed vehicles but they are not always marked. Unfortunately, signs are sometimes vandalized. Forest maps are often outdated and confusing. To be sure a trail is open, call the nearest ranger station (see appendix for addresses and phone numbers). They can provide you with the latest closure information. Otherwise, if a trail is not marked, consider it closed.

*Some out-of-state ATVs are licensed. This does not mean they can go anywhere a car goes. Licensed out-of-state ATVs generally must follow the same rules as in-state ATVs. Use common sense. Colorado recognizes out-of-state registrations and licenses for 30 days. After that, you must register in Colorado.

Irresponsible use of ATVs and dirt bikes is one of the biggest concerns of the Forest Service, BLM and other land management agencies and a major reason for trail closures. It is your responsibility to understand and obey laws wherever you ride. You must stay on designated routes at all times.

For up-to-date information on OHV laws, fees and registering your unlicensed vehicle, contact Colorado State Parks. They have an online registration form. (See appendix for contact information.) *Tread Lightly* offers a free 20-page pamphlet on ATV riding that is very helpful.

IMPORTANT FACTS ABOUT COLORADO

Although similar to other Rocky Mountain states, Colorado is unique in many ways. If you are new to mountain driving, read this part carefully.

It's a big place. Colorado is a large state by eastern standards. When I first moved here from Ohio 25 years ago, I was surprised at how long it took to get from one place to another. When traveling to trails, check the scale of the map and determine the total number of miles to your destination. Then allow plenty of time to get there.

When to go. The length of the four-wheel-drive season in Colorado depends on the elevation of the trail and the amount of snow received over the winter. Some trails at low elevations open in late May. More trails open in June. High mountain passes typically can be crossed the first or second week in July; however, extremely high passes like Pearl Pass (Trail #24) Mosquito Pass (Trail #48) and Argentine Pass (Trail #52) may open much later. Some years, these trails may not open at all. Trails in Area 1 may open earlier because the roads are plowed to encourage earlier participation by tourists. The best time of year to find most trails open is in August and September. September also is the peak time to enjoy the changing colors of the aspens. You may squeeze in some very late season wheeling in early October if no early winter snow has fallen. But be aware the regular Colorado hunting season begins in October. Start as early as possible in the day. Mornings are usually clear while afternoons are often cloudy with a greater chance of thunderstorms.

The weather. Colorado weather is often very pleasant and more moderate than people expect. Low humidity at high elevations keeps temperatures cool in the summer. In the winter, the sun shines most of the time and it stays relatively warm. There are few flies and mosquitoes except around wetlands. The downside to Colorado weather is that it is very unpredictable and can be extreme at times. Although it doesn't happen frequently, it can snow anytime during the summer, especially at higher elevations and at night when temperatures drop. Colorado can also be very windy. Pack plenty of warm clothing regardless of how hot it might be when you depart. Also, make sure you drink plenty of fluids to help you adapt to the dry thin air. Use sunscreen because you will sunburn quicker.

Changing road conditions. Colorado loves to surprise you. Watch for unexpected ice, snow, landslides, avalanches, fallen trees, washouts, deep water, and leaping deer. A clay surface road can be passable when dry but very slippery if wet.

Lightning. Thunderstorms, hail, and lightning are very common in Colorado, especially in the late afternoon. Stay below timberline if you see a storm approaching. If you get stuck above timberline, a hardtop vehicle offers more safety from lightning than being outside. Lightning can strike from a distant storm even when it is sunny overhead.

Fires and floods. You must be aware of the possibility of forest fires and flash floods. Fires can move quickly, so watch for smoke when you are at higher points. At certain times of year, fire danger can be extremely high and the Forest Service will post fire danger warnings. During these times, campfires may be prohibited. Fines can be very steep for violators. Heavy rainstorms can cause flash floods at any time during the spring and summer. The danger is particularly acute if you are in a narrow canyon. If you have reason to believe a flash flood is imminent, do not try to outrun it. Abandon your vehicle and climb to higher ground.

Altitude sickness. Some people experience nausea, dizziness, headaches, or weakness the first time at high altitude. This condition usually improves over time. To minimize symptoms, give yourself time to acclimate, drink plenty of fluids, decrease salt intake, reduce alcohol and caffeine, eat foods high in carbohydrates, and try not to exert yourself. If symptoms become severe, the only sure remedy is to return to a lower altitude. Consult your doctor if you have health problems.

Hypothermia. Hypothermia is possible even in the summer. If you get caught in a sudden shower at high altitude, your body temperature can drop suddenly. Always take rain gear and extra clothing.

Don't drink the water. No matter how cool, clear, or refreshing a mountain stream may appear, never drink the water without boiling it, using a filter or iodine tablets. Best to carry your own.

RULES OF THE ROAD
The laws of Colorado.
• Most trails require that you be licensed, street legal, and carry a valid driver's license if driving. (Exceptions: ATVs and dirt bikes.)
• Vehicles traveling uphill always have the right of way, but use common sense. If you are closer to a wide spot, move over for the other vehicle.
• Don't drink and drive.
• Motorized vehicles are prohibited in Wilderness areas.
Forest Service rules.
• Travel only on roads with signs displaying a Forest Service number, or in some forests, a white arrow. Consider a road closed if you see no signs.
• Stay on the trail at all times. Don't take shortcuts at switchbacks, or

16

drive around bad spots.

• Trails are closed for valid reasons that may not be apparent to you. Do not under any circumstances enter a closed trail.

• Forest Service roads frequently pass through private property. If a gate is unlocked, and there are no "no trespassing" signs on the gate, it is usually okay to pass through, but make sure you leave the gate the way you found it. Close gate if indicated. When following a Forest Service road across private property, stay on the trail at all times.

• Pack out your trash except in fee areas that have approved receptacles. Never throw your trash into pit toilets.

• Never drive across open meadows. Do not walk or drive on delicate tundra, pick wildflowers, or remove anything from historical sites.

• Camp within 300 feet of the road.

• Don't park your vehicle in tall grass. The intense heat from your catalytic converter may start a fire.

• Human waste should be buried 6 to 8 inches deep at least 200 feet from any water source, campsite, or trail. Keep a small shovel handy for this purpose. If possible carry a portable camping toilet.

• Consult Forest Service maps for special land use regulations.

Trail Etiquette.

• Drive cautiously at all times, especially around blind curves.

• Try to be as quiet as possible. Don't play your radio loudly, gun your engine, or spin your tires. Use your horn sparingly for emergencies only. Proudly represent the 4-wheeling community by being courteous to all.

• Always pull over to the side of the road when you are out of your vehicle or not moving. Pull over for bikers and hikers. Stop and shut off your engine for horses and pack animals.

• Avoid crossing streams if possible, but if you must cross, do it at designated crossings only.

• If someone overtakes you, pull over and let them pass.

• Control your pets at all times. Don't let them bark or chase wildlife.

Camping guidelines.

• Use developed or existing campsites whenever possible.

• Camp away from streams, lakes, hiking trails, and historical mining sites. Leave as much distance as possible between you and other campers.

• Use a gas stove if possible and try to avoid fires. If you must have a fire, build it inside a fire ring of rocks, preferably one that is already there. Bring your own firewood if possible. Don't cut trees or branches. Let the fire burn itself out so only ashes remain. Spread the ashes to make sure they are cold. If you must douse the fire, do it thoroughly. If you've thrown bottles or cans into the fire that have not disintegrated, pack them as trash.

• Avoid using soap if at all possible and never around lakes or streams. Heat water to clean utensils. If you must use soap to bathe, use as little as possible. Do not bathe in or near a lake or stream.

17

• Plan your trip carefully and prepack your food in plastic bags or reusable containers. There will be less trash to haul away.

• Inspect the area thoroughly before leaving and make sure nothing is left lying around. The goal is to leave the area the way you found it.

SAFETY TIPS

Mines and mine structures. Getting close to mines and mine buildings is very dangerous. Vertical mine shafts, hundreds of feet deep, may be hidden just below the surface. They've been known to collapse, killing people and pets. Rusty nails, splinters, sharp objects, rotten boards, awkward climbs, contaminated soils and deadly gases are just a few other hazards. In addition, most mines are privately owned and closed to the public. Gates and "no trespassing" signs are often vandalized or removed. It is best to assume you are not allowed on the property. Always view mines from a distance. STAY OUT—STAY ALIVE.

Wear your seat belt. You might think that because you are driving slowly, it's not necessary to wear your seat belt or use child restraints. I've learned through experience that you are much safer with a seat belt than without. Buckle up at all times.

Keep heads, arms, and legs inside moving vehicle. Many trails are narrow. Brush, tree limbs, and rock overhangs may come very close to your vehicle. The driver must make it clear to every passenger to stay inside the vehicle at all times. Children, in particular, must not be allowed to stick their heads, arms, or legs out the windows.

Extra maps. The maps in this book will clearly direct you along the trail. However, if you get lost or decide to venture down a spur road, you'll need additional maps with more detail. At the end of each trail description, I have listed other helpful maps. *National Forest Service maps* are the most commonly used. More than one map may be necessary if the trail crosses forest boundaries. Forest Service maps are usually the least expensive but are not frequently updated. More expensive but worth the money are *Trails Illustrated Topo Maps*. These maps are updated every year and are made of durable waterproof plastic. They include topographic information and the graphics are outstanding. The maps cover a smaller area, so you may need more of them. Another map I strongly recommend is the *DeLorme Colorado Atlas & Gazetteer*. It covers the entire state. Most of the back roads are shown if you look closely. Maps can be purchased at bookstores, map stores and at your local National Forest Service office.

Today, many people are using mapping software on their computers. You can carry your computer or just print out the area you need. You can also download maps to a good GPS unit. For more information on mapping software and GPS, see page 264.

Spend a little time looking over the maps before you head out. Familiarize yourself as much as possible with the area. When you get on the trail, don't be surprised to find inaccuracies. Signs don't always match the map. Trail markers are often vandalized or missing.

Travel with another vehicle. Travel with other vehicles whenever possible. If you must go alone, stay on easier, more traveled routes. Never travel alone on difficult trails. Make sure you tell someone where you are going and when you plan to return.

If you don't have a 4WD friend, join a four-wheel-drive club. Select a club with similar trail preferences.

If you get lost or stuck, stay with your vehicle unless you are very close to help. Your vehicle will provide shelter and is easier to see.

Inspect your vehicle carefully. Before you start into the backcountry, make sure your vehicle is in top operating condition. If you have a mechanic do the work, make sure he is reliable and understands four-wheeling. Tell him where you plan to take your vehicle. Pay particular attention to fluids, hoses, belts, battery, brakes, steering linkage, suspension system, driveline, and anything exposed under the vehicle. Tighten anything that may be loose. Inspect your tires carefully for potential weak spots and tread wear.

Supplies and equipment to take. No single list can be all inclusive. You must be the final judge of what you need. Here's a list of basic items:

❑ Plenty of food and water. Allow enough water for drinking and extra for the vehicle. Carry water purification tablets or a water filter.

❑ Rain gear plus extra clothing, shoes, socks, coats, and hats even in the summer. It gets very cold at night at higher elevations.

❑ Sleeping bags in case you get stuck overnight even if you are not planning to camp.

❑ A good first aid kit including sunscreen and insect repellent.

❑ Candle, matches, and a lighter

❑ An extra set of keys and glasses.

❑ Toilet paper, paper towels, wet wipes, and trash bags.

❑ A large plastic sheet or tarp.

❑ Detailed maps, GPS unit or compass, watch, and a knife.

❑ If you plan to make a fire, carry your own firewood.

❑ Work gloves.

❑ A heavy duty tow strap.

❑ A good fire extinguisher. Make sure you can reach it quickly.

❑ Jumper cables.

❑ Replacement fuses and electrical tape.

❑ Flashlight and extra batteries.

❑ A full tank of gas. If you carry extra gas make sure it is in an approved container and properly stored.

❑ A good set of tools.

❑ Baling wire and duct tape.

❑ An assortment of hose clamps, nuts, bolts, and washers.

❑ A full-size spare tire. Small emergency tires are not adequate in the backcountry.

❑ A tire pressure gauge, electric tire pump that will plug into your cigarette lighter, and a can of nonflammable tire sealant.

❑ A jack that will lift your vehicle fairly high off the ground. Take a small board to place under the jack. Carry a high lift jack if you can, especially on more difficult trails. Test your jack before you leave.

❑ Shovel and axe. Folding shovels work great.

❑ Tire chains.

❑ CB radio and/or cellular phone.

❑ Portable toilet.

❑ If you have a winch, carry a tree strap, clevis, and snatch block.

Store these items in tote bags or large plastic containers so they can be easily loaded into your vehicle when it's time to go. Make sure you tie everything down thoroughly so it doesn't bounce around or shift.

Maintenance. Backroad travel puts your vehicle under greater stress than normal highway driving. Follow maintenance directions in your owners manual for severe driving conditions. This usually calls for changing your oil, oil filter, and air filter more frequently as well as more frequent fluid checks and lubrications. Inspect your tires carefully; they take a lot of extra abuse. After your trip, make sure you wash your vehicle. Use a high pressure spray to thoroughly clean the underside and wheel wells. Automatic car washes usually are not adequate. Do it yourself, if you want your vehicle in good shape for the next trip.

YOUR RESPONSIBILITIES AS A BACKCOUNTRY DRIVER

It is imperative that we educate ourselves on minimum impact driving techniques and diligently practice what we learn. If we don't, we will eventually lose our rights to use our remote lands. Fortunately, there are organizations whose goal is to educate the public on low impact recreational techniques. Two of the largest and most respected organizations are *Tread Lightly!, Inc.* and the *BlueRibbon Coalition.*

Tread Lightly!,® Inc. This national non-profit organization was established in 1990 to protect public and private lands by educating as many people as possible in the proper use of off-highway vehicles. It is supported by donations from corporate members including manufacturers of off-highway vehicles, environmental groups, user associations including many four-wheel drive clubs, government agencies, and people like you and me who are fighting to keep the backcountry open to enjoy. The suggestions of *Tread Lightly* are simple. Please read them, abide by them and pass them along to others.

• Travel and recreate with minimum impact.

• Respect the environment and the rights of others.

- Educate yourself, plan and prepare before you go.
- Allow for future use of the outdoors, leave it better than you found it.
- Discover the rewards of responsible recreation.

Join today. You'll receive educational materials and be supporting a great cause. Call or write to the address shown in appendix.

BlueRibbon Coalition. No group fights harder to keep public lands open for responsible vehicular use. Their motto is "Preserving Our Natural Resources For the Public Instead of From the Public." This organization has people in Washington constantly watching over your rights. They frequently testify at hearings on land use issues and constantly work to convince your congressmen of the importance of keeping the backcountry open. They publish the informative monthly *BlueRibbon Magazine,* which is full of interesting articles on the latest governmental actions affecting land use. It also includes educational articles and reports of fun vehicular activities that are happening all over the country. Join today. See appendix for address and phone number.

Four-wheel-drive organizations. Other information specific to four-wheeling is available from the Colorado Association of 4 Wheel Drive Clubs, Inc. and the national United Four Wheel Drive Associations, Inc. Both of these organizations publish informative monthly newsletters. See appendix for addresses and phone numbers.

BACKCOUNTRY DRIVING TECHNIQUES

The basics. It may surprise you to learn that some SUV owners have never shifted their vehicles into low range. I once encountered an SUV on the most dangerous part of Devil's Punchbowl (Trail #19). There were four vehicles in our group going uphill. Since he was a single vehicle and we had the right of way, we assumed he would back up and let us by. When he didn't, we asked him why. When he said he didn't have enough power to back up, we looked inside and noticed that he was not in low gear. When we pointed this out he seemed a little embarrassed. Apparently it never occurred to him what that other lever was for. It is situations like this that have provided extra motivation for me to write this book. I'd like to prevent others from getting themselves in such dangerous and helpless situations. If you read this book carefully, a similar situation is unlikely to happen to you. You'll recognize dangerous trails for which you are not yet ready, and when you are ready, you will know how to drive them safely.

If you have never shifted into low, grab your owner's manual now and start practicing. Read the rest of this book, then try some of the easy trails. Gradually you'll become more proficient and eventually you'll be ready to move up in difficulty.

Low and slow. Your vehicle was designed to go over rocky and bumpy terrain but only at slow speed. Get used to driving slowly in first gear low range. This will allow you to idle over obstacles without stalling. You don't need to shift back and forth constantly. Get into a low gear and stay there as much as possible so your engine can operate at a higher RPM and at maximum power. If you have a standard transmission, your goal should be to use your clutch as little as possible. As you encounter resistance on an obstacle or an uphill grade, just give it a little gas. As you start downhill, allow the engine's resistance to act as a brake. If the engine alone will not stop you from accelerating, then help a little with the brake. When you need more power but not more speed, press on the gas and feather the brake a little at the same time. This takes a little practice, but you will be amazed at the control you have. This technique works equally well with automatic transmissions.

Rocks and other high points. Never attempt to straddle a rock that is large enough to strike your differentials, transfer case or other low-hanging parts of your undercarriage. Instead, drive over the highest point with your tire, which is designed to take the abuse. This will lift your undercarriage over the obstacle. As you enter a rocky area, look ahead to determine where the high points are, then make every effort to cross them with your tires. Learn the low points of your undercarriage. Many newer vehicles have independent wheel suspension. This is not quite as effective offroad as a solid axle because the differential isn't lifted as high when the wheel goes up. You should still use the same technique of driving over the obstacle with your tire. Just be a little more careful.

Using a spotter. Sometimes there are so many rocks you get confused about which way to go. In this case, have someone get out and guide you. They should stand at a safe distance in front, watching your tires and undercarriage. With hand signals, they can direct you left or right. If you are alone, don't be embarrassed to spot for yourself by getting in and out of your vehicle several times.

Those clunking sounds. Having made every attempt to avoid dragging bottom, you'll find it's not always possible. It is inevitable that a rock will contact your undercarriage eventually. The sound can be quite unnerving the first time it happens. If you are driving slowly and have proper skid plates, damage is unlikely. Look for a different line, back up and try again. If unsuccessful, see "Crossing large rocks" below.

Crossing a log. If the log is higher than your ground clearance, you will likely become high centered. Sometimes crossing at an angle helps. If you can't make it, build a ramp by stacking rocks on each side of the log. When done, put the rocks back where you found them. It might be possible to avoid driving over the log altogether by simply pulling the log to the side of the road with a tow strap or winch.

Crossing large rocks. Sometimes a rock is too large to drive over or at such a steep angle your bumper hits the rock before your tire. The solution is the same as crossing a log. Stack rocks on each side to form a ramp. Once over the obstacle, make sure you put the rocks back where you found them.

The next driver to come along may prefer the challenge of crossing the rock in its more difficult state.

Getting high centered. You may drive over a large rock or into a rut, causing you to get lodged on the object. If this happens, don't panic. First ask your passengers to get out to see if less weight helps. Try rocking the vehicle. If this doesn't work, jack up your vehicle and place a few rocks under the tires so that when you let the jack down, you take the weight off the high point. Determine whether driving forward or reverse is best and try again. You may have to repeat this procedure several times if you are seriously high centered. Eventually you will learn what you can and cannot drive over.

Look in all directions. Unlike highway driving in which your primary need for attention is straight ahead, backcountry driving requires you to look in all directions. Objects can block your path from above, below, and from the sides. Trees fall, branches droop, and rocks slide, making the trail into an ever-changing obstacle course.

Scout ahead. If you are on an unfamiliar trail and are concerned that the trail is becoming too difficult, get out of your vehicle and walk the trail ahead of you. This gives you an opportunity to pick an easy place to turn around before you get into trouble. If you have to turn around, back up or pull ahead until you find a wide flat spot. Don't try to turn in a narrow confined area. This can damage the trail and perhaps tip over your vehicle.

Anticipate. Shift into four-wheel drive or low range before it is needed. If you wait until it is needed, conditions might be too difficult, e.g., halfway up a hillside.

Blind curves. When approaching blind curves, always assume that there is a speeding vehicle coming from the opposite direction. This will prepare you for the worst. Be aware that many people drive on the wrong side of the road to stay away from the outer edge of a trail. Whenever possible, keep your windows open and your radio off so that you can hear an approaching vehicle. You can usually hear motorcycles and ATVs. Quiet SUVs are the biggest problem. Collisions do occur so be careful.

Driving uphill. Use extreme caution when attempting to climb a hill. The difficulty of hill climbing is often misjudged by the novice 4-wheeler. You should have good tires, adequate power, and be shifted into four-wheel drive low. There are four factors that determine difficulty:

Length of the hill. If the hill is very long, it is less likely that momentum will carry you to the top. Short hills are easier.

Traction. A rock surface is easier to climb than dirt.

Bumpiness. If the road surface undulates to the point where all four tires do not stay on the ground at the same time, you will have great difficulty climbing even a moderately steep hill.

Steepness. This can be difficult to judge, so examine a hill carefully before you attempt it. Walk up the hill if necessary to make sure it is not steeper at the top. If you are not absolutely sure you can climb a hill, don't attempt it. Practice on smaller hills first.

If you attempt a hill, approach it straight on and stay that way all the way to the top. Do not turn sideways or try to drive across the hill. Do not use excessive speed but keep moving at a steady pace. Make sure no one is coming up from the other side. Position a spotter at the top of the hill if necessary. Do not spin your tires because this can turn you sideways to the hill. If you feel you are coming to a stop due to lack of traction, turn your steering wheel back and forth quickly. This will give you additional grip. If you stall, use your brake and restart your engine. You may also have to use your emergency brake. If you start to slide backwards even with your brake on, you may have to ease up on the brake enough to regain steering control. Don't allow your wheels to lock up. If you don't make it to the top of the hill, shift into reverse and back down slowly in a straight line. Try the hill again but only if you think you learned enough to make a difference. As you approach the top of the hill, ease off the gas so you are in control before starting down the other side.

Driving downhill. Make sure you are in four-wheel drive. Examine the hill carefully and determine the best route that will allow you to go straight down the hill. Do not turn sideways. Use the lowest gears possible, allowing the engine's compression to hold you back. Do not ride the clutch. Feather the brakes slightly if additional slowing is needed. Do not allow the wheels to lock up. This will cause loss of steering and possibly cause you to slide sideways. The natural reaction when you begin to slide is to press harder on the brakes. Try to stay off the brakes. If you continue to slide despite these efforts, turn in the direction of the slide as you would on ice or snow and accelerate slightly. This will help maintain steering control.

Parking on a steep hill. Put your vehicle in reverse gear if pointing downhill and in forward gear if pointing uphill. For automatic transmissions, shift to park. Set your emergency brake hard. For extra insurance, block your tires.

Driving side hills. Side hill situations are dangerous so try to avoid them if possible. In Colorado, this will be difficult because off-camber situations are a fact of life. No one can tell you how far your vehicle can safely lean. You must learn the limitations through practice. Remember that sport utility vehicles have a higher center of gravity and are less stable than a passenger car. However, don't get paranoid. Your vehicle will likely lean a lot more than you think. Drive slowly to avoid bouncing over. A good way to learn is to watch an experienced driver with a vehicle similar to yours. This is an advantage to traveling with a group. Once you see how far other vehicles can lean, you will become more comfortable in these situations. Use extreme caution if the road surface is slippery from loose gravel, mud, or wet clay. Turn around if necessary.

Passing on narrow shelf roads. When two vehicles meet on a narrow shelf road, it can be very dangerous. Try to avoid the situation by waiting at a wide spot for oncoming traffic. Don't endanger yourself by driving too close to the outer edge if you are the outside vehicle. But equally important, if you are the inside vehicle, don't ride the bank so high that you tip excessively. If you tip over, you can roll all the way across the road and over the edge, especially if weight shifts inside your vehicle. Don't take a chance if there is not enough room to pass. Take your time and back up to a wide spot. Backing on a narrow shelf road is dangerous but not as dangerous as trying to pass when it's too narrow. When backing, use a spotter if you don't feel comfortable. Remember, uphill traffic has the right-of-way.

Crossing streams and water holes. You must know the high water point of your vehicle before entering any body of water. Several factors can determine this point, including the height of the air intake and the location of the computer module (newer vehicles). Water sucked into the air intake is a very serious matter. If you don't know where these items are located, check with your dealer or a good four-wheel-drive shop. A low fan can throw water on the engine and cause it to stall. You may have to briefly disconnect your fan belt. Water can be sucked into your differentials so check them regularly after crossing deep streams.

After you understand your vehicle's capabilities, you must assess the stream conditions. First determine the depth of the water. If you are with a group, let the most experienced driver cross first. Follow his line if he is successful. If you are alone, you might wait for someone else to come along. Sometimes you can use a long stick to check the depth of small streams or water holes. Check for deep holes, large obstacles, and muddy sections. If you can't determine the water depth, don't cross. A winch line or long tow strap can be used as a safety line to pull someone back if he gets into trouble, but it must be attached before entering the water. It must also be long enough for him to reach shallow water on the other side. Once in the water, drive slowly but steadily. This creates a small wake which helps form an air pocket around the engine. I've seen people put a piece of cardboard or canvas over the front of their vehicle to enhance the wake affect. This only works if you keep moving. After exiting a stream, test your brakes. You may have to ride them lightly for a short distance until they dry.

Always cross streams at designated water crossings. Don't drive in the direction of the stream. Try to minimize disruption of the water habitat.

Mud. Don't make new mud holes or enlarge existing ones. Stay home if you have reason to believe the trail will be too wet. Some trails, however, have permanent mud holes that you must cross. Mud can build up suction around your tires and be very difficult to get through. Always check a mud hole carefully to see how deep it is. Take a stick and poke around. Check the other side. If there are no tracks coming out, don't go in. If you decide to cross, keep moving at a steady pace and if necessary, turn the steering wheel back and forth quickly for additional traction. If you get stuck, dig around the tires to break the suction and place anything hard under the tires for traction. It may be necessary to back out. If you are with a friend, and you are doubtful if you can get through without help, attach a tow strap before you enter so that you can be pulled back. But beware, sometimes the mud can be so bad, even a friend can't pull you out. Your only protection against this happening is to use your head and not go in the mud in the first place. When I've seen people stuck this badly it is usually due to a total disregard for the obvious. If you can't get through the mud, search for an alternate route but don't widen the trail.

Gullies or washouts. If you are running parallel to a washed out section of the trail, straddle it. If it becomes too large to straddle, drive down the middle. The goal is to center your vehicle so you remain as level as possible. This may require that you drive on the outer edges of your tires, so drive slowly and watch for any sharp objects. If you begin to tilt too far in one direction, turn in the direction of the tilt until you level out again. Sometimes it helps to have a spotter. To cross a gully, approach at a 45-degree angle and let each tire walk over independently.

Ravines. Crossing a ravine is similar to crossing a gully. Approach on an angle and let each tire go through independently. If the ravine is large with steep sides, you may not be able to cross at an angle because it could cause a rollover. If you don't cross at an angle, two things can happen. You will drag the front or rear of your vehicle, or you will high center on the edge of the ravine. If this is the case, ask yourself if you really need to cross the ravine. If you must cross, your only solution is to stack rocks to lift the vehicle at critical points.

Sand. Except for the Great Sand Dunes National Park, Colorado has few desert areas. Sandy soil situations are mostly encountered around dry creek beds. Not all sand is a problem. Some can be quite firm and easy to drive over. Unfortunately, you can never be sure until you are in the middle of it. The trick is to keep moving so that your momentum helps carry you through. Stay in a higher gear and use a little extra power but don't use excessive power and spin your tires. If necessary, turn your steering wheel back and forth quickly to give your tires a fresh grip. Airing down your tires can also help. Experiment with different tire pressures. Some tires can go as low as 8 to 10 pounds, although use caution below 15 pounds. Make sure you have a way to air up after you get through the sand. If you do get stuck, wet the sand in front of your tires. Try rocking the vehicle. If necessary, use your floor mats under the tires.

Snow and ice. The best advice is to avoid snow and ice completely. Call ahead for trail conditions. (See appendix.) If you encounter ice or snow on a shelf road, use extreme caution. If it is drifted over and there are no tire tracks, turn around. If other vehicles have safely crossed and there is some melting to the dirt surface, it is probably all right to cross provided you feel comfortable and have proper tires. If you are not sure, get out of your vehicle and walk the route. Be careful late in the day as the road surface may be in the process of refreezing. If you encounter any place where ice is completely across the trail, turn around.

If you are starting down a slope that is snow covered or icy, go slowly until you have some idea of how slippery the surface is. Some snow can have relatively good traction. Other snow can be too slippery to walk across. If you find your vehicle sliding, steer in the direction of the slide. Pump your brakes lightly so your wheels do not lock. This will allow your wheels to turn a little which will give you some steering capability. Don't pump antilock brakes.

Use extreme caution before starting up a slippery grade. If the road surface is tippy, you may slide off the road. If you find yourself losing traction, try turning your steering wheel back and forth quickly for a fresh grip.

If you get stuck in the snow, dig around the tire and rock your vehicle back and forth. Try shoveling some fresh dirt, gravel, or small rocks into the hole. If no other alternative, try putting your floor mats under the tires. Don't spin your tires.

Tire chains. Many of the situations described above can be eliminated with the use of tire chains, which I recommend you carry at all times. Learn how to put them on before you need them. Chains should be properly fitted to your vehicle because they can cause damage to wheel wells or steering mechanisms.

Dust and washboard roads. Dust and washboard roads are a part of Colorado travel. Vibration from these roads can be annoying. It is a problem for everybody so don't think there is something wrong with your vehicle. Experiment with different speeds to find the smoothest ride. Slowing down is usually best, but some conditions may be improved by speeding up a little. Be careful around curves where you could lose traction and slide. Check your tires to make sure they are not over-inflated. Dust is less of a problem for closed SUVs. You simply roll up your windows and turn on the air conditioner or fan. The inside pressure will help keep out most dust. With an open vehicle, there is not much you can do. At slow speeds, you can fold down your windshield if you have this option. The dust will pass through rather than collect behind the windshield.

Thumbs up. Make a habit of not wrapping your thumbs inside the steering wheel when crossing over rocky terrain. If you hit a large rock, your steering wheel could spin suddenly and injure your thumbs. This is more of a problem for vehicles without power steering.

Airing down. There may be times when you need to let air out of your tires to get more traction or improve your ride, e.g., when driving through sand, going up a steep hill, or driving on washboard roads. It is usually safe to let air out of your tires until they bulge slightly, provided you are not traveling at high speed. If you let out too much air, your tires may come off the rims, or the sidewalls may become vulnerable to damage by sharp objects. Consider how or where you will reinflate. A small air pump that plugs into your cigarette lighter is handy for this purpose. Airing down on hard-core trails is essential. I've seen some wheelers with larger tires air down to as little as 3-5 lbs. A typical SUV can usually be aired down to 18 to 20 lbs. without noticeable handling difficulties at low speeds.

Winching. Next to tow points and skid plates, a winch is one of the best investments you can make. If you drive more difficult trails and you don't have a winch, travel with someone who does. I've known some hard-core wheelers who have gone for years without owning a winch but they always travel with a group. If you never intend to buy a winch, carry a high lift jack or come-along. Although these tools are slow and inconvenient, they can get you out of difficulty when there is no other way.

If you own a winch, make sure you also have these four basic winch accessories:

1. Heavy-duty work gloves.

2. A tree strap - Looks like a tow strap but is shorter. It has a loop on each end.

3. A snatch block - A pulley that opens on the side so you can slip it over your winch cable.

4. A clevis - A heavy U-shaped device with a pin that screws across one end. This enables you to connect straps together and to your vehicle. It has many other uses.

Winching tips:

• Your winch cable should be lined up straight with the pulling vehicle. If you can't pull straight, attach a snatch block to a tree to form an angle. This technique also works for pulling a fallen tree off the trail.

• If your winch cable bunches up at one end of the spool, let it go as long as possible without jamming and rewind it later.

• Attach your winch line to the largest tree possible using your tree strap and clevis. If no tree is large enough, wrap several smaller trees. The strap should be put as low as possible on the tree.

• Keep your engine running while winching to provide maximum electrical power to the battery.

• Help the winch by driving the stuck vehicle slowly. Be in the lowest gear possible and go as slowly as possible. Don't allow slack in the winch cable. This can start a jerking motion that could break the cable.

• If there is not enough power to pull the stuck vehicle, attach a snatch block to the stuck vehicle and double the winch cable back to the starting point. This block-and-tackle technique will double your pulling power.

• Set the emergency brake on the anchor vehicle and block the wheels if necessary. In some cases, you may have to connect the anchor vehicle to another vehicle or tree.

• Throw a blanket or heavy coat over the winch cable while pulling. This will slow the end of the winch cable if it breaks and snaps back.

• Make sure there are at least 5 wraps of the winch cable left on the spool.

• Never hook the winch cable to itself. Use a tree strap and clevis. Never allow the winch cable to kink. This creates a weak spot in the cable.

• If tow points are not available on the stuck vehicle, attach the winch cable to the frame not the bumper. If you are helping a stranger, make sure he understands that you are not responsible for damage to his vehicle.

• Never straddle or stand close to the winch cable while it is under stress.

• If you are stuck alone with no place to attach your winch cable, bury your spare tire in the ground as an anchor point. When you are finished, repair any damage to the ground.

• When finished winching, don't let the end of the cable wind into the spool. It can become jammed and damage your winch. Attach the hook to some other part of your vehicle like a tow point.

OTHER ACTIVITIES

To make the trip more enjoyable for everyone, especially if children are along, plan frequent stops with a variety of activities including picnics, hiking, biking, camping, rafting, and fishing. Go to the library before your trip and learn a little history about the area or stop at museums in towns along the way. Museums like the ones in Cripple Creek, Ouray and Silverton are outstanding. Share maps with the kids and let them trace your route. Carry binoculars to look at mines, wildlife and distant landmarks. Allow your adult passengers an opportunity to drive appropriate parts of the trail if they are so inclined. Some portions of the trail provide driving opportunities for responsible licensed teenagers. They will be eager to learn proper off-highway driving techniques and will grow up to be responsible backcountry drivers.

FINAL COMMENTS

Don't forget to check our Web site at **www.funtreks.com** for new books and latest trail updates. If you know of changes to trails, please contact us so we can get them posted.

If you are dissatisfied with this book in any way, regardless of where you bought it, please call our toll-free number during business hours at **1-877-222-7623**. We promise to do whatever it takes to make you happy.

We've made every effort to make this book as accurate and as easy to use as possible. If you have ideas for improvements or find any significant errors, please write to us at FunTreks, Inc., P.O. Box 3127, Monument, CO 80132-3127 or E-mail to *books@funtreks.com*. We hope this book makes your backcountry experiences safer, easier, and more fun.

Map Legend

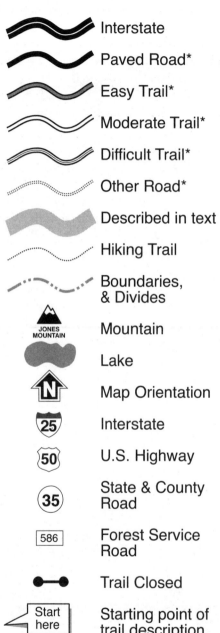

Interstate

Paved Road*

Easy Trail*

Moderate Trail*

Difficult Trail*

Other Road*

Described in text

Hiking Trail

Boundaries, & Divides

Mountain

Lake

Map Orientation

Interstate

U.S. Highway

State & County Road

Forest Service Road

Trail Closed

Starting point of trail description.

Public Toilet

Gas, Service

Parking

Picnic Area

Camping Area

Mine or Mill

Hiking Trailhead

Mountain Biking

Fishing

Water Crossing

Bridge

Falls

Cabin

Ghost Town

Scenic Point

Major Obstacle

Unlicensed Vehicles Allowed

Scale indicated by grid

Scale is different for each map; check grid size at bottom of map.

These items repeated on each map for your convenience. See Mini Key.

30

THE TRAILS

Holy Cross, Trail #44, difficult. Crossing at French Creek.

AREA 1

Ouray, Silverton, Lake City, Telluride

1. Last Dollar Road
2. Yankee Boy Basin
3. Governor Basin
4. Imogene Pass
5. Black Bear Pass
6. Ophir Pass,
   Alta Lakes
7. Clear Lake
8. Mineral Creek
9. Poughkeepsie
   Gulch
10. Corkscrew Gulch
11. Red Mountain
    Mining Area
12. California Gulch
13. Engineer Pass
14. Cinnamon Pass,
    Wager Gulch
15. Picayne & Placer
    Gulches
16. Eureka Gulch
17. Stony Pass

MINI KEY
Paved
Easy
Moderate
Difficult
Other

EASY ●
MODERATE ■
DIFFICULT ◆

TO GUNNISON

149

LAKE CITY

149

TO CREEDE

WAGER GULCH

Carson

Grid size - 5 miles

© 2005 FunTreks, Inc.

TO CREEDE

Animas Forks

14

13

Eureka

Howardsville

17

Kite Lake

12

8

9

10

11

15

16

Gladstone

110

550

550

550

550

SILVERTON

TO DURANGO

RIDGWAY

550

OURAY

4

2

3

TELLURIDE

5

550

6

7

TO MONTROSE

62

PLACERVILLE

62

1

145

145

145

TO CORTEZ

N

32

Ouray, Silverton, Lake City, Telluride

America has many beautiful mountain ranges, but most can only be seen at a distance from crowded paved highways. Close-up views are reserved for a fortunate few strong enough to hike and climb above timberline. Not so in the beautiful San Juan Mountains of southwestern Colorado. Here, you are allowed to drive deep into the backcountry, visit historic mine buildings, cross high, rugged passes and enjoy views you never thought possible. Even better, you can drive most of the roads in an ordinary 4-wheel-drive, high-clearance sport utility vehicle or pickup truck. Only a few roads in the area require more aggressive Jeep-like vehicles. With the privilege of driving, of course, comes the responsibility to leave the area exactly as you find it and to pass through unobtrusively so that others can find the same serenity as you. Don't take safety for granted. Danger lurks for the reckless and ill prepared.

When you're finished in the backcountry, return to the quaint but lively mountain towns of Ouray, Silverton, Lake City and Telluride. Here you'll find pleasing shops, hotels, restaurants, campgrounds and museums.

Animas Forks Ghost Town, left. Easy California Gulch, Trail #12, right.

Family loads up SUV after camping at great spot west of Telluride.

ATVs ok on marked forest roads.

Seasonal abundant wildflowers cover hillsides.

Easy drive when dry.

34

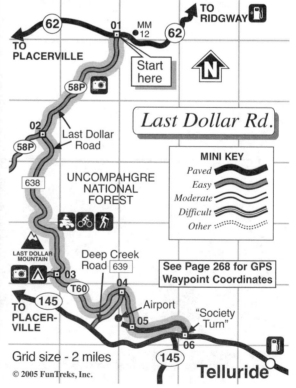

TO RIDGWAY

62   01   MM 12   62

TO PLACERVILLE

Start here

N

58P

Last Dollar Rd.

02   Last Dollar Road

58P

638

UNCOMPAHGRE NATIONAL FOREST

MINI KEY

Paved
Easy
Moderate
Difficult
Other

LAST DOLLAR MOUNTAIN

Deep Creek Road   639

03

T60   04

See Page 268 for GPS Waypoint Coordinates

TO PLACER-VILLE   145

Airport

05

"Society Turn"

06

Grid size - 2 miles

© 2005 FunTreks, Inc.

145

Telluride

Last Dollar Road ❶

Location: Southwest of Ridgway and northwest of Telluride.

Difficulty: Easy. Rutted dirt road suitable for high-clearance, 2-wheel-drive vehicles when dry. Slick clay can be impassable when wet even for four-wheel-drive vehicles.

Features: This scenic ranchland and forest backroad is a great alternative to the paved drive between Ridgway and Telluride. Enjoy abundant wildflowers through early summer, great fall color and stunning mountain views. Camp, hike, bike or ride ATVs on designated routes in forest. Plan plenty of time to visit Telluride, a great summer destination. The town can get very crowded during special events, so call ahead to find out what's going on.

Time & Distance: Almost 21 miles. Allow about 2 hours.

To Get There: Head west on Hwy. 62 from Ridgway about 12 miles. Turn left on well-marked Last Dollar Road 0.8 miles west of mile marker 12.

Trail Description: Reset trip odometer as you turn off Hwy. 62 (01). Last Dollar Road follows well-maintained County Road 58P for first part of journey. Bear left at 2.1 miles, then slightly right at 2.5. Turn left at 5.0 miles (02) where Last Dollar Road narrows and heads towards forest. Bear right and cross small creek at 6.5 miles. Continue straight at 10.5 where Alder Creek Trail goes left. Cross broad talus slopes at 12.4. Road twists downhill with beautiful mountain views and intersects with better T60 at 13.0 miles (03). Great camp spot to right. Turn left and head downhill through residential area. Avoid turning on numerous, well-marked private roads. Stay left at 16.7 miles (04) where Deep Creek Road (not signed) goes right. You'll see Telluride Airport on the right before reaching paved road at 18.8 miles (05). Turn left and descend to Hwy. 145, reached at 20.8 miles (06).

Return Trip: Left at Hwy 145 goes into Telluride. Right goes to Placerville and connects to Hwy. 62 back to Ridgway.

Services: Full services in Ridgway and Telluride. Dispersed camping along route in forest. Respect all private lands.

Maps: Drake Map. Trails Illustrated Map #141. Uncompahgre National Forest. DeLorme Atlas & Gazetteer.

"Drinking Cup" photo spot.   Looking downhill from the area around Twin Falls.

The Atlas Mill. (Enjoy from a distance.)   Below Twin Falls.

Stock SUVs galore reach the parking area for Blue Lakes Hiking Trailhead.

Yankee Boy Basin 2

Location: Immediately south of Ouray off U.S. 550.

Difficulty: Moderate. The lower portion of the trail is easy. Beyond the toilet, the trail gets rocky, narrow and steep, but is still suitable for aggressive, high-clearance, stock SUVs. This becomes apparent when you reach the often-crowded parking area at the Blue Lakes Hiking Trailhead. A gate for the upper portion of the trail is closed until the snow melts, usually in late June or early July.

Features: One of the most popular destinations in the Ouray area due to its stunning natural beauty, rich history, and colorful wildflower display. At the height of spring color, amateur and professional photographers flock to the area. (Please do not pick the wildflowers. Over the years, their numbers have decreased, threatening closure of the area.) Popular landmarks include Twin Falls, Atlas Mill and Camp Bird Mine. (View mine structures from a distance. They are all on private land.) Because the area is used so heavily, camping is restricted to designated dispersed areas only. A fee is charged to camp. ATVs are permitted on this trail including most of Camp Bird Road. A large staging area is located a couple of miles up from the bottom.

Time & Distance: A total of 9.6 miles if you make it all the way to the top. Allow 3 to 5 hours for the round trip.

To Get There: Head south from Ouray on U.S. 550. Just 0.4 miles from the Beaumont Hotel on Main Street, turn right on Camp Bird Road, C.R. 361.

Trail Description: Set odometer to zero as you turn at Camp Bird Road (01). This road is easy and wide with some car traffic. Don't become complacent, however, as there are many blind curves and high cliffs. The top left picture on opposite page was taken after going more than 3 miles. This is a popular photo spot called the "Drinking Cup"—a natural spring is located at this point. (Be particularly careful at this curve coming back down. People have missed this turn and driven off the cliff.) Around 4.6 miles, stay right past Camp Bird as the road becomes C.R. 26. After Camp Bird, you'll pass under a dramatic overhang.

Continue straight at 6.1 miles (02) where Imogene Pass Road goes left. You'll pass through Sneffels Townsite (not obvious) before reaching the turn for Governor Basin, Trail #3, at 7.0 miles (03). Stay right on F.S. 853.1B as the road gets a bit rougher and steeper. You'll soon see Twin Falls on the left. Flowers are abundant in this area and many people stop here for pictures. Last chance to use public toilet is at 7.8 miles. After the toilet, the road forks and gets rockier. You can go either way; I went right.

Continue to climb until you reach a gate at 8.5 miles (04). If it is open, you may continue. Many people elect to turn around here; however, the best part of the trip remains for those looking for a bit more adventure. The narrow road climbs steeply uphill past more wildflowers (when in season). Stay right at 9.3 miles. (The road to the left goes to a lake, but is not open to motor vehicles.) The main road ends at a parking area for the Blue Lakes Hiking Trail at 9.6 miles (05). At this point you've climbed to above 12,400 feet where views are incredible.

Return Trip: Retrace your steps back to Ouray. On the way down, consider the slightly more difficult but outstanding trip up to Governor Basin, Trail #3. You can also reach Telluride by taking the long but spectacular trip over Imogene Pass, Trail #4.

Services: Full services in Ouray. Primitive toilet above Twin Falls. Camp in designated dispersed fee areas only.

Other Activities: This is a very popular high-elevation hiking area. To hike, you must be in good shape and accustomed to the altitude. If you enjoy wildflowers, you can spend many delightful hours identifying flowers within a short walk of your vehicle.

Historical Highlights: One of most obvious features of this road is the Camp Bird Mine. In its heyday, this mine had advanced creature comforts including hot and cold running water, electric lights, and steam heat. It was discovered in 1896 by Tom Walsh, who felt that the 400 miners who worked there should be treated to a decent lifestyle. He required only eight hours of work per day rather than the standard 12 hours. His humanitarian approach brought big rewards as he made over 4 million dollars by 1900. He sold the mine in 1902 for 5.2 million dollars. The mine continued to operate until 1911 and made over 26 million dollars. The road up to Camp Bird was built by the legendary Otto Mears in 1891 after others had tried and failed.

Maps: Drake Map. Uncompahgre National Forest. Trails Illustrated Silverton, Ouray #141. DeLorme Atlas & Gazetteer. I also recommend folded pocket-size maps published by Backcountry Travelers, Inc, available in local stores. The maps are very handy and have a lot of detailed information (see appendix for listing of three maps).

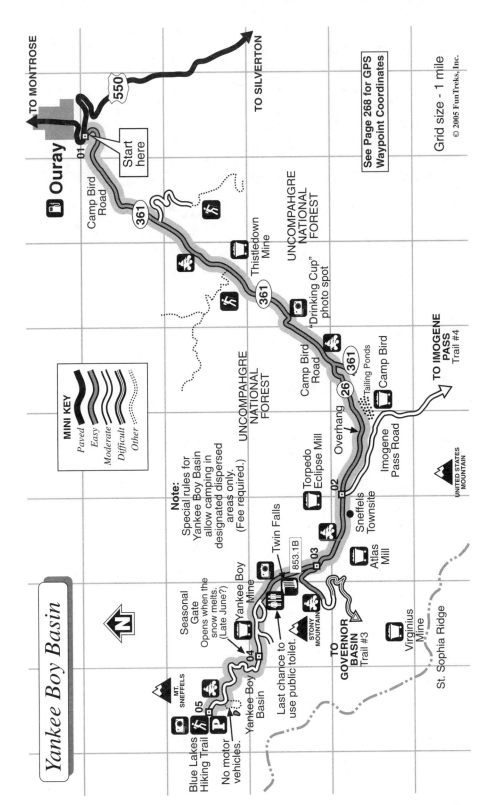

Yankee Boy Basin

MINI KEY
Paved
Easy
Moderate
Difficult
Other

N

TO MONTROSE

Ouray

550

TO SILVERTON

01

Start here

Camp Bird Road

361

361

Thistledown Mine

UNCOMPAHGRE NATIONAL FOREST

"Drinking Cup" photo spot

UNCOMPAHGRE NATIONAL FOREST

Camp Bird Road

Camp Bird

361

26

Tailing Ponds

Overhang

02

Imogene Pass Road

TO IMOGENE PASS Trail #4

Sneffels Townsite

UNITED STATES MOUNTAIN

Atlas Mill

Virginius Mine

St. Sophia Ridge

Torpedo Eclipse Mill

03

853.1B

Twin Falls

Note:
Special rules for Yankee Boy Basin allow camping in designated dispersed areas only. (Fee required.)

STONY MOUNTAIN

TO GOVERNOR BASIN Trail #3

Seasonal Gate Opens when the snow melts. (Late June?)

Yankee Boy Mine

04

Yankee Boy Basin

Last chance to use public toilet.

No motor vehicles.

MT. SNEFFELS

05

Blue Lakes Hiking Trail

See Page 268 for GPS Waypoint Coordinates

Grid size - 1 mile

© 2005 FunTreks, Inc.

39

Looking down at Camp Bird Road.

Mountain Top Mine (Private, keep out.)

Great spot for photos and lunch at 2.3 miles (03).

Thick wildflowers everywhere.

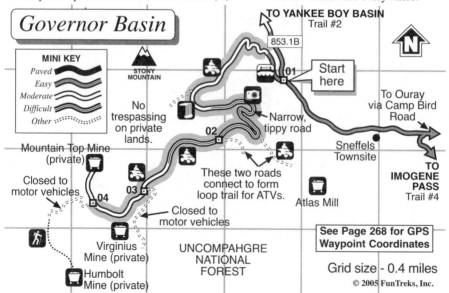

Governor Basin

MINI KEY
Paved
Easy
Moderate
Difficult
Other

STONY MOUNTAIN

No trespassing on private lands.

Mountain Top Mine (private)

Closed to motor vehicles

Virginius Mine (private)

Humbolt Mine (private)

These two roads connect to form loop trail for ATVs.

Closed to motor vehicles

Atlas Mill

Sneffels Townsite

TO YANKEE BOY BASIN
Trail #2

853.1B

Start here

01

02

03

04

To Ouray via Camp Bird Road

TO IMOGENE PASS
Trail #4

Narrow, tippy road

N

UNCOMPAHGRE NATIONAL FOREST

See Page 268 for GPS Waypoint Coordinates

Grid size - 0.4 miles

© 2005 FunTreks, Inc.

Governor Basin ◆3◆

Location: Immediately south of Ouray off U.S. 550.

Difficulty: Difficult. Rocky, narrow and tippy in spots, but the main trail is suitable for high-clearance, aggressive stock SUVs. Side trails are more difficult. Experienced drivers only.

Features: Gorgeous high-elevation scenery, incredible wildflowers and standing mine buildings. Trail accesses historic mines including the massive Virginius Mine. Mines are on private land—no trespassing. Consider taking a Jeep tour if you are afraid of heights. ATVs are allowed on the trail.

Time & Distance: The main portion of the trail is less than 3 miles one way and takes about an hour. Allow 3 to 4 hours for the round trip from Ouray. Add more time to explore side roads.

To Get There: Head south from Ouray on U.S. 550. Just 0.4 miles from the Beaumont Hotel, turn right on Camp Bird Road, C.R. 361. Bear right after 4.6 miles past the Camp Bird Mine on C.R. 26. The turn for Governor Basin is a total of 7.0 miles from U.S. 550.

Trail Description: Reset trip odometer as you turn left towards Governor Basin (01). Stay right after crossing a small bridge. Stay left and go by a waterfall after 0.7 miles. Climb steeply on a narrow shelf road with several tippy spots. (Upper left photo, opposite page, was taken at 1.2 miles at a narrow switchback.) Stay right at 1.5 and right again at a T at 1.8 miles (02). A photogenic spot with large boulders is reached at 2.3 miles (03). This great lunch spot has abundant wildflowers and views of the entire basin. Left is a closed road to the Virginius Mine. Right takes you across the valley where a fork at 2.7 miles (04) goes right to structures of the Mountain Top Mine (private property). Left is a closed road to the Humbolt Mine.

Return Trip: Return the way you came. Other trips in the area include Yankee Boy Basin, Trail #2, and Imogene Pass, Trail #4.

Services: Full services in Ouray. Camp in designated dispersed areas only on main road below start of trail (fee required).

Maps: Drake Map. Trails Illustrated Map #141. Uncompahgre National Forest. DeLorme Atlas & Gazetteer.

41

Road improvements on south side have made it safer.

Tunnel adds to fun of drive.

Dangerous mining debris at Tomboy Townsite.

Lonely cabin (keep out).

Clouds gather at the pass. Note SUV is parked next to historic lineman's shack.

Popular overlook on north side.

Wildflowers still present in early August.

42

Imogene Pass 4

Location: Between Telluride and Ouray.

Difficulty: Moderate. Do not take this trip lightly. The road is rocky, steep and narrow in places and passing can be dangerous. In the summer of 2004, an SUV rolled off the mountain while attempting to pass at a narrow spot. Tragically, several people were killed. Stock SUVs should have low-range gearing, 4WD, high clearance and skid plates. Experienced drivers only.

Features: Imogene Pass is the second highest drivable pass in Colorado. The drive is one of the most thrilling in the state. At Savage Basin, you'll pass through Tomboy Townsite, once one of most active mining towns in Colorado. Production lasted until 1927 so a great deal of mining debris is still scattered about. The townsite is private land and very dangerous so stay on main road and view it from a distance. The trail is blocked by snow until it is plowed, usually in early July. ATVs are permitted on north side of pass. On south side, San Juan County restricts unlicensed vehicles to forest roads only. ATVs can not travel on county roads that cross private property.

Time & Distance: 18 miles from Telluride to Ouray. Allow 4 to 5 hours.

To Get There: Although this trip can be driven in either direction, I find it easier starting in Telluride. This allows you to drive downhill on the steeper, rockier north side. Take the first part of the day to reach Telluride via Ophir Pass, Trail #6, or difficult Black Bear Pass, Trail #5.

In Telluride, find Oak Street on the north side of town. It does not intersect with Colorado (Main Street) so it must be accessed from Aspen or Fir Streets. (See map detail on page 45.) Tomboy Road goes to the right at the very end of Oak after Gregory.

Trail Description: Set odometer to zero at start of Tomboy Road (01). The narrow road climbs above a residential area, then a series of switchbacks begins a long uphill climb. At 1.6 miles, there's a wide, shady spot where a group of vehicles can pull to the side and have lunch without blocking traffic. As you climb, you can look across the valley and see the switchbacks of Black Bear Pass, Trail #5. You continue to wind up the canyon walls with each turn bringing ever more breathtaking views. Around 4.5 miles, you approach Savage Basin and the Tomboy Townsite. The road winds back and forth along the north side of the townsite in a general southeast direction. You can choose routes of varying difficulty, but eventually all roads merge back into one before climbing toward the pass.

As you pass through the townsite, the need for high-clearance, four-wheel drive becomes apparent. Often snow remains above this area. With the exception of a few muddy spots, road traction remains good even in the wettest weather. At 6.8 miles (02), you reach the top of the pass and the line-man's shack. Temperatures are very brisk at this elevation, even on the warmest summer day. About a quarter mile past the summit, a short side road goes right uphill to a popular overlook. The steepest and roughest part of the trail continues to the left after the overlook. Vehicles with minimal ground clearance may scrape bottom. Choose a route best suited for your vehicle. All roads merge back together and by 8.0 miles you descend steeply on a narrow, rocky shelf road. Allow any uphill traffic to pass before you descend. Passing along this stretch is very dangerous. After crossing this narrow section, you can pull over to the left at a dramatic overlook. Small children and pets should be left in the car because a sheer cliff is nearby.

Past the overlook, the road winds downhill into beautiful Imogene Basin and crosses Imogene Creek several times. A bridge at 9.6 miles (03) is no longer in service. Find a spot to cross the creek and bear left downhill. (Richmond Basin is right.) You'll cross the creek again as you continue downhill. (Note waterfalls on both sides of road.) Bear left at a fork at 10.7 miles (04). You wind through the woods over rocky terrain with intermittent views of Camp Bird Mine on the right. Bear right alongside a bridge and cross the creek one last time before reaching Camp Bird Road at 11.9 miles (05). Left goes to Governor and Yankee Boy Basins. Right connects to Hwy. 550 in another 6.1 miles.

Return Trip: Left on Hwy. 550 takes you immediately into Ouray. North of Ouray at Ridgway, follow paved Hwy. 62 west to Placerville. From there, Hwy. 145 heads southeast back to Telluride.

Reverse Directions: Follow directions for Yankee Boy Basin, Trail #2. *Reset odometer* and turn left off Camp Bird Road at 6.1 miles (05) following sign for Imogene Pass. Stay right uphill at 1.2 miles (04). At 2.3 miles (03), a road goes straight toward Richmond Basin. Bear right and cross Imogene Creek. (The bridge here is no longer in service.) The pass is reached at 5.1 miles (02). Continue over the pass through Savage Basin and follow the well-defined road into Telluride reached at 11.9 miles (01).

Services: Full services in Ouray and Telluride. No toilets along route.

Other Activities: Telluride is a fantastic town to visit in the summer, offering many hiking trails and numerous other activities. Stop at the Visitors Center on the west end of town for information. It's open all year.

Maps: Drake Map. Uncompahgre National Forest. Trails Illustrated Silverton, Ouray #141. DeLorme Atlas and Gazetteer.

44

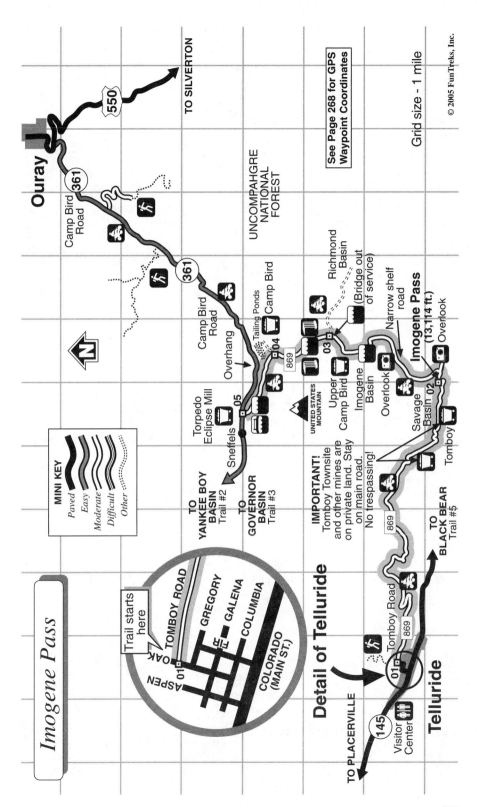

Imogene Pass

MINI KEY
Paved
Easy
Moderate
Difficult
Other

N

Ouray

550

TO SILVERTON

361

Camp Bird Road

361

Camp Bird Road

Overhang

Torpedo
Eclipse Mill

Sneffels

05

Tailing Ponds

Camp Bird

704

869

UNCOMPAHGRE
NATIONAL
FOREST

Richmond
Basin

(Bridge out
of service)

03

Upper
Camp Bird

Imogene
Basin

Narrow shelf
road

Imogene Pass
(13,114 ft.)

Overlook

Overlook

Savage
Basin

02

Overlook

Tomboy

UNITED STATES
MOUNTAIN

TO
YANKEE BOY
BASIN
Trail #2

TO
GOVERNOR
BASIN
Trail #3

IMPORTANT!
Tomboy Townsite
and other mines are
on private land. Stay
on main road.
No trespassing!

869

TO
BLACK BEAR
Trail #5

Tomboy Road

869

Detail of Telluride

TOMBOY ROAD

Trail starts
here

OAK

ASPEN

01

GREGORY

GALENA

COLUMBIA

FIR

COLORADO
(MAIN ST.)

TO PLACERVILLE

145

Visitor
Center

Telluride

01

Tomboy Road

869

See Page 268 for GPS
Waypoint Coordinates

Grid size - 1 mile

© 2005 FunTreks, Inc.

45

Trail is dangerous and not for inexperienced drivers.

View of east side.

Four-wheel-drive club gathers at Black Bear Pass.

Switchbacks, Bridal Veil Falls.

Backing required to make tight turns.

Black Bear Pass ◆5◆

Location: South of Ouray between Red Mountain Pass and Telluride.

Difficulty: Difficult. Most of the trail is easy to moderate. The difficult rating is based on a mile-long stretch of dangerous switchbacks above Bridal Veil Falls. (One way, downhill only.) Hardly a summer passes without some kind of accident. The latest accident occurred in July of 2004. A couple died when their Jeep went off the road and plummeted about 900 ft.

    Your vehicle must have low-range 4WD, good tires, good brakes and an excellent emergency brake. In addition, it must have excellent articulation or a differential locker. Without these last two features, your tires may come off the ground when you back up to make the tight turns. This situation could lead to ultimate terror as you become stuck at a point when you are literally hanging over the edge. **If you do not understand this paragraph, stay off this trail!** (Both Grand Cherokees pictured have modified suspensions.)

Features: Incredible views from high above Red Mountain Pass and Telluride. Close-up views of historic mines and dramatic waterfalls. Pass by the top and bottom of spectacular Bridal Veil Falls. This road is closed November through May 1st. ATVs are allowed, but remember, if you go down the one-way switchbacks, you can't go back up. A pick-up vehicle would have to be waiting at the bottom.

Time & Distance: It is about 12 miles from the start at U.S. 550 to the edge of Telluride. Allow 2 to 3 hours.

To Get There: Head south from Ouray on U.S. 550 about 13 miles. Turn right on well-marked Black Bear Road just after the summit of Red Mountain Pass, near mile marker 80.

Trail Description: Reset odometer to zero as you turn right off 550. The road starts climbing quickly, so shift immediately into four-wheel drive low. Bear right at 1.0 miles. Subsequent forks eventually come back to the main trail. There are a few steep, narrow, rocky sections as you quickly climb above timberline. Views of the highway below are impressive. At 2.3 miles it begins to level out as you cross a flatter, more barren area. Watch for heavy equipment at all times because this area is still an active mining area. Bear left at 2.9 miles (02) to stay on the main trail. Right is illegal shortcut. Continue uphill after the two roads come back together. Generally, stay left until you reach the top of the ridge at approximately 3.2 miles (03). This is Black Bear Pass. If you get too far right, you'll climb the ridge and miss the point where the road descends over the other side.

Reset your odometer as you begin your descent from the pass. After you cross the ridge, the road turns to the right as it starts down. From this point, the road is one-way downhill all the way to Bridal Veil Falls. The entire valley opens up into view and is quite impressive. At 1.7 miles, a road coming up from Ingram Lake joins on the left. You continue straight. Stay left where a closed road goes right to Black Bear Mine and begin your descent toward Telluride. By 2.4 miles, the road begins to split, but all ways lead to the bottom. Pick the best line for your vehicle.

At 3.3 miles (04), you encounter perhaps the scariest spot on the trail. A road of loose shale seems to fall off the mountain (top photo, page 46). Before you descend, make sure your tires are not over inflated and that you are in low-range 4WD. The road descends past Ingram Falls and several collapsed mine buildings. The switchbacks are extremely narrow and tight. You may have to back up several times to make the turns.

At 4.3 miles, you reach the powerhouse for Bridal Veil Falls. Turn right here where 2-way traffic begins. There is no one correct way to get to the bottom. I went left at 4.9, right at 5.8 and 6.6, and left at 6.7. The Pandora Mine is reached at 6.9 miles (05). From here, licensed vehicles can continue on the paved road into Telluride.

Return Trip: To get back to Ouray on a paved road: Take Rt. 145 to Placerville, 62 to Ridgway, and 550 to Ouray. This is a relaxing and scenic 50-mile drive. You can also return via Imogene Pass, Trail #4, Ophir Pass, Trail #6, or Last Dollar Road, Trail #1.

Services: Full services in Ouray and Telluride.

Other Activities: Telluride has more activities in the summer than in the winter. There are hiking and mountain biking trails in every direction. Stop in at the Visitors Center at the west end of town for a complete list of trails and activities. The center is open all year long.

Maps: Drake Map. Uncompahgre National Forest. Trails Illustrated Silverton, Ouray #141. DeLorme Atlas and Gazetteer.

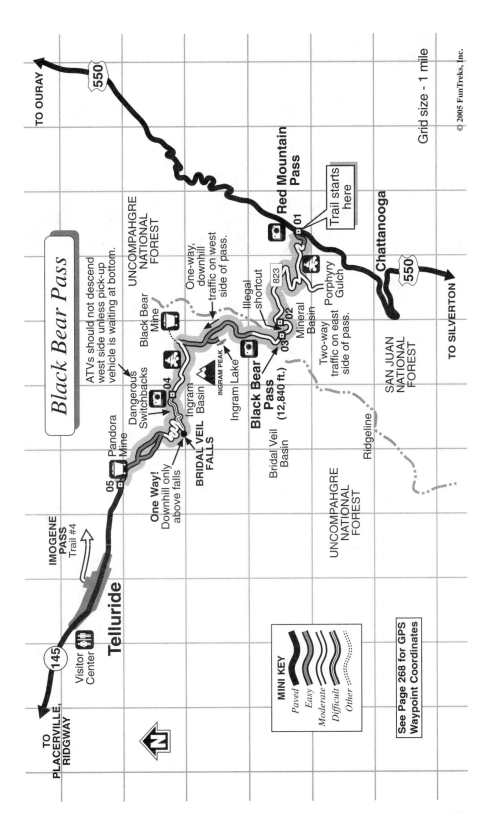

Black Bear Pass

ATVs should not descend west side unless pick-up vehicle is waiting at bottom.

TO OURAY

550

UNCOMPAHGRE NATIONAL FOREST

Black Bear Mine

One-way, downhill traffic on west side of pass.

Dangerous Switchbacks

04

Illegal shortcut

823

Red Mountain Pass

01 — Trail starts here

Chattanooga

02

INGRAM PEAK

Ingram Lake

Ingram Basin

03

Mineral Basin

Porphyry Gulch

Pandora Mine

05

One Way! Downhill only above falls

BRIDAL VEIL FALLS

Black Bear Pass (12,840 ft.)

Two-way traffic on east side of pass.

550

IMOGENE PASS Trail #4

Telluride

Visitor Center

Bridal Veil Basin

SAN JUAN NATIONAL FOREST

TO SILVERTON

145

TO PLACERVILLE, RIDGWAY

N

UNCOMPAHGRE NATIONAL FOREST

Ridgeline

MINI KEY

Paved
Easy
Moderate
Difficult
Other

See Page 268 for GPS Waypoint Coordinates

Grid size - 1 mile

© 2005 FunTreks, Inc.

49

Moderate stretch of road on west side of Ophir Pass. Note columbines in foreground.

Small residential community of Ophir. Ophir Pass Road can be seen in distance.

Passing is tight in a few places.

Camp and fish at Alta Lakes.

Ophir Pass, Alta Lakes 6

Location: Ophir Pass is between Silverton and Telluride. Alta Lakes is south of Telluride, east of Hwy. 145 and north of Ophir.

Difficulty: Moderate. Applies to one section of narrow, rocky shelf road on the west side of Ophir Pass. Everything else is easy, including all of Alta Lakes Road. Passing an oncoming vehicle along the narrow shelf road west of Ophir Pass can be a little scary for a novice driver. Wait for traffic to clear before starting across. Snowplows usually clear the road in June.

Features: Ophir Pass is a convenient and scenic way to get from Silverton to Telluride. Seasonal wildflowers grow thick at higher elevations. Pass through ghost town of Alta on way to great camping, picnicking and fishing in beautiful mountain setting of Alta Lakes. Take insect repellent. ATVs are allowed on Ophir Pass Road east of the town of Ophir. You can not ride unlicensed vehicles through town. ATVs are also allowed on the primary Alta Lakes Road. Side roads are closed to all vehicles.

Time & Distance: Ophir Pass is about 10 miles from U.S. 550 to 145 and takes less than 2 hours. Alta Lakes is 4.4 miles one way and takes 1/2 hour.

To Get There: Ophir Pass: Head north from Silverton on U.S. 550 about 4.8 miles. Turn left on C.R. 8 near mile marker 75. *Alta Lakes:* After completing Ophir Pass going east to west, head north on Hwy. 145 about 2 miles and turn right at sign for Alta Lakes Road. To reach Alta Lakes from Telluride, turn south on Hwy. 145 west of Telluride and go 5.3 miles.

Trail Description: Ophir Pass: Reset odometer to zero as you turn west onto CR 8 (01). Head downhill into a small valley crossing Mineral Creek and immediately begin climbing up the other side. C.R. 8 is a well-graded road all the way to the pass reached at 4.2 miles (02).

As you start down the other side, there are spectacular views of the valley below. I found a huge field of columbines (Colorado's state flower) on the south side of the road just west of the pass. After the first switchback to the right, the road narrows and passing becomes difficult. Wait until the road is clear before continuing. Remember, uphill traffic has the right-of-way.

After coming down off this rocky section, you pass through a section of tall aspen trees, which makes this trip particularly dramatic in the fall. There are several shallow stream crossings that add to the enjoyment. Watch for a series of beaver ponds on the left before reaching the town of Ophir, a small, growing residential community. Follow signs as the road zigzags through town. After Ophir, the road is well graded until you reach highway 145 at 10.1 miles (03). Turn right and go 1.9 miles to the start of Alta Lakes Road on the right.

Trail Description, Alta Lakes: *Reset odometer as you turn east on Alta Lakes Road* (04). Follow well-marked C.R. 64F. At 3.6 miles, the road swings right uphill and winds through remains of the old mining town of Alta. All buildings are privately owned, so observe from a distance. Stay left at 4.2 miles at sign for Gold King Basin. At 4. 4 miles (05) you reach a pit toilet next to a lake. Left or right takes you around the lake to great camping and picnic spots. Explore other roads in the area that dead end at two other lakes.

Return Trip: From start of Alta Lakes Road (04), take Hwy. 145 north 5.3 miles to a major T intersection. Right goes into Telluride where you can take Imogene Pass, Trail #4, to Ouray. Left at T intersection takes you to Placerville on Hwy. 145 where you can take Hwy. 62 back to Ridgway and 550 to Ouray. The quickest way back to Silverton is to retrace your route back over Ophir Pass.

Services: Full services in Silverton and Telluride. Primitive pit toilet at Alta Lakes. Camping at Alta Lakes is limited to 7 days within a 30-day period.

Other Activities: Hiking, mountain biking, camping, and fishing remain the most popular summertime activities. Both Telluride and Silverton have large and helpful visitor centers.

Historical Highlights: Built in 1891, Ophir Pass was originally a toll road between Silverton and Telluride. The town of Ophir was a supply town for hundreds of mines in the area. Today it is a quaint residential community.

Alta was once a bustling mining town serving the Alta-Gold King area from 1877 to 1948 when the mill was destroyed by fire. Over the years, vandals have destroyed many of the remaining buildings. This was one of the first towns where alternating electrical current was used for power. In 1891, electricity was transmitted from the Ames Power Plant on the San Miguel River some distance away.

Maps: Drake Map. Uncompahgre National Forest. Trails Illustrated Silverton, Ouray #141. DeLorme Atlas & Gazetteer.

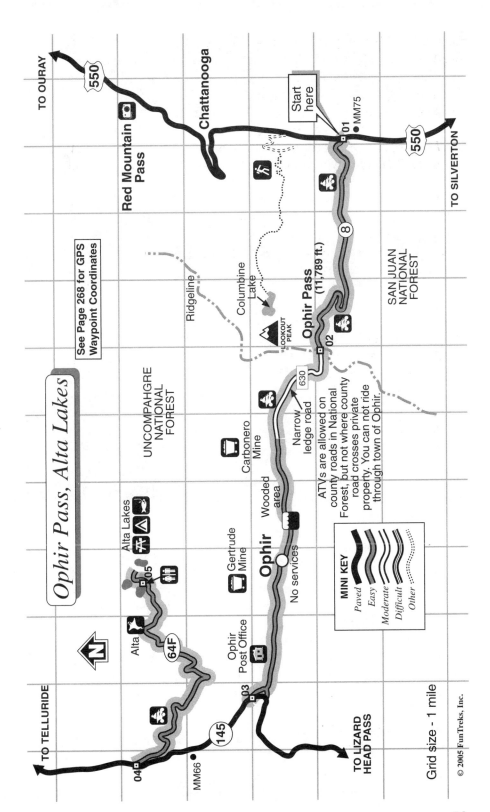

Ophir Pass, Alta Lakes

TO OURAY

550

Red Mountain Pass

Chattanooga

Start here

MM75

01

550

TO SILVERTON

8

Ophir Pass (11,789 ft.)

SAN JUAN NATIONAL FOREST

See Page 268 for GPS Waypoint Coordinates

Ridgeline

Columbine Lake

LOOKOUT PEAK

02

630

UNCOMPAHGRE NATIONAL FOREST

Carbonero Mine

Narrow ledge road

ATVs are allowed on county roads in National Forest, but not where county road crosses private property. You can not ride through town of Ophir.

Alta Lakes

05

Alta

64F

Gertrude Mine

Ophir

Wooded area

No services

Ophir Post Office

03

145

MM66

04

TO LIZARD HEAD PASS

TO TELLURIDE

N

MINI KEY
Paved
Easy
Moderate
Difficult
Other

Grid size - 1 mile

© 2005 FunTreks, Inc.

53

Plenty of room to dry camp at various points along South Mineral Creek.

South Mineral Creek.

Easy trip for stock SUVs.

Upper switchbacks are narrow but manageable.

Clear Lake

See Page 268 for GPS
Waypoint Coordinates

TO OURAY

550

N

Start
here

Clear Lake 03 P

SAN JUAN
NATIONAL
FOREST

01

Island Lake

815

7

P

Ice Lake

12

TO SILVERTON

Lower Ice
Lake Basin

02 585

P

BEAR MTN.

MINI KEY

Great waterfalls, walk
upstream 1/4 mile
from campground.

South Mineral
Campground

585

Paved
Easy
Moderate
Difficult
Other

To Bandora Mine
& Silverton Trail

Grid size - 1 mile

© 2005 FunTreks, Inc.

Clear Lake 7

Location: West of Silverton.

Difficulty: Easy. Steep and narrow at the top but suitable for any high-clearance stock SUV.

Features: Beautiful valley close to Silverton offers great hiking, biking and fishing. Large open campgrounds along South Mineral Creek suitable for motorhomes. Spectacular climb to high mountain lake with beautiful wildflowers. Great area to camp and ride ATVs on marked forest roads.

Time & Distance: 8.1 miles from U.S. 550 to Clear Lake. Allow about an hour one way.

To Get There: Head north from Silverton on U.S. 550 about 2 miles. Turn left on well marked County Road 7.

Trail Description: Reset odometer as you turn off U.S. 550 (01). Head west on C.R. 7 passing several camping areas along South Mineral Creek. Turn right uphill at 3.7 miles (02) at sign for Clear Lake 4WD Road, C.R. 12 (F.S. 815). The first 3 miles of this road do not require 4-wheel drive. Once the road narrows and starts winding up the mountain, you'll want to shift into 4WD low range for power and security. This part of the trip may be intimidating to a novice driver, but the drive is quite easy. At 7.8 miles, you reach a flat area and a small lake. Bear right around this lake to reach larger Clear Lake at 8.1 miles (03). Stay in designated parking area at lake. Do not drive vehicles into grassy areas around lake.

Return Trip: Go back the way you came.

Services: In Silverton and Ouray. Several modern vault toilets at designated campgrounds.

Other Activities: Silverton is a must-see town. Residents here take real pride in their community. It has a rich mining history with many great stores and restaurants. Visit the museum or take a ride to Durango on the famous "Durango and Silverton Railroad."

Maps: Drake Map. Uncompahgre National Forest. San Juan National Forest. Trails Illustrated Silverton, Ouray #141. DeLorme Atlas & Gazetteer.

Sign at start.

Mountain goat on road.

Turn right here for Poughkeepsie Gulch. Engineer Pass is uphill.

Waterfall at turn for Poughkeepsie Gulch.

San Juan Chief Mill. Mineral Point in distance.

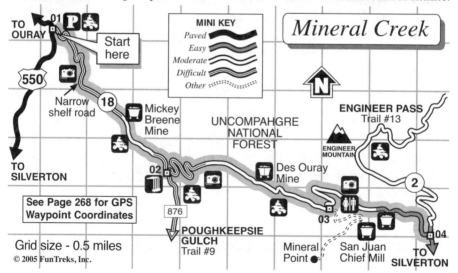

Mineral Creek

MINI KEY
Paved
Easy
Moderate
Difficult
Other

N

TO OURAY
01 P

Start here

550

Narrow shelf road
18

Mickey Breene Mine

UNCOMPAHGRE NATIONAL FOREST

ENGINEER PASS
Trail #13

ENGINEER MOUNTAIN

TO SILVERTON

02

Des Ouray Mine

2

876

See Page 268 for GPS Waypoint Coordinates

POUGHKEEPSIE GULCH
Trail #9

03

Mineral Point

San Juan Chief Mill

04

TO SILVERTON

Grid size - 0.5 miles

© 2005 FunTreks, Inc.

56

Mineral Creek ◆8◆

Location: South of Ouray. East of U.S. Highway 550.

Difficulty: Difficult. Rocky and steep in places, especially at the beginning. Stock 4WD SUVs can do it with careful tire placement and patience. One stretch of narrow ledge road. High clearance and skid plates recommended.

Features: Quickest but most difficult way to reach Engineer Pass, Trail #13 (part of Alpine Loop), from Ouray. Road climbs up scenic narrow canyon. Accesses Poughkeepsie Gulch and San Juan Chief Mill. Seasonal wildflowers at higher elevations. Hidden waterfall by road. ATV staging area at start.

Time & Distance: Total of 7.2 miles from U.S. 550 to Engineer Pass Road (C.R. 2). Allow 1-1/2 to 2 hours one way.

To Get There: Head south on U.S. 550 from Beaumont Hotel in Ouray 3.8 miles and turn left at sign for Alpine Loop and Engineer Pass (C.R. 18).

Trail Description: Reset odometer as you turn off Hwy. 550 (01). Follow wide but rocky road uphill. Before first mile, the road goes down to one lane and crosses a narrow ledge across a sheer rock face. Check ahead because passing here is impossible. Mickey Breene Mine on left at 1.6. Stay left uphill over large rock outcrop at 2.4 miles (02). Poughkeepsie Gulch goes right here. (To see dramatic waterfall, pictured at left, climb downhill southwest of sign for Poughkeepsie Gulch. Falls are only about 70 feet away but are totally hidden.) Bear left uphill on switchbacks at 5.2 miles (03). A road goes right here to San Juan Chief Mill near Mineral Point. (I did not redrive this road, but it used to be very rocky.) Toilet on right at 6.0 miles at overlook for Mineral Point. Road flattens out before intersecting with C.R. 2 (04) to Engineer Pass, Trail #13.

Return Trip: Left on C.R. 2 goes uphill over Engineer Pass to Lake City. Right takes you downhill past Animas Forks and west end of Cinnamon Pass Road. Connect to Silverton on paved road south of Animas Forks.

Services: Full services in Ouray, Silverton and Lake City. Vault toilet at overlook for Mineral Point.

Maps: Drake Map. Uncompahgre National Forest. San Juan National Forest. Trails Illustrated Silverton, Ouray #141. DeLorme Atlas & Gazetteer.

Looking down Poughkeepsie Gulch from Hurricane Pass. Lake Como in foreground.

One of several rocky ledges to climb.

Lower part of trail.

Wildflowers remain in late August.

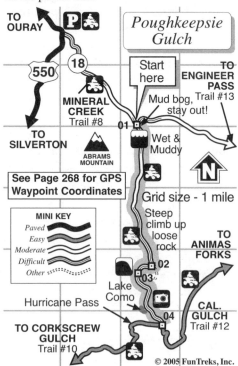

Poughkeepsie Gulch

TO OURAY

550

18

MINERAL CREEK
Trail #8

TO SILVERTON

ABRAMS MOUNTAIN

Start here

Mud bog, stay out!

TO ENGINEER PASS

Trail #13

Wet & Muddy

N

Grid size - 1 mile

See Page 268 for GPS Waypoint Coordinates

MINI KEY
Paved
Easy
Moderate
Difficult
Other

01

Steep climb up loose rock

TO ANIMAS FORKS

02

03

Lake Como

Hurricane Pass

04

CAL. GULCH
Trail #12

TO CORKSCREW GULCH
Trail #10

© 2005 FunTreks, Inc.

Poughkeepsie Gulch ◆ 9

Location: South of Ouray. East of U.S. Highway 550.

Difficulty: Difficult. Uphill direction described here. Easier going downhill. Can be muddy at the bottom during wet periods. One long, steep climb of loose rock is challenging without lockers. Other rocky climbs may require winching. Not recommended for stock SUVs going uphill.

Features: Scenic valley offers variety of challenges for hard-core enthusiast. Snow is not plowed, so trail opens later in the season. Fun but difficult trail for ATVs. Stay off trail during wet periods.

Time & Distance: Trail is only 4.1 miles long and can be done in an hour if all goes well. Allow an extra half hour to reach start from U.S. 550.

To Get There: Head south on U.S. 550 from Beaumont Hotel in Ouray 3.8 miles and turn left at sign for Alpine Loop and Engineer Pass (C.R. 18). Follow Mineral Creek, Trail #8, uphill 2.4 miles and turn right at sign for Poughkeepsie Gulch. (Stay out of mud bog at start of trail.)

Trail Description: Reset odometer as you turn right off Mineral Creek (01). Trail weaves through dark, wet wooded area then begins to climb. Stay right at 1.5 miles to avoid illegal shortcut to left. Climb a long, steep hill of loose rock. An important turn at 2.6 miles (02) requires that you bear right and head west for a short distance. If you miss this turn, the road dead ends up a steep valley. The road gets rougher as it turns south again and begins a series of tall rock ledges. A rocky play area at 3.0 miles (03) is a good place to test your rock climbing skills. The road splits frequently but remerges as you continue uphill. Lake Como, at 3.7 miles, is a great place for lunch on a sunny day. Select from various routes heading southeast until you intersect with California Gulch, Trail #12, at 4.1 miles (04).

Return Trip: Turn right to return to Ouray via Corkscrew Gulch, Trail #10 (quickest way). Left takes you over California Pass and down into California Gulch to Animas Forks and eventually Silverton.

Services: Full services in Ouray and Silverton. Toilets at Animas Forks and at top of Corkscrew Gulch. Nothing on Poughkeepsie.

Maps: Drake Map. Uncompahgre N. F. San Juan N. F. Trails Illustrated Silverton, Ouray #141. DeLorme Atlas & Gazetteer.

59

County Roads 10 and 11 converge at upper starting point of Corkscrew Gulch.

Start of County Road 11 at top of trail.

Descending the switchbacks.

One of several tight turns down the switchbacks.

Corkscrew Gulch 🔟

Location: North of Silverton and Gladstone. South of Ouray.

Difficulty: Easy. The road is wide and graded most of the way; however, one section of narrower switchbacks may be intimidating to a novice driver. The lower section of the trail has a great deal of clay in the soil which makes it very slippery when wet. Stay off the trail during wet periods.

Features: This scenic trail cuts through the heart of old mining country as it winds between Red Mountain No. 1 and No. 2. You may encounter large trucks on the lower half of the route because the area is still actively logged. ATVs are allowed on this trail and staging is permitted at the north end of the trail just off U.S. 550. You can also park and enter the area from the Gladstone end if you are coming from Silverton via C.R. 110. There are many legal side roads to explore between Gladstone and Hurricane Pass.

Time & Distance: About 5 miles in length. Allow a minimum of one hour in good weather.

To Get There:

Starting at the Top: If you are using this trail to exit Poughkeepsie Gulch, Trail #9, or California Gulch, Trail #12, head west to Hurricane Pass. Follow the best defined road downhill 1.8 miles and turn right on County Road 11 (01). From Silverton, take C.R. 110 north to Gladstone. Turn left uphill on well-marked C.R.10. After approximately 1.5 miles, turn left on C.R.11.

Starting at the bottom: From the Beaumont Hotel in Ouray, head south 7.8 miles on U.S. 550 and turn left at what appears to be a dam (04). (This is actually a containment wall for a mining area that is being reclaimed.) You'll also see a parking area on the left.

Trail Description:

Starting at the Top: Set odometer to zero at start (01). Follow C.R. 11 uphill. Stay left at 0.2 where a lesser road goes right. There's a modern vault toilet at 0.3. Stay right at 1.1 miles (02) where a road goes left uphill. The main road drops downhill steeply on long, narrow switchbacks. At the bottom, stay right past another toilet at 2.1 miles. Bear left at 3.4 miles (03) where a lesser road goes right. Continue straight at 3.8. The road drops downhill and bends left around the reclaimed mining area. Ignore roads that branch off to the right. You'll pass through a wooded area where people like to camp. You'll head northwest along the dam-like structure before reaching U.S. 550 at 4.9 miles (04). Turn right for Ouray or left for Silverton.

     Starting at the Bottom: *Set odometer to zero as you turn southeast off U.S. 550* (04). Follow a wide road along the dam-like structure past a parking area and into the woods. Ignore roads that go left. At 0.2 miles, turn right around the corner of the tailings area. Bear left uphill when the road forks again. Continue uphill, ignoring lesser roads closed to motor vehicles. At 1.5 miles (03) bear right where a lesser road goes left. Bear to the left when you reach a toilet at 2.8 miles and climb the mountain on long, narrow switchbacks. Continue straight at 3.8 miles (02) where a road goes right uphill. Go by another toilet at 4.6 then bear right at 4.7. C.R.10 is reached at 4.9 miles (01). Right takes you downhill to Gladstone and Silverton. Left takes you uphill to Hurricane Pass. Beyond the pass lies California Gulch, Trail #12, and Poughkeepsie Gulch, Trail #9.

Services: Full services in Silverton and Ouray. Two modern vault toilets along trail.

Other Activities: There are a few hiking trails off the lower section of Corkscrew, but the primary activity in this area is four-wheeling.

Historical Highlights: Just south of where Corkscrew Gulch leaves U.S. 550, several roads wind around in the trees. Here and there, a building can be found. This is all that remains of the once important mining town of Ironton. In 1890, the town provided supplies for many rich mines in the area and had a population of over 300. The town had its own water system, an electric plant, fire department and post office. The town managed to survive long after the silver market collapsed around the turn of the century. People actually lived in Ironton until the 1960s. The lumber from the buildings was carted off over the years, so not much remains.

Maps: Drake Map. Uncompahgre National Forest. Trails Illustrated Silverton, Ouray #141. DeLorme Atlas & Gazetteer.

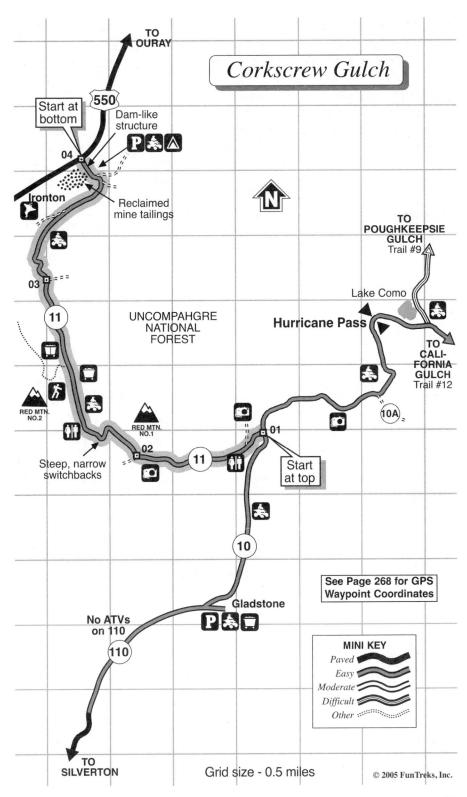

TO
OURAY

Corkscrew Gulch

550

Start at
bottom

Dam-like
structure

P

04

Ironton

Reclaimed
mine tailings

N

TO
POUGHKEEPSIE
GULCH
Trail #9

03

Lake Como

11

Hurricane Pass

UNCOMPAHGRE
NATIONAL
FOREST

TO
CALI-
FORNIA
GULCH
Trail #12

10A

RED MTN.
NO.2

RED MTN.
NO.1

01

02

11

Steep, narrow
switchbacks

Start
at top

10

See Page 268 for GPS
Waypoint Coordinates

Gladstone

No ATVs
on 110

P

110

MINI KEY

Paved
Easy
Moderate
Difficult
Other

TO
SILVERTON

Grid size - 0.5 miles

© 2005 FunTreks, Inc.

63

Shaft-house of Yankee Girl Mine.   National Bell Mine. (Road to left of picture exits early.)

The roads are SUV friendly and fun to drive.   Two-track road in places.

Longfellow Mine.   View of Hwy. 550 at Chattanooga.

Road south of U.S. Basin traverses 12,000-ft. ridge. Great views all the way.

Red Mountain Mining Area ⑪

Location: East of U.S. Highway 550 and Red Mountain Pass between Ouray and Silverton.

Difficulty: Easy. A fun, meandering road covering a variety of terrain from graded gravel to narrow two-track. Suitable for all 4x4 SUVs with moderate ground clearance. Low-range gearing helpful on some of the steeper grades at higher elevations. Do not drive this route during wet periods.

Features: The northern portion of this route takes you on a tour of the Red Mountain mining district and a townsite once known as Guston. Some of the road follows an old grade of the Silverton Railroad. The southern portion continues south on U.S. Basin Road and provides impressive high views of U.S. 550 and all surrounding mountains. Pick a clear day for this trip. ATVs are allowed on entire trail but southern half of trail is better suited for unlicensed vehicles. View mines from a distance.

Time & Distance: The upper portion measures about 3 miles; the lower portion about 6 miles. Allow about 3 hours.

To Get There: From the Beaumont Hotel in Ouray, head south 10.0 miles on U.S. 550. Turn left 0.8 miles south of mile post 84 on marked C.R. 31 at the end of a tight switchback. The southern exit point is 5.5 miles north of Silverton and 0.7 miles north of the turn for Ophir Pass, Trail #6.

Trail Description: Reset odometer at the start of C.R. 31 (01). The road winds downhill and crosses a modern steel bridge and then a smaller wooden bridge. Swing left after the wooden bridge and climb uphill. You'll pass several interesting mine structures on the left at 0.6 miles. Bear right where a closed road goes left at 0.9. When you reach the shaft house for the Yankee Girl Mine at 1.1 miles, continue straight then follow the road as it swings left then right up a switchback. The road heads south and gets a bit rougher. Watch carefully for the National Bell Mine on the right at 2.1 miles (02). (See top, right photo opposite page.) At this point, turn left and climb over a small ridge, then immediately turn right heading south again. If you miss this little jog, you'll end up exiting too soon and going back out to U.S. 550. Stay right at 2.3 miles. You'll soon exit the woods and pass a pond on the left. Beyond the pond is the Longfellow Mine (pictured at left). Just past the mine, turn right to reach U.S. 550 at 3.0 miles (03). Right on 550 goes back to Ouray. To continue on the second half of this trip, turn left on 550, then, immediately, left again on marked C.R. 14.

Reset your odometer as you start C.R. 14. Go a few hundred feet and turn right following sign for U.S. Basin Forest Road 825 (04). Head south ignoring a road that goes right back out to 550. After the road swings east, turn right at 0.6 miles (05). Continue south past what appears to be a private residence. At 1.0 miles, jog left then right around a rental cabin. The road gets rougher as you drop down and cross a small creek at 1.3 miles. The valley uphill to your left is U.S. Basin. You may need low range to climb out of the creek. You continue to climb as the road winds uphill then begins a long traverse across a high ridge. From the ridge, you can see the big curve of U.S. 550 at Chattanooga.

At 3.0 miles, the road turns right and heads steeply downhill. At 3.8 miles (06), a lesser road forks to the left to some buildings above the Brooklyn Mine. Bear right dowhhill to continue through the mine. When I passed through, workers were in the process of reclaiming the land around the mine, but the road was not affected. Several more miles of wide, graded road continue downhill to U.S. 550 at 5.9 miles (07).

Return Trip: Turn left for Ophir Pass, Trail #6, and Silverton. Right takes you back over Red Mountain Pass to Ouray.

Services: Full services in Ouray and Silverton. No toilets along trail.

Historical Highlights: Don't miss an opportunity to see the Red Mountain Peaks at sunset. Their fluorescent red and yellow glow is unlike anything you've ever seen. To prospectors back in 1879, that glow was the promise of vast riches. Indeed, over the next two decades, fortunes were extracted from these mountains in the form of gold, silver, lead and copper. No less than six towns—Chattanooga, Red Mountain City, Guston, Hudson Town, Rogerville and Ironton—grew out of this promising valley. Fortunately, many important mine buildings from that golden era are still standing. They are surprisingly easy to reach if you know where to look.

To better understand the area, I highly recommend you pick up a copy of "Exploring the Historic San Juan Triangle" (formerly Mountain Mysteries) by P. David Smith. It's filled with great pictures and detailed history that will help you visualize what this area was like over 120 years ago.

Maps: Drake Map. Uncompahgre and San Juan National Forests. Trails Illustrated Silverton, Ouray #141. DeLorme Atlas & Gazetteer.

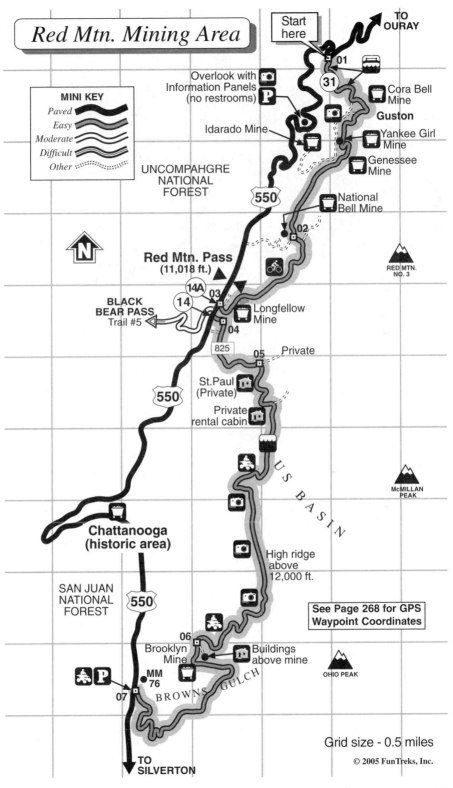

Red Mtn. Mining Area

MINI KEY
- Paved
- Easy
- Moderate
- Difficult
- Other

Start here

TO OURAY

01

31

Cora Bell Mine

Guston

Yankee Girl Mine

Genessee Mine

Overlook with Information Panels (no restrooms)

Idarado Mine

UNCOMPAHGRE NATIONAL FOREST

550

National Bell Mine

02

Red Mtn. Pass (11,018 ft.)

RED MTN. NO. 3

N

14A
14
03

BLACK BEAR PASS Trail #5

Longfellow Mine

04

825

05   Private

St. Paul (Private)

550

Private rental cabin

U S   B A S I N

McMILLAN PEAK

High ridge above 12,000 ft.

Chattanooga (historic area)

SAN JUAN NATIONAL FOREST

550

See Page 268 for GPS Waypoint Coordinates

06

Brooklyn Mine

Buildings above mine

OHIO PEAK

MM 76

07

B R O W N S   G U L C H

TO SILVERTON

Grid size - 0.5 miles

© 2005 FunTreks, Inc.

67

Summit of California Pass still has snow in late August.

East end of California Gulch.

Jeep club passes mill near Frisco Tunnel.

Duncan House at Animas Forks.

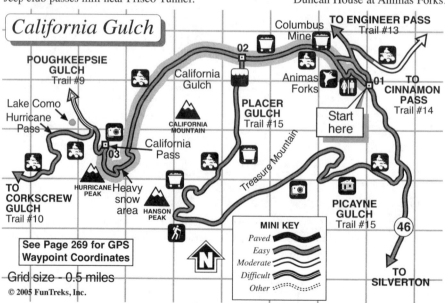

California Gulch

TO ENGINEER PASS
Trail #13

Columbus
Mine

POUGHKEEPSIE
GULCH
Trail #9

California
Gulch

02

Animas
Forks

01

TO
CINNAMON
PASS
Trail #14

Lake Como
Hurricane
Pass

PLACER
GULCH
Trail #15

Start
here

CALIFORNIA
MOUNTAIN

California
Pass

03

TO
CORKSCREW
GULCH
Trail #10

HURRICANE
PEAK

Heavy
snow
area

HANSON
PEAK

Treasure Mountain

PICAYNE
GULCH
Trail #15

46

See Page 269 for GPS
Waypoint Coordinates

N

MINI KEY
Paved
Easy
Moderate
Difficult
Other

TO
SILVERTON

Grid size - 0.5 miles

© 2005 FunTreks, Inc.

68

California Gulch ⑫

Location: Northeast of Silverton, west of Animas Forks.

Difficulty: Easy. Road is in good condition most of the summer. Heavy snow on east side of California Pass is usually plowed by late June.

Features: East end of trail starts at historic Animas Forks Ghost Town, gateway to the Alpine Loop. A remote, memorable drive with many well-preserved mine buildings. Awesome views. ATVs allowed.

Time & Distance: As described here it's 4.7 miles to California Pass. This portion can be done in less than an hour under dry conditions. Allow extra time if you go beyond California Pass.

To Get There: From northeast end of Silverton, bear right on C.R.2 (some maps still show this road as 110). Follow signs to Alpine Loop. Turn left when you see a restroom on the left at 11.4 miles.

Trail Description: Reset odometer when you turn left for Animas Forks (01). Climb uphill past second restroom and Animas Forks parking lot. Continue north a short distance before the trail heads west past a large mill. Continue straight at 1.8 miles (02) where Placer Gulch, Trail #15, goes left. The road swings south and meanders up a broad valley. After a couple of miles, a shelf road begins a steep westward climb towards the pass. You might find high walls of snow on each side of the road in early summer. The pass is reached at 4.7 miles (03).

Return Trip: You can return the way you came or continue west past California Pass. When you drop down the other side of the pass, difficult Poughkeepsie Gulch, Trail #9, goes downhill to the right. Left takes you uphill across a long shelf road to Hurricane Pass. Beyond is Corkscrew Gulch, Trail #10, Gladstone and Silverton.

Services: Full services Silverton. Toilets at Animas Forks.

Historical Highlights: Animas Forks was active between 1875 and the early 1920s. In 1885, its summer population reached a high of 450 people. The Silverton Northern Railroad reached the town in 1904 when the giant Gold Prince Mill was built. The mill lasted only six years before it was closed.

Maps: Drake Map. Trails Illustrated Silverton, Ouray #141. DeLorme Atlas.

69

SUV stopped at Engineer Pass on an overcast day.

BLM cabin below pass on east side.

Road follows Henson Creek.

Bonanza Empire Chief Mill.

Lingering snow in early August.

70

Engineer Pass

Location: Northeast of Silverton, southeast of Ouray and west of Lake City.

Difficulty: Moderate. Most of the route is easy, but there are still a few narrow, steep places on the west side of the pass that will get your attention. The trail climbs to an elevation of 12,800 ft. Caution should be used at all times especially in wet weather. Any 4x4 with moderate ground clearance and low-range gearing can do it.

Features: This trail, combined with Cinnamon Pass, Trail #14, constitutes the famous Alpine Loop. It is an exhilarating trip for drivers of all experience levels. There are many mines and points of historical interest along the route. The east side of the trail follows Henson Creek where you'll find excellent places to camp and fish. The entire route is open to ATVs. You'll find staging areas on the west, south and eastern entry points. Unlicensed vehicles must display an OHV permit and riders must possess a valid drivers license or vehicle operator's license. Ouray and San Juan Counties require proof of liability insurance for unlicensed vehicles.

Time & Distance: The portion described here is about 21 miles. Allow about 3 hours one way. Allow additional time to reach the start.

To Get There: There are three basic ways to reach the western starting point shown here:
From Ouray: First drive Mineral Creek, Trail #8. This route is officially marked as part of the Alpine Loop, but, it is the most difficult approach. Read Mineral Creek trail description carefully.
From Silverton: Head northeast 14.1 miles following signs for the Alpine Loop. You'll go by the road to Cinnamon Pass about 2 miles before the start of Engineer. This is the easiest way.
From Lake City: Drive over Cinnamon Pass, Trail #14, from east to west.

Trail Description: Reset your odometer to zero at the start (01). Head north on County Road 2 following signs to Engineer Pass. Bear left at 0.8 miles. Low-range gearing will give you the confidence you need to climb the intermittent steep sections. Stay right at 1.9 miles where a scenic overlook, called "Oh Point" goes to the left. The road wraps around the northern side of the mountain and descends gradually to Engineer Pass at 2.3 miles (02). Turn right at the pass and head downhill. Information panels are positioned along the route to explain points of interest.

Stop at 4.5 miles to examine the tiny cabin on the right maintained by the BLM for public use. It's a fun spot for the kids with a small stream and seasonal wildflowers. Don't confuse this with "Thoreau's Cabin" on the left at 4.7 miles. This is private property. Bear left at 5.2, 5.5 and 6.2 miles where roads go right. A primitive toilet was on the right at 6.4 miles. You'll pass Bonanza Empire Chief Mill and the Rose Lime Kiln before reaching Whitmore Falls at 9.7 miles. It's a short but very steep hike down to the falls but worth the effort if you have the time and strength. At 11.6 miles (03) you'll see historic Capitol City cabins on the left. North Henson Road goes left here to the Matterhorn Creek Hiking Trail. Continue straight at 15.6 miles (04) where Nellie Creek Trail goes left. This is an enjoyable moderate 4x4 route. Pass through a small town surrounding the Ute-Ulay Mine. At 20.7 miles the road is paved just before Second Street. Turn right on Second Street to reach State Hwy. 149 at 20.9 miles (05) in the center of Lake City.

Return Trip: For Gunnison, turn left at 149. To complete the second part of the Alpine Loop, Cinnamon Pass (Trail #14), turn right at Hwy. 149.

Reverse Directions: Reset odometer (05) and turn north on Second Street from Hwy. 149 in Lake City. Turn left after a 10th of mile and continue west after pavement ends. Follow signs for Alpine Loop. Continue straight past Nellie Creek Trailhead at 5.3 miles (04). Stay left at 9.3 miles (03) where North Henson Road goes right. Whitmore Falls on left at 11.2. Restroom on left at 14.5 miles. Stay right at 14.7, 15.4 and 15.7 miles. Climb to Engineer Pass reached at 18.6 miles (02). Turn left at pass following wide shelf road around mountain. Stay left at "Oh Point" and descend the mountain. Stay right at 20.1 before reaching intersection at 20.9 miles (01). Straight takes you downhill on C.R. 2 past Animas Forks and into Silverton. Right takes you down difficult Mineral Creek, Trail # 8, to U.S. 550 south of Ouray.

Services: Full services in Ouray, Lake City and Silverton. Several public toilets along the route.

Other Activities: Lake City is a quiet little town with quaint log cabins and old Victorian churches. There were several interesting restaurants along the main highway and a large RV park with full hookups. South of Lake City is the beautiful Lake San Cristobal, popular for fishing, boating, and camping. I saw signs for rental cabins around the lake.

Maps: Drake Map, Trails Illustrated Silverton, Ouray #141. DeLorme Atlas & Gazetteer.

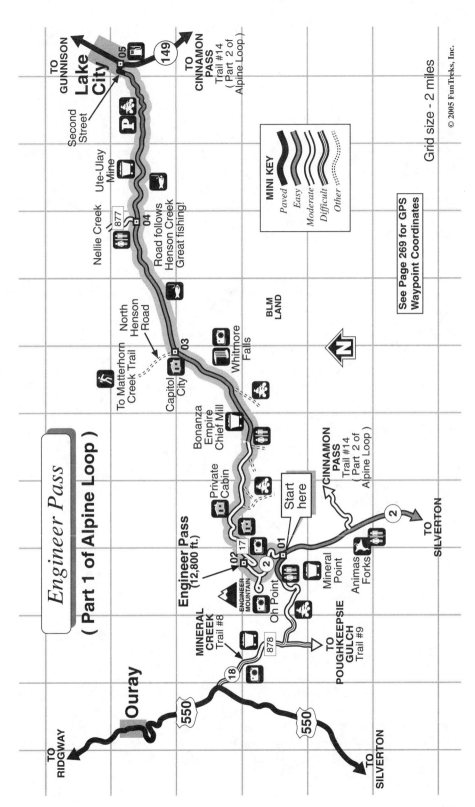

Engineer Pass
(Part 1 of Alpine Loop)

TO
GUNNISON

TO
CINNAMON
PASS
Trail #14
(Part 2 of
Alpine Loop)

Lake
City

149

05

Second
Street

P

Ute-Ulay
Mine

Nellie Creek

877

04

Road follows
Henson Creek
Great fishing!

North
Henson
Road

To Matterhorn
Creek Trail

03

Capitol
City

Bonanza
Empire
Chief Mill

Private
Cabin

Whitmore
Falls

BLM
LAND

MINI KEY

Paved
Easy
Moderate
Difficult
Other

Engineer Pass
(12,800 ft.)

02

17

01

Start
here

CINNAMON
PASS
Trail #14
(Part 2 of
Alpine Loop)

2

TO
SILVERTON

**MINERAL
CREEK**
Trail #8

ENGINEER
MOUNTAIN

Oh Point

2

Mineral
Point

Animas
Forks

878

TO
POUGHKEEPSIE
GULCH
Trail #9

18

Ouray

550

550

TO
RIDGWAY

TO
SILVERTON

N

See Page 269 for GPS
Waypoint Coordinates

Grid size - 2 miles

© 2005 FunTreks, Inc.

73

Looking east from Cinnamon Pass.

Climbing towards Cinnamon Pass. American Basin in background.

Start of County Road 36.   ATVs arrive at Carson Ghost Town. Note new metal roofs.

Cinnamon Pass, Wager Gulch 14

Location: Between Lake City and Silverton.

Difficulty: Moderate. Most of this trail is easy; however, the western half is steep and rocky in a few places. The side trip up Wager Gulch is slightly more difficult than Cinnamon Pass. All roads, when dry, are suitable for any stock 4x4 SUV with moderate ground clearance. The side trip up American Basin (shown on map) is borderline difficult.

Features: This trail, combined with Engineer Pass (Trail #13), constitutes the famous Alpine Loop. The western half of the trip passes many historic points and climbs to outstanding views. Side trip up Wager Gulch takes you to Carson Ghost Town. Cinnamon Pass Road also accesses beautiful American Basin, one of the best places in the area for wildflowers. There's a large staging area for ATVs soon after the pavement ends on C.R. 30. This is a popular ATV area. Unlicensed vehicles must display an OHV permit and riders must possess a valid driver's license or vehicle operator's license. Ouray and San Juan Counties require proof of liability insurance for unlicensed vehicles.

Time & Distance: As described here, about 24.7 miles. Allow 3 to 4 hours. The side trip up Wager Gulch is 3.7 miles one way and takes about half an hour each way. The entire Alpine Loop, counting Engineer Pass, is a long trip and takes a full day.

To Get There: Take State Hwy. 149 south 2.3 miles from Second Street in Lake City. Turn right on County Road 30 just after mile marker 70.

Trail Description: Reset odometer as you turn right on C.R. 30 (01) at large sign for the Alpine Loop. The paved road passes along the western side of beautiful Lake San Cristobal, Colorado's largest natural lake. Red Mountain Gulch Picnic Area with primitive toilet is on the right at 3.4 miles. Stay right where the pavement ends at 4.2 miles (02). An ATV staging area is reached at 5.3 miles. After passing the Williams Creek Forest Service Campground at 7.0, you reach the turn for Wager Gulch at 9.3 miles (03).

   Side trip up Wager Gulch: *Reset odometer and turn south on C.R. 36* (03). Continue straight through 4-way intersection at 0.1. Avoid private drives. Stay right uphill at 1.7. The road gets rougher and steeper as it enters Gunnison National Forest and becomes F.S 568. Bear left at 3.5 before arriving at Carson Ghost Town at 3.7 miles (04). If you wish, you can explore other roads above Carson. Return to start of C.R. 36.

75

Once you get back down to C.R. 30 (03), *reset odometer and turn left.* Go by a toilet on left, then Mill Creek Forest Service Campground. Bear right uphill at 3.0 miles (05) where road goes left to Sherman Townsite. As you continue uphill, an overlook on left at 4.0 miles has information boards describing Sherman as it once was. No buildings remain.

As you proceed towards Cinnamon Pass, the road becomes a narrow, scenic shelf road with embedded rock. The shelf road ends before Burrows Park at 7.1 miles. Here you'll find a toilet, parking and camping spots for various hiking trails. You'll pass a mine building on right at 8.7 before reaching the turn for American Basin at 10.8 miles (06). This is a fun side trip for those seeking more challenge. Stay right and continue to climb before reaching Cinnamon Pass at 13.0 miles. A good road descends west through broad valley before connecting to County Road 2 at 15.4 miles (07) just above Animas Forks.

Return Trip: Right goes uphill to Engineer Pass, Trail #13, and Mineral Creek, Trail #8. Left goes downhill to Silverton in 12.1 miles.

Services: Full services in Lake City and Silverton. Several public toilets along the route.

Reverse Directions: From east side of Silverton, bear right on C.R. 2 following signs to Alpine Loop. Stay right past the restroom at Animas Forks and make a sharp right up the road to Cinnamon Pass at 12.1 miles (07). Drop down other side, then stay left at 4.6 miles (06) where American Basin joins on right. Continue straight at 12.4 miles (05) where road to Sherman Townsite joins on right. Restroom on right at 14.2. Wager Gulch (C.R. 36) goes right at 15.4 miles (03). See previous page for description of Wager Gulch to Carson Ghost Town (04). *Reset odometer* (03) and proceed east on C.R. 30. Stay left at 5.1 (02) where pavement begins. Red Mountain Gulch Picnic Area with toilet is on left at 5.9 before reaching Hwy. 149 at 9.3 miles (01). Left 2.3 miles takes you into Lake City where a left turn on Second Street goes to Engineer Pass, Trail #13.

Historical Highlights: The town of Carson was established in 1882 with an operating post office between 1889 to 1903. The town served the St. Jacobs Mine and others in the area which produced gold, silver, lead, copper and zinc. The few buildings that remain are only a tiny part of the town that, at one time, was large enough to straddle the Continental Divide.

Maps: Trails Illustrated Silverton, Ouray #141. DeLorme Atlas & Gazetteer. The Drake Map shows only western half of the Alpine Loop.

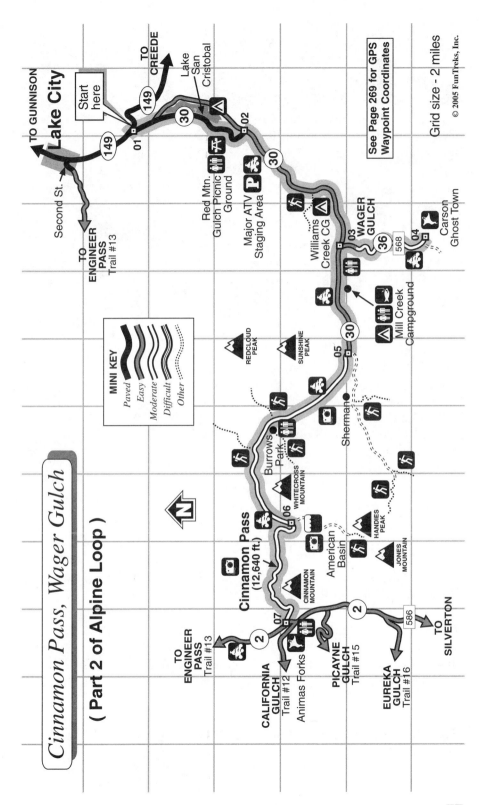

Cinnamon Pass, Wager Gulch

(Part 2 of Alpine Loop)

TO GUNNISON

Lake City

Start here

149

149

TO CREEDE

149

Lake San Cristobal

01

30

02

Second St.

TO ENGINEER PASS
Trail #13

Red Mtn. Gulch Picnic Ground

Major ATV Staging Area

30

Williams Creek CG

WAGER GULCH

03

36

568

04

Carson Ghost Town

Mill Creek Campground

30

05

Sherman

REDCLOUD PEAK

SUNSHINE PEAK

MINI KEY
Paved
Easy
Moderate
Difficult
Other

Burrows Park

WHITECROSS MOUNTAIN

06

N

Cinnamon Pass
(12,640 ft.)

American Basin

HANDIES PEAK

JONES MOUNTAIN

CINNAMON MOUNTAIN

07

2

2

586

TO SILVERTON

TO ENGINEER PASS
Trail #13

CALIFORNIA GULCH
Trail #12

Animas Forks

PICAYNE GULCH
Trail #15

EUREKA GULCH
Trail #16

See Page 269 for GPS Waypoint Coordinates

Grid size - 2 miles

© 2005 FunTreks, Inc.

77

Remaining buildings of Treasure Mtn. Gold Mining Co.

Trail below Hanson Peak.

Sheep graze in Picayne Gulch.

Descending into Placer Gulch.

Picayne & Placer Gulches

CALIFORNIA GULCH
Trail #12

Columbus Mill

TO ENGINEER PASS
Trail #13

04

POUGHKEEPSIE GULCH
Trail #9

Lake Como

Hurricane Pass

California Gulch

CALIFORNIA MOUNTAIN

Placer Gulch

Animas Forks

TO CINNAMON PASS
Trail #14

California Pass

Treasure Mountain

Start here

01

TO CORKSCREW GULCH
Trail #10

HURRICANE PEAK

Heavy snow area

HANSON PEAK

02

Picayne Gulch

03

2

See Page 269 for GPS Waypoint Coordinates

MINI KEY
Paved
Easy
Moderate
Difficult
Other

TO SILVERTON

N

Grid size - 0.5 miles

© 2005 FunTreks, Inc.

78

Picayne & Placer Gulches

Location: Northeast of Silverton, southwest of Animas Forks.

Difficulty: Easy. High shelf road may be intimidating to anyone afraid of heights. The road is wide in most places except near the start where it can be difficult to pass.

Features: Remote route passes interesting mine buildings. Beautiful high-elevation views. Several side roads to explore. Fun area for ATVs.

Time & Distance: 6.4 miles as described here. Allow 1.5 hours.

To Get There: Bear right on C.R. 2 (some maps still show as 110) on the northeast side of Silverton and follow signs to Alpine Loop. Turn left up tight switchback at 10.6 miles before you reach the turn for Animas Forks.

Trail Description: *Reset odometer at start* (01). The first quarter mile is the narrowest and steepest part of trail. Watch for vehicles coming downhill because it is difficult to pass. Stay right at 0.4. At 1.0 miles, continue straight past a group of buildings on left owned by the Treasure Mountain Gold Mining Company (top left picture, opposite page). Make a hard right at 1.4 miles (02) and begin the climb up Treasure Mountain. Stay left at 2.3. Bear right at 3.6 as you cross over the ridge and start down into Placer Gulch. Left takes you to a scenic overlook. Stay right at 4.1 miles (03) where a lesser road goes left. The main road is obvious all the way down the mountain until you run into California Gulch, Trail #12, at 6.4 miles (04).

Return Trip: Right at California Gulch takes you to Animas Forks. Left heads to California Pass and connects to Poughkeepsie Gulch, Trail #9, and Corkscrew Gulch, Trail #10. Left also connects to Gladstone and Silverton.

Reverse Directions: Follow directions for California Gulch, Trail #12. *Reset odometer at 1.8 miles and turn south at Placer Gulch* (04). Follow good road as it climbs toward Hanson Peak. Bear left at 2.3 miles (03). Stay left at 2.8 and start down other side. Stay right at 4.1. Make a hard left at 5.0 miles (02). Stay left until you reach C.R. 2 at 6.4 miles (01). Silverton is right 10.6 miles.

Services: Full services in Silverton. Toilets at Animas Forks.

Maps: Drake Map. Trails Illustrated Silverton, Ouray #141. DeLorme Atlas & Gazetteer.

Eureka Townsite is now popular campground.

Main road is fairly wide most of the way.

Upper section is desolate and treeless.

Angle tram station located on steep hillside.

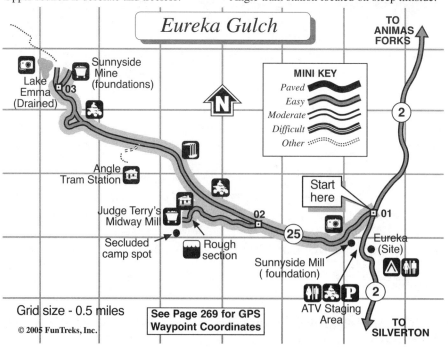

Eureka Gulch

TO ANIMAS FORKS

Sunnyside Mine (foundations)

Lake Emma (Drained)

03

MINI KEY
Paved
Easy
Moderate
Difficult
Other

N

2

Angle Tram Station

Judge Terry's Midway Mill

Secluded camp spot

Rough section

02

Start here

01

25

Eureka (Site)

Sunnyside Mill (foundation)

ATV Staging Area

2

Grid size - 0.5 miles

See Page 269 for GPS Waypoint Coordinates

© 2005 FunTreks, Inc.

TO SILVERTON

Eureka Gulch ⑯

Location: Northeast of Silverton and south of Animas Forks.

Difficulty: Easy. Road is mildly rocky and rutted but fairly wide even at top of mountain. Side trip on lower portion of trail is somewhat overgrown with one rocky water crossing just before Midway Mill. Main road is suitable for any 4x4 SUV. High clearance recommended for lower side trip.

Features: Large campground at Eureka Townsite at base of trail. Trip passes historically significant Sunnyside Mill on way to Sunnyside Mine (only foundations remain). There is no clear hiking path up to the tram station, so take a telephoto lens if you want close-up pictures. ATVs are allowed on trail. A staging area is located near the trail start. Most of the land, beyond the road, is private reclaimed mining land and is not open to the public.

Time & Distance: 3.6 miles one way. Allow 1 to 1-1/2 hours for round trip. Add extra time for side trips.

To Get There: Bear right on C.R. 2 (some maps show as 110) on the northeast side of Silverton and follow signs to Alpine Loop. Turn left uphill (C.R. 25) at 8.2 miles just after campground and ATV parking area.

Trail Description: Reset odometer at start (01). Lesser roads go left at 0.8 and 1.1 miles (02). First road is private drive; second road is side trip to Judge Terry's Midway Mill. At 2.5 miles, short road goes left to flat area below tram station. Hiking to tram station not recommended. Stay right at 3.1 before reaching fork at 3.6 miles (03). Right goes to Sunnyside Mine. Left dead ends in desolate dry lake bed. Return the way you came.

Services: Full services in Silverton. Toilets below start of trail.

Historical Highlights: Eureka was established in 1875 with an active post office until 1942. Sunnyside Mine produced over $50 million. Mines under Lake Emma collapsed in 1978 and the lake drained. No one was hurt, but it took 2 years to clean up the damage. Judge Terry's Midway Mill was the final destination for ore in the early tramway system. The Angle Tram Station was part of a 2nd tram system to carry ore to the newer Sunnyside Mill. The foundations of this mill can be seen on left as you start up the trail.

Maps: Drake Map. Trails Illustrated Silverton, Ouray #141. DeLorme Atlas & Gazetteer.

Historic Silverton is a popular tourist destination.

Crossing Pole Creek.

Descending east side of Stony Pass.

Buffalo Boy Tram House.

Beautiful setting with cabin at Kite Lake. Take a fishing pole.

ATV rider and friend stop to say hello.

County Road 3B is narrow and steep, but easy.

Stony Pass 🄗

Location: East of Silverton.

Difficulty: Easy. Mildly rocky and steep in a few places but suitable for any high clearance, 4WD SUV. Pole Creek, on the far east side of the pass, can get quite deep in the spring. The side trip up to Buffalo Boy Tram House is very steep and narrow in places but stock vehicles with low-range gearing can do it. The road to Beartown and Kite Lake is narrow and potentially muddy in spots. The last quarter mile before Kite Lake has some moderate rocky ledges. You may wish to walk this section if your vehicle does not have skid plates.

Features: This trail crosses the continental divide through an area rich in mining history. There are kiosks all along the route that explain points of interest. At one point, you cross under an aerial tramway with an ore bucket suspended over the road. You can reach the origination point of this bucket by taking the side trip up C.R. 3B to the Buffalo Boy Tram House.

   Just outside of Silverton, where the pavement ends on C.R. 2, stop and read the kiosks that explain the fascinating history of Arrastra Gulch and the Mayflower Mill. To take a self-guided tour of the mill (small fee required), bear left uphill following signs. You can also drive through Arrastra Gulch by turning right on C.R. 21 just after the bridge where the pavement ends.

   South of Howardsville, on C.R. 4A, you'll find the "Old Hundred Gold Mine Tour." The one-hour tour transports you 1/3 mile into an actual gold mine. (See appendix for contact information.)

   ATVs are permitted on this trail. The road to Kite Lake is particularly fun. There's a parking area just before Howardsville. Please note that San Juan County requires operators of off-highway vehicles to carry a valid driver's license and liability insurance.

Time & Distance: It is only 6 miles to Stony Pass. The entire trip to Kite Lake is 18.6 miles. The up-and-back side trip on C.R. 3B to the Buffalo Boy Tram House adds 3 miles. Allow full day for all routes.

To Get There: Northeast of Silverton, bear right on C.R. 2 (many maps still show as 110). After 4 miles, turn right on C.R. 4 at Howardsville.

Trail Description: Reset your odometer at Howardsville (01). Head south on County Rd. 4, following signs to Stony Pass. Stay right at 0.2 miles unless

83

you are heading to the Old Hundred Gold Mine Tour. Make a soft left uphill at 1.8 miles (02) on C.R. 3. If the ore bucket hasn't fallen down, you'll cross under it at 2.5 miles. County Road 3B joins on left at 3.5 miles (03). (See description of this side trip below.) A beautiful climb remains to Stony Pass reached at 6.0 miles (04).

The road narrows somewhat as you descend the other side but is still quite easy. Views are spectacular, especially in early morning. Pole Creek is reached at 12.2 miles. In August, I found it only 6 inches deep, but in the spring it may be too deep to safely cross. An important fork is reached at 12.4 miles (05). Turn right for Kite Lake. Left takes you to Rio Grande Reservoir in 10 miles. Creede is a very long, slow trip of 47 miles.

After turning right for Kite Lake, you cross Pole Creek again at a wider crossing. The road is eventually marked as C.R. 3A and later, F.S. 506. At 15.1 miles, you enter the forest and the road gets narrower and rougher. At 16.9 miles (06), the Colorado Hiking Trail departs from the road to the right. The map showed this point as the site of Beartown, but I could find no evidence of the town, except for a couple of cabins on the hillside way off in the trees to the left. Continue uphill, bearing right at 17.3, 17.5 and 17.9 miles. Roads to left dead end at camp spots. The road gets quite steep and rocky before ending at Kite Lake at 18.6 miles (07).

Side Trip to Buffalo Boy Tram House: Reset odometer and head uphill on C.R. 3B (This turn (03) is 3.5 miles from start.) Bear right at 0.1 miles. Left goes to an interesting mine with a short section of railroad track. As you continue to climb, the road climbs steeply up several tight switchbacks then eases up before reaching the Buffalo Boy Tram House at 1.5 miles (08). On the way, you'll pass a cabin and several large tram towers. The road is closed to all vehicles beyond the tram house. Please do not go any farther. Doing so could result in closure of the entire trail.

Return Trip: Return the way you came.

Services: Full services at Silverton. Nothing along route.

Historical Highlights: Stony Pass was once a major supply route between Del Norte and Silverton. In 1882, the Denver and Rio Grande narrow gauge railroad was completed into Silverton and Stony Pass was abandoned. In recent years the road has been improved primarily for tourist use.

Maps: The northern portion of this route is shown on the Drake Map and Trail Illustrated Map #141. I used my National Geographic computer software for detail on the area around Beartown and Kite Lake.

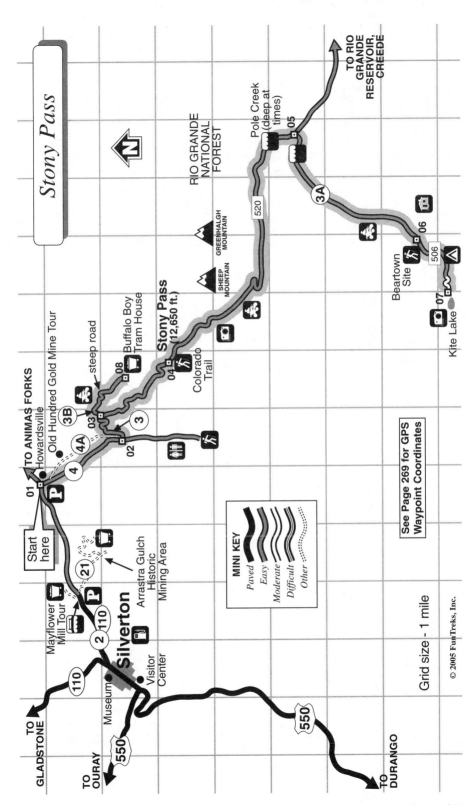

Stony Pass

RIO GRANDE NATIONAL FOREST

TO RIO GRANDE RESERVOIR, CREEDE

Pole Creek (deep at times)

520

3A

05

06

506

Beartown Site

07

Kite Lake

GREENHALGH MOUNTAIN

SHEEP MOUNTAIN

Buffalo Boy Tram House

steep road

Old Hundred Gold Mine Tour

Stony Pass (12,650 ft.)

08

04

Colorado Trail

TO ANIMAS FORKS

Howardsville

3B

03

3

4A

4

02

01

P

Start here

Mayflower Mill Tour

P

110

2

110

Silverton

Museum

Visitor Center

Arrastra Gulch Historic Mining Area

21

550

110

TO GLADSTONE

TO OURAY

550

550

TO DURANGO

MINI KEY

Paved

Easy

Moderate

Difficult

Other

See Page 269 for GPS Waypoint Coordinates

Grid size - 1 mile

© 2005 FunTreks, Inc.

N

85

18. Lead King Basin
19. Devil's Punchbowl
20. Paradise Divide
21. Aspen Mountain,
    Richmond Hill
22. Lincoln Creek Road
23. Montezuma Basin
24. Pearl Pass
25. Taylor Pass
26. Italian Creek,
    Reno Divide

© 2005 FunTreks, Inc.

Grid size - 5 miles

TO
INDEPENDENCE
PASS,
LEADVILLE,
BUENA VISTA

82 22

ASPEN

Aspen Mountain
Road

21

82 TO
    GLENWOOD
    SPRINGS

Midnight
Mine Road

Little Annie
Road

Castle
Creek
Road

23

Ashcroft
Ghost Town

Italian Creek
Road

25

Lower Reno
Divide

742

TO
COTTONWOOD
PASS, TINCUP

Taylor
Reservoir

Upper Reno
Divide

26

Reno
Divide
Road

Cement
Creek Road

135

TO
GUNNISON

24

MT.
CRESTED
BUTTE

738

Airport

135

CRESTED
BUTTE

12

TO
GUNNISON

Schofield
Pass

Gothic

20

20

Slate River
Road

Kebler
Pass

Ohio
Pass

732

MINI KEY
Paved
Easy
Moderate
Difficult
Other

19

18

19

MARBLE

N

314

133

TO
GLENWOOD
SPRINGS

Paonia
Reservoir

133

TO
DELTA

12

● EASY
■ MODERATE
◆ DIFFICULT

86

Crested Butte, Aspen, Marble, Gunnison

Crested Butte and Aspen are internationally known for winter activities. Summer visitors, however, will tell you much of the beauty is buried under winter snows. Only in summer can this area be explored and appreciated to its fullest extent. Surrounded by four wilderness areas, including the fabulous Maroon Bells-Snowmass Wilderness, this area dishes out a massive dose of unspoiled beauty. When a wilderness is created, most four-wheel-drive trails are lost forever. Here, however, some wilderness boundaries were made contiguous with existing roads so that a few of the best roads could remain open. Because of this, it is critically important that you stay on course. Any deviation could send you into a federally-protected wilderness which could result in a substantial fine as well as contempt from responsible four wheelers.

This second edition includes more trails in the Aspen area. Trail #21 climbs through the heart of Aspen Ski Area, while Trail #22 follows rock-carved Lincoln Creek through a non-wilderness corridor of the Collegiate Peaks Wilderness. Trail #23 goes to the top of daunting Montezuma Basin.

Pearl Pass, Trail #24, difficult.

87

Descending narrow switchbacks into Lead King Basin.

Rocky shelf road above river.

Colorado columbines.

Rocky but doable in aggressive, stock SUV.

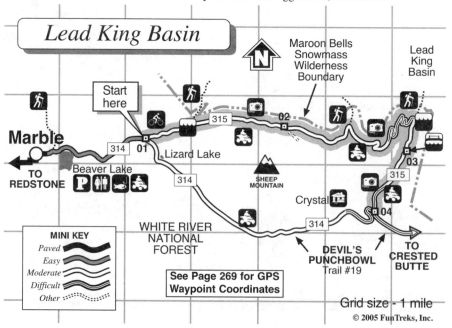

Lead King Basin

N

Maroon Bells
Snowmass
Wilderness
Boundary

Lead
King
Basin

Start
here

315

02

Marble

314

01

Lizard Lake

TO
REDSTONE

Beaver Lake

314

SHEEP
MOUNTAIN

03

315

Crystal

04

WHITE RIVER
NATIONAL
FOREST

314

DEVIL'S
PUNCHBOWL
Trail #19

TO
CRESTED
BUTTE

MINI KEY
Paved
Easy
Moderate
Difficult
Other

See Page 269 for GPS
Waypoint Coordinates

Grid size - 1 mile

© 2005 FunTreks, Inc.

Lead King Basin ◆18◆

Location: East of Marble. Northwest of Crested Butte.

Difficulty: Difficult. Rating based on a few rocky spots and stretches of narrow shelf road where it is difficult to pass. An experienced driver can get a stock, high-clearance, 4x4 SUV through when the trail is dry. West end is steep and very slippery when wet.

Features: Absolutely spectacular scenery. Abundant seasonal wildflowers. Great hiking and mountain biking. Fun for ATVs, but stay on marked roads.

Time & Distance: Allow 2 hours plus return time for this 8.1-mile trip.

To Get There: From Glenwood Springs, take Hwys. 82 and 133 south past Redstone. Follow signs east to Marble on F.S. 314 before McClure Pass. Zigzag through Marble and climb rough road east beyond Beaver Lake to sign for Lead King Basin, F.S. 315. From Crested Butte, follow directions for difficult and dangerous Devil's Punchbowl, Trail #19.

Trail Description: Reset odometer as you head northeast on 315 (01). At 0.7 miles, continue straight across stream after hiking trailhead. Narrow road climbs steeply. It's dusty when dry and slippery when wet. Passing is difficult. Bear left at 2.1 miles (02). After long descent down narrow switchbacks, cross small stream and head south at 6.3. Ignore roads to left. At 6.9 miles (03), cross bridge, then turn right. Trail weaves through trees then follows high, rocky shelf road above north fork of Crystal River. Trail gets rocky just before connecting with Devil's Punchbowl, Trail #19 at 8.1 miles (04).

Return Trip: Right goes back to Marble. Left takes you up difficult Devil's Punchbowl, Trail #19, to Schofield Pass and eventually Crested Butte.

Reverse Directions: Reset odometer and head north on F.S. 315 from Trail #19 (04). Bear left and cross bridge at 1.2 miles (03). At 1.8, trail turns west and climbs series of narrow switchbacks. Bear right at 6.0 miles (02) where road joins on left. Descend narrow switchbacks and cross stream before connecting with F. S. 314 at 8.1 miles (01).

Services: General store in Marble but no gas. Public toilet at Beaver Lake.

Maps: White River National Forest. Trails Illustrated Maroon Bells, Redstone, Marble #128. DeLorme Atlas & Gazetteer.

The much-photographed Crystal Mill

Novice drivers stop here.

The Devil's Punchbowl.

Tricky ledge above the Devil's Punchbowl.

Road above Crystal is very narrow and passing is difficult.

Stock Cherokee crosses Crystal River.

F.S. Road 317 north of Schofield Pass.

Devil's Punchbowl ◀19▶

Location: Between Crested Butte and Marble.

Difficulty: Difficult. The first portion of the trail to the Crystal Mill is rocky but doable in a stock 4x4. East of the town of Crystal, the road becomes extremely narrow as it climbs steeply along the daunting vertical walls of Crystal Canyon. You may have to back up a long distance if you meet an oncoming vehicle. Rock slides are common and occasionally close the trail. Snow lingers in the shadows of the canyon most of the summer. There have been years when this part of the trail has not opened at all. Novice drivers should not go past the signs shown at left (Waypoint 03). The group with which I traveled included a stock Cherokee. It struggled in spots but managed, with an experienced driver, to complete the entire trail without damage. *(Note: Several fatal accidents have occurred on this trail, including the worst in Colorado history. In July of 1970, nine tourists died when their vehicle plummeted off the ledge above the Devil's Punchbowl.)*

Features: Every year, thousands of tourists drive their SUVs to the famous Crystal Mill and the historic town of Crystal. Only the most serious four-wheelers continue up through the Devil's Punchbowl. Drivers with some experience, who don't wish to tackle the Devil's Punchbowl, can loop back to Marble via Lead King Basin, Trail #18. This should not be attempted when the trail is wet. Both the Devil's Punchbowl and Lead King Basin are open to ATVs. Stay on marked routes at all times.

Time & Distance: 10.7 miles as described here. Allow at least 2 hours one way. More time is needed on holiday weekends when traffic is heavier.

To Get There: **From Glenwood Springs:** Take Hwys. 82 and 133 south past Redstone. Follow signs east to Marble on F.S. 314 before McClure Pass. Zigzag through Marble on 314 until you reach the parking area next to Beaver Lake. **From Crested Butte:** Follow directions for Paradise Divide, Trail #20, and turn left on F.S. 317 at Schofield Pass. Follow reverse directions next page.

Trail Description: Set your odometer to zero as you leave the parking lot at Beaver Lake (01). Head east uphill 1.5 miles (02) and bear right on F.S. 314 following signs to the town of Crystal. Bear right at 1.8 miles around Lizard Lake. The famous Crystal Mill is reached at 5.3 miles, followed by the town of Crystal at 5.5. Bear left at 5.7 before reaching the turn for Lead King

Basin, Trail #18, at 6.1 miles (03). Left takes you on a loop back to Marble. Right continues uphill past the dangerous Devil's Punchbowl. The road becomes extremely narrow as it clings to the steep canyon walls. Passing is very tricky so proceed with caution. You may want to send a scout on foot to check around blind curves. A short bridge at 7.4 miles (04) is just below the Devil's Punchbowl. The rockiest and scariest part of the trail is just above the bridge. Even though uphill vehicles have the right of way, make sure the trail is clear before proceeding. Downhill vehicles don't have much room to pull over. The worst is over when you reach the top of the canyon at 7.9 miles. There is a water crossing at this point as the trail turns left. It stays rocky with tight brush until you cross another bridge at 8.3 miles. Note beautiful waterfall on left. Continue uphill on an easier road until you reach Schofield Pass at 10.7 miles (05).

Return Trip: Stay left at Schofield Pass following F.S. 317 into Crested Butte. Or turn right just before Schofield Pass on F.S. 519. This will take you across Paradise Divide, Trail #20, to Crested Butte. Both ways are very scenic.

Reverse Directions: Reset odometer and head north on F.S. 317 from Schofield Pass (05). Warning signs mark end of the maintained road at 2.2 miles. Trail gets rougher with tight brush after bridge and waterfall at 2.4. Cross Crystal River at 2.8 miles as trail turns right and heads downhill past the dangerous Devil's Punchbowl. Test your brakes after crossing river. At 3.1 miles, there's a short wide spot where two vehicles can barely pass. Stop here and check around corner to make sure no one is coming up. Go by Devil's Punchbowl and cross bridge at 3.3 miles (04). At 4.6 miles (03), stay left on F.S. 314 for Crystal Mill. (Right goes to Marble via Lead King Basin, Trail #18.) Stay right at 5.0 and pass through town of Crystal. Go by Crystal Mill at 5.4. Rocky road follows along edge of Crystal River. Bear left at 8.9 miles after Lizard Lake and left again at 9.2 miles (02) where F.S. 315 goes right to Lead King Basin. The parking lot at Beaver Lake is reached at 10.7 miles (01). To reach Hwy. 133, continue west, zigzagging through Marble on F.S. 314. The road becomes paved west of Marble. Right at Hwy. 133 takes you to Redstone and Carbondale.

Services: Full services in Crested Butte. General store but no gas in Marble. Redstone, north of Marble on Hwy. 133, has gas. Toilet at Beaver Lake.

Maps: White River National Forest. Trails Illustrated Maroon Bells, Redstone, Marble #128. DeLorme Atlas & Gazetteer.

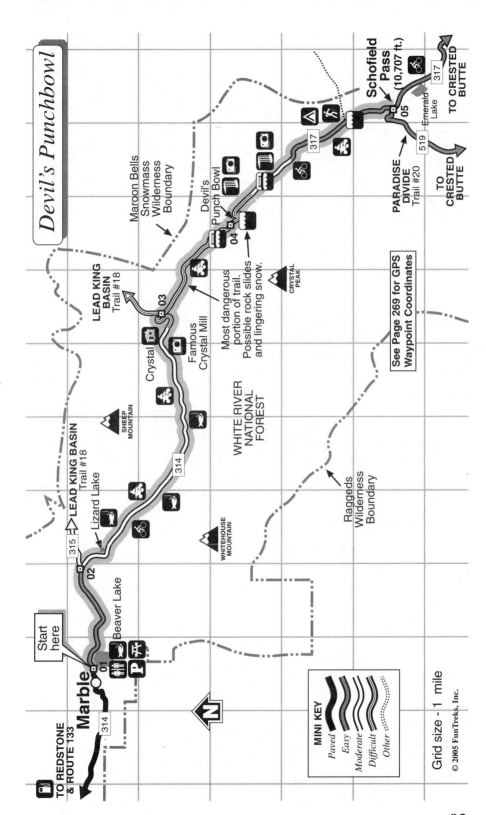

Devil's Punchbowl

TO REDSTONE & ROUTE 133

Marble

314

Start here

01

Beaver Lake

02

315

LEAD KING BASIN
Trail #18

Lizard Lake

WHITEHOUSE
MOUNTAIN

314

SHEEP
MOUNTAIN

Crystal

Famous
Crystal Mill

03

LEAD KING BASIN
Trail #18

WHITE RIVER
NATIONAL
FOREST

Most dangerous
portion of trail.
Possible rock slides
and lingering snow.

CRYSTAL
PEAK

Raggeds
Wilderness
Boundary

Devil's
Punch Bowl

04

Maroon Bells
Snowmass
Wilderness
Boundary

317

Schofield Pass
(10,707 ft.)

317

TO CRESTED
BUTTE

05

Emerald
Lake

519

PARADISE
DIVIDE
Trail #20

TO
CRESTED
BUTTE

See Page 269 for GPS
Waypoint Coordinates

N

MINI KEY

Paved
Easy
Moderate
Difficult
Other

Grid size - 1 mile

© 2005 FunTreks, Inc.

93

Climbing towards Paradise Divide on F.S. 734.

Alternate route up Washington Gulch Road, F.S. 811.   F.S. 519 through Paradise Basin.

Lake, camping, hiking and beautiful views at Paradise Divide.   Note seasonal closure.

The town of Gothic is inhabited by employees of the Rocky Mountain Biological Laboratory.

Paradise Divide ⑳

Location: Immediately north of Crested Butte.

Difficulty: Easy. Slate River Road road is a wide graded road. As it climbs towards Paradise Divide, it becomes a narrower shelf road but there is still plenty of room to pass. Any high-clearance vehicle can reach Schofield Pass via Gothic Road when everything has dried out. In early summer, however, Gothic Road can be blocked by snow below Emerald Lake.

Features: One of the most beautiful and stressless drives in the state. In season, wildflowers are everywhere. Limited designated camping spots within sight of the road in addition to Gothic Forest Service Campground. Washington Gulch, F.S. 811, is a beautiful alternate way to reach Paradise Divide. Northern portion of Gothic Road is closed between March 1 and May 30 depending on snow and mud conditions. ATVs are allowed north of Nicholson Lake on Slate River Road and north of Gothic Campground on Gothic Road. The side trip to Gunsight Pass is a great ATV trip.

Time & Distance: The main loop, as described here, is 27.2 miles. Allow about 2 hours driving time. After you've driven this route, you'll want to come back and spend more time in the area. Washington Gulch Road measures 9.1 miles and takes about 30 minutes.

To Get There: Take Hwy. 135 north 0.8 miles from the visitor center in Crested Butte and turn left on Slate River Road 734. To drive the loop in the opposite direction described here, follow signs to the Mt. Crested Butte Ski Area and continue on to Gothic and Schofield Pass. Just after the pass, turn left on F.S. 519.

Trail Description: Reset your odometer as you turn left on Slate River Road (01). Stay right at 2.5 miles after private Nicholson Lake. At 3.5 miles, the road to Gunsight Pass can be seen below on the left. This is a great side trip after you cross the river. On the left at 4.6 miles is popular *Oh-Be-Joyful* Campgournd. You'll enter the Gunnison National Forest before reaching the site of Pittsburgh at 6.6. If it weren't for the sign, you'd never know there was once a town here. Continue straight at 7.2 miles where a road goes left to Daisy Hiking Trail. Make a hard right up a tight switchback at 9.0 miles and begin the climb to Paradise Divide. Although the road is wide, there are no guard rails, so don't get complacent. Continue straight at 10.8 miles (02) where Washington Gulch Road F.S. 811 joins on the right.

95

Paradise Divide is reached at 11.9 miles (03). Views are outstanding from an elevation of 11,250 ft. A small lake and several side trails make this a popular place to camp. Stay right and drop down into Paradise Basin. Cross a creek at the bottom of the basin, then bear right at 13.8 miles. F.S. 317 is reached at 14.4 miles (04). Left takes you to the Devil's Punchbowl, Trail #19. *Reset your odometer and turn right* (04). You immediately reach Schofield Pass. Continue downhill on a wide gravel road past Emerald Lake (another great place to camp and fish). In early summer, people are sometimes surprised to find a giant wall of ice and snow blocking the road at this point. In this case, you must turn around and go back the way you came or via Washington Gulch.

Continue downhill on what can be a very dusty road in the dry summer months. Please slow down when you pass mountain bikers. Continue straight at 3.2 miles (05) where Rustlers Gulch goes to the left. Gothic F.S. Campground is on the right at 3.8 miles. Just after a bridge at 4.2 miles is a seasonal closure gate. More hiking trails branch off before reaching the historic town of Gothic at 5.8 miles (06). A small store here, with limited hours, sells refreshments. You can also pick up a free brochure that explains the Rocky Mountain Biological Laboratory which owns and inhabits the town.

Gothic Road becomes paved at 9.9 miles before reaching Mt. Crested Butte Ski Area. You can see the ski slopes on the mountainsides above the town. Washington Gulch Road, F.S. 811, goes right at 11.9 miles. You return to the start of Slate River Road at 12.8 miles (01).

Return Trip: Continue downhill into Crested Butte. Make sure you obey the extremely slow speed limits as you pass through town.

Other Activities: Beyond the roadside camping areas lie the Maroon Bells-Snowmass Wilderness and the Raggeds Wilderness, offering some of the most incredible hiking and backpacking anywhere. Mountain biking is very popular on the main roads in addition to the Trail Riders Trail that descends from Schofield Pass. Plenty of fishing is available in several lakes along the route. Fly fishing is also very popular in the Slate River along 734 and the East River along Gothic Road. For more information on the area, stop in at the Crested Butte Visitor Center.

Services: Full services in Crested Butte and Mt. Crested Butte. Toilets at Oh-Be-Joyful, Gothic Campground and Avery Picnic Ground. Gothic had a portable toilet by the general store when I drove through town.

Maps: Gunnison and White River National Forests. DeLorme Atlas & Gazetteer. Three Trails Illustrated Maps are required to cover the whole route: #128, #131, and #133.

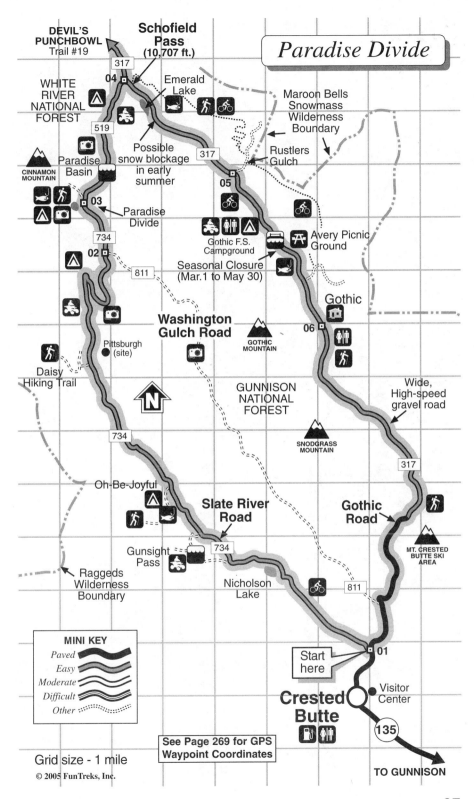

DEVIL'S PUNCHBOWL Trail #19

Schofield Pass (10,707 ft.)

Paradise Divide

317

04

WHITE RIVER NATIONAL FOREST

519

Emerald Lake

Maroon Bells Snowmass Wilderness Boundary

317

CINNAMON MOUNTAIN

Paradise Basin

Possible snow blockage in early summer

Rustlers Gulch

05

03

Paradise Divide

734

02

811

Gothic F.S. Campground

Avery Picnic Ground

Seasonal Closure (Mar.1 to May 30)

Gothic

06

Washington Gulch Road

Pittsburgh (site)

GOTHIC MOUNTAIN

GUNNISON NATIONAL FOREST

Wide, High-speed gravel road

N

Daisy Hiking Trail

734

SNODGRASS MOUNTAIN

317

Oh-Be-Joyful

Slate River Road

Gothic Road

MT. CRESTED BUTTE SKI AREA

Gunsight Pass

734

Raggeds Wilderness Boundary

Nicholson Lake

811

MINI KEY

Paved
Easy
Moderate
Difficult
Other

Start here

01

Visitor Center

Crested Butte

135

See Page 269 for GPS Waypoint Coordinates

Grid size - 1 mile

© 2005 FunTreks, Inc.

TO GUNNISON

97

The road climbs through Aspen Mountain Ski Area.

Start of Aspen Summer Road.

View of Aspen Highlands from Sundeck Restaurant.

Pull over and allow mountain bikers to pass.

South end Richmond Hill Road.   Narrow shelf road coming down Express Creek Road.

Aspen Mtn., Richmond Hill

Location: Immediately south of Aspen.

Difficulty: Moderate. Aspen Summer Road and the first part of Richmond Hill Road are easy although 4-wheel drive is needed because the road is steep in places. The southern end of Richmond Hill Road, as you near Taylor Pass, is rough and steep with possible mud holes. There is one quarter-mile section of high, narrow shelf road as you start down Express Creek Road from Taylor Pass. Overall, the trail is suitable for stock SUVs with high clearance and low-range gearing. Best to go with another vehicle.

Features: Climb through the heart of beautiful Aspen Ski Area. At the summit of Aspen Mountain, have lunch at the Sundeck Restaurant with gondola-riding tourists or picnic at a separate picnic spot nearby. After lunch, escape the crowds with a backcountry drive along remote Richmond Ridge. Much of mountain top is private land so stay on main road at all times. Visit Historic Ashcroft Townsite at end of trip. Aspen Summer Road is sometimes temporarily closed for construction. If this should occur, you can still get to the top of Aspen Mountain via Midnight Mine Road. See separate directions next page. ATVs are allowed on entire route but Richmond Hill Road is better suited for unlicensed vehicles. ATV riders can walk into town from bottom of Aspen Summer Road. Do not ride on paved streets.

Time & Distance: Aspen Summer Road is 4.6 miles and takes about 45 minutes. Richmond Hill Road is 12.1 miles and takes about 2 hours. Add another 4.8 miles and 30 minutes for Express Creek Road.

To Get There: Head south on Hwy. 82 (Main Street) all the way through Aspen to Original Street and turn right (south). Continue straight on Original Street at the 4-way stop where Hwy. 82 goes left (east). Keep going south past Durant and East Ute Street as the road narrows and enters what appears to be a driveway between condominiums. Bear right around back of building and make short climb to start of Aspen Summer Road. Gate will be open if road is open. If gate is not open, see directions for Midnight Mine Road, next page.

Trail Description: Reset odometer at start of Aspen Summer Road (01). (See top left photo opposite page.) Road immediately passes under gondola and starts up mountain. Stay left uphill at 0.3 where a wide road goes back downhill. Follow road as it curves around a restaurant at 1.8 miles. Bear left downhill when you reach a T intersection at 3.3 miles. At 4.5 miles, you reach the top end of the gondola. Bear left along the end of the building and pass through an opening in a fence. You'll see a parking area on the left at 4.6 miles (02). Walk uphill to the right behind the gondola building to the Sundeck Restaurant. There's also a picnic spot a short walk down the hill by the restaurant.

To continue on Richmond Hill Road, *Reset your odometer* (02) and head south through parking area. Watch for hikers and bikers. Before long, the hustle and bustle at the mountaintop is left behind. Stay left at 1.5 miles where a road joins on the right. Follow sign to Taylor Pass. Continue straight at 1.6 miles where a better road goes right uphill and another road curves downhill to the left. At 4.3 miles, signs indicate that the Collegiate Peaks Wilderness Boundary parallels the road on the left. You may see people camped in the woods on the right. After 5 miles, a steep descent begins the moderate portion of the route—nothing too bad, but definitely rougher. Eventually, you come out of the woods and begin a series of long climbs and descents through an area called Gold Hill. At 9.7 miles, you reach a high point at 12,300 feet. Drop steeply downhill and bear right at 10.5 miles. Tighter, downhill switchbacks mark the approach of Taylor Pass at 12.1 miles (03).

Left at Taylor Pass takes you downhill to Taylor Lake, described in Taylor Pass, Trail #25. To return to Aspen, *reset odometer* and bear right downhill on Express Creek Road. After a steep, narrow section of shelf road, it widens and descends more gradually. The upper portion of the road has the best views. Paved Castle Creek Road, F.S. 102, is reached after 4.8 miles. A short distance to the left is the Ashcroft Historic Townsite. A small fee is charged to keep the area manned and maintained.

Return Trip: Right on Castle Creek Road takes you back to Hwy. 82 west of Aspen. When you reach the busy roundabout in less than 11 miles, right goes to Aspen, left goes to Basalt and Glenwood Springs.

Directions to top of Aspen Mountain via Midnight Mine Road: From the roundabout west of Aspen on Hwy. 82, take Castle Creek Road south 2.7 miles. *Reset odometer* and turn left on Midnight Mine Road, F.S. 118 (05). Pass the Midnight Mine at 2.4, then bear left at 4.1 (06). Continue straight uphill at 4.2 before reaching gondola building and parking area at 5.4 miles (02).

Services: Full services in Aspen. Gas prices in Aspen are extremely high. Aspen has several public parks with restrooms, including Paepcke Park along Main Street. Take time to walk or drive through the beautiful and quaint downtown section. The town has many great outdoor cafes and restaurants but no fast food restaurants.

Maps: White River N.F. Trails Illustrated Map #127. DeLorme Atlas.

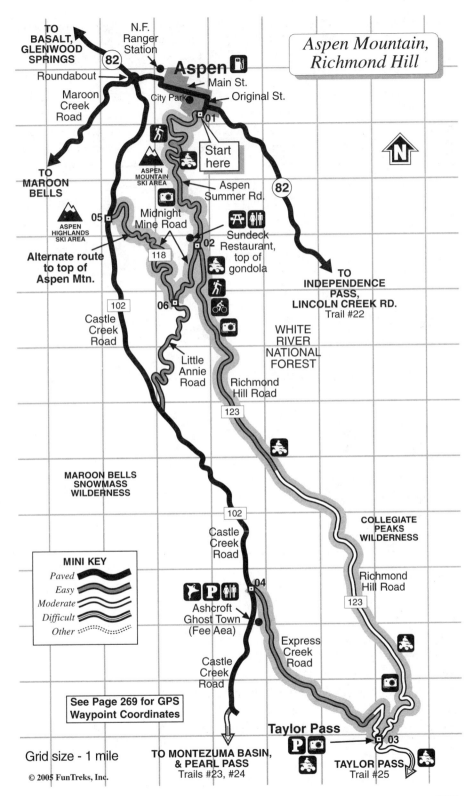

TO
BASALT,
GLENWOOD
SPRINGS

82

N.F.
Ranger
Station

*Aspen Mountain,
Richmond Hill*

Aspen

Roundabout

Main St.

Maroon
Creek
Road

City Park

Original St.

01

Start
here

TO
MAROON
BELLS

ASPEN
MOUNTAIN
SKI AREA

Aspen
Summer Rd.

82

N

05

ASPEN
HIGHLANDS
SKI AREA

Midnight
Mine Road

Sundeck
Restaurant,
top of
gondola

Alternate route
to top of
Aspen Mtn.

118

02

TO
INDEPENDENCE
PASS,
LINCOLN CREEK RD.
Trail #22

102

06

WHITE
RIVER
NATIONAL
FOREST

Castle
Creek
Road

Little
Annie
Road

Richmond
Hill Road

123

MAROON BELLS
SNOWMASS
WILDERNESS

102

COLLEGIATE
PEAKS
WILDERNESS

Castle
Creek
Road

Richmond
Hill Road

123

MINI KEY

Paved
Easy
Moderate
Difficult
Other

Ashcroft
Ghost Town
(Fee Aea)

04

Express
Creek
Road

P

Castle
Creek
Road

See Page 269 for GPS
Waypoint Coordinates

Taylor Pass

P

03

Grid size - 1 mile

© 2005 FunTreks, Inc.

TO MONTEZUMA BASIN,
& PEARL PASS
Trails #23, #24

TAYLOR PASS
Trail #25

101

Road is easy most of the way.

Rock-carved section of Lincoln Creek near Camp Spot #7.

Grizzly Reservoir.

John Nichols Cabin.

Lincoln Gulch Campground.

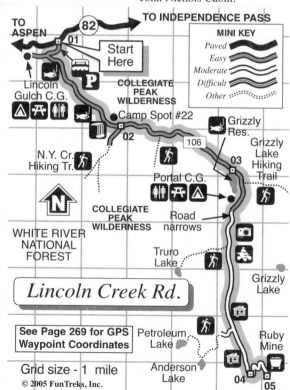

TO ASPEN

TO INDEPENDENCE PASS

MINI KEY
Paved
Easy
Moderate
Difficult
Other

82

01

Start Here

P

Lincoln Gulch C.G.

COLLEGIATE PEAK WILDERNESS

Camp Spot #22

02

Grizzly Res.

106

N.Y. Cr. Hiking Tr.

Grizzly Lake Hiking Trail

03

Portal C.G.

N

COLLEGIATE PEAK WILDERNESS

Road narrows

WHITE RIVER NATIONAL FOREST

Truro Lake

Grizzly Lake

Lincoln Creek Rd.

See Page 269 for GPS Waypoint Coordinates

Petroleum Lake

Ruby Mine

Grid size - 1 mile

© 2005 FunTreks, Inc.

Anderson Lake

04

05

Narrow road at Ruby Mine.

102

Lincoln Creek Road

Location: Southeast of Aspen, west of Independence Pass.

Difficulty: Moderate. The northern portion of this trail is easy. South of Grizzly Reservoir the trail narrows and gets a bit rockier. The last 0.7 miles before Ruby Mine is rocky, narrow and steep. Suitable for any stock 4x4 with high clearance and low-range gearing.

Features: Road follows beautiful Lincoln Creek and is surrounded by wilderness. Stay on road at all times. Popular mountain biking, hiking and fishing area. Road accesses Historic Lincoln Creek Mining District. Camp in one of 22 designated sites along trail or in two F.S. Campgrounds. Swimming in Lincoln Creek is allowed but very dangerous. ATVs are allowed, but it is absolutely critical to stay on main road at all times.

Time & Distance: Just under 12 miles. Allow 1-1/2 to 2 hours each way.

To Get There: About 10 miles east of Aspen on Hwy. 82. Turn south 0.3 miles east of mile marker 51 at sign for Lincoln Creek Road, F.S. 106.

Trail Description: Reset odometer as you turn off Hwy. 82 (01). Cross bridge and follow road to right. Stay left at 0.4 where road goes right to Lincoln Gulch F.S. Campground. Parking on right at 0.5. Camp Spot #7 at 2.0 miles is near beautiful rock-carved section of Lincoln Creek. Stay left at 3.0 miles (02) where road goes right to New York Creek Hiking Trail. Road smoothes out until you reach Grizzly Reservoir at 6.2 miles. Continue past dam, then bear left on lesser road at 6.3 miles (03). Go past hiking trail to Grizzly Lake, then bear left after Portal Campground at 6.6 miles. Follow narrow, rocky road south past Frenchman's Cabin and enter Historic Lincoln Creek Mining District. Stay left at 10.0 where road goes right to Petroleum Lake Hiking Trail. After John Nichols Cabin, stay on road through Ruby Townsite at 10.8 miles (all buildings are private property). Turn left uphill at 11.1 miles (04) and climb narrow, steep road to Ruby Mine at 11.9 miles (05). Road after mine becomes impassable before ending at wilderness boundary.

Return Trip: Return the way you came.

Services: Vault toilets at Lincoln Gulch and Portal Campgrounds.

Maps: White River National Forest. Trails Illustrated Aspen, Independence Pass #127. DeLorme Atlas & Gazetteer.

Flat parking area at end of trail at 12,700 feet. Note stock pickup truck made it to the top.

Don't miss waterfall.

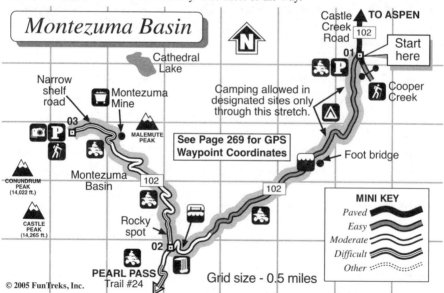

Road is fairly wide most of the way.

Montezuma Basin

N

Cathedral Lake

Castle Creek Road 102

TO ASPEN

01

Start here

Cooper Creek

Narrow shelf road

Montezuma Mine

Camping allowed in designated sites only through this stretch.

03

P

MALEMUTE PEAK

See Page 269 for GPS Waypoint Coordinates

Foot bridge

CONUNDRUM PEAK (14,022 ft.)

Montezuma Basin

102

102

CASTLE PEAK (14,265 ft.)

Rocky spot

02

PEARL PASS Trail #24

Grid size - 0.5 miles

MINI KEY

Paved
Easy
Moderate
Difficult
Other

© 2005 FunTreks, Inc.

104

Montezuma Basin 23

Location: South of Aspen, northeast of Crested Butte.

Difficulty: Difficult. Rating based on one rocky spot at the bottom and one stretch of narrow shelf road near the top. Most of the road is fairly wide and moderate. Stock vehicles should have high clearance, low-range gearing and skid plates. Novice drivers may find the last half mile intimidating.

Features: Follow old mining road to flat parking area above 12,700 feet. Austere and beautiful route is mostly above timberline. Provides hiking access to two 14,000-ft. mountain peaks. Camping on lower portion of trail must be done in designated camping spots. Wildflowers. ATVs allowed.

Time & Distance: As described here, trail is 5.3 miles. Takes about an hour to reach the top in properly equipped vehicle.

To Get There: From roundabout on Hwy. 82 west of Aspen, turn south on Castle Creek Road, F.S. 102. Follow paved road south about 13 miles and bear right at signs to Pearl Pass and Montezuma Basin.

Trail Description: Reset odometer as you turn right off paved road (01). A small parking area is located at start of trail. If you wish to camp, continue uphill to numbered camping spots. At 1.3 miles, the trail bends to left and crosses Castle Creek next to a foot bridge. Cross the creek again at 2.8 miles over small wooden bridge. Note impressive waterfall high above on the left. You can see it better as you go around the next switchback. You may see SUVs parked here as trail gets rougher from this point. Turn right at 3.0 miles (02) for Montezuma Basin. Pearl Pass is left.

The rockiest part of the trail is encountered at 3.2 miles. Stock vehicles may bottom out through this section if the driver is not careful. Stay right at 3.4. Follow switchbacks uphill past the Montezuma Mine at 4.9 miles. The road narrows to one lane as it turns across the face of the mountain. A short rocky section remains before the trail ends at 5.3 miles (03). Plenty of room to park and turn around. Serious hiking above parking area.

Return Trip: Return the way you came.

Services: Public toilet at Ashcroft Townsite on F.S. 102. Nothing along trail.

Maps: White River National Forest. Trails Illustrated Aspen, Independence Pass #127. DeLorme Atlas & Gazetteer.

105

Aspens provide fall color.   Numerous water crossings.   Toughest spot on north side.

Incredible views at Pearl Pass, 12,705 ft.   Starting down from north side of Pearl Pass.

Still some snow in mid-August.

Narrow shelf road on south side of pass.   Abundant late season wildflowers.

Pearl Pass ◆24◆

Location: Between Crested Butte and Aspen.

Difficulty: Difficult. Many boulder fields, steep climbs, water crossings, and narrow shelves. These conditions are magnified by snow and ice that are present well into late summer at higher elevations. During years of heavy snowpack, the summit can be blocked for the entire year. Always travel with another vehicle or group of vehicles. Trail is not well suited for stock SUVs but an experienced driver can get an aggressive vehicle through with patience and a little luck.

Features: Located between two of the most famous recreational areas in the state, this long trail offers an unmatched variety of different landscapes from rolling hillsides to challenging rock ledges. High elevation sections of the trail follow the border of the Maroon Bells-Snowmass Wilderness and pass through some of the most remote and strikingly beautiful areas of Colorado. I drove the trail in mid August and found wildflowers at lower elevations and snow at higher elevations. ATVs are allowed on entire trail, but it is absolutely critical to stay on main road at all times.

Time & Distance: About 22 miles from Route 135 in Crested Butte to Castle Creek Road on the Aspen side. The south side of Pearl Pass is about 16 miles compared to 6 miles on the north side. Due to the ruggedness of the trail, you should allow 3 to 5 hours for the complete trip. Allow adequate time to get back down if trail is blocked by snow at the top.

To Get There: **From Crested Butte:** From Hwy. 135 south of town, head northeast on Brush Creek Road, F.S. 738 (same road that goes to airport and country club). **From Aspen:** From the roundabout on Hwy. 82 on the west side of Aspen, take paved Castle Creek Road, F.S. 102 south about 13 miles and turn right at sign for Pearl Pass and Montezuma Basin.

Trail Description: **From Crested Butte:** *Reset odometer as you turn off Hwy. 135 south of Crested Butte* (01). Pavement soon ends as you head northeast. Stay right at sign at 5.6 miles (02) on 738. Stay left at 5.8 miles past camping and staging area. Drop downhill and bear right across creek at 6.2. Continue straight past popular camping and fishing area on right next to creek at 8.0 miles. Cross creek again then bear left at 8.8 miles (03). Turn right uphill at 10.6 miles (04) as trail gets more difficult. Stay right again at 11.9. After a repaired bog area, the trail begins a long climb up rocky talus

107

slopes. Cross over high ridge with great views at 15.5 miles. If road is clear of snow, continue up narrow shelf road to Pearl Pass at 16.2 miles (05).

Once you reach top of pass, look down other side to make sure road is not blocked by snow. This is the last place where the snow lingers. Follow road downhill through boulder fields. Most of the road is moderate but there are a couple of challenging rocky sections. Montezuma Basin, Trail #23 goes left at 19.2 miles (06). Stay right downhill and the road soon gets easier. Note waterfall on right as you approach small bridge at 19.4 miles. Cross Castle Creek next to foot bridge and proceed past designated camping spots. Paved Castle Creek Road is reached at 22.2 miles (07).

Return Trip: Stay left on Castle Creek Road about 13 miles to roundabout on Hwy. 82 west of Aspen. If you wish to drive Taylor Pass, Trail #25, turn right on Express Creek Road just north of Ashcroft Townsite.

Reverse Directions from Aspen: Reset odometer as you turn off paved Castle Creek Road at sign for Pearl Pass (07). Stay left across Castle Creek near foot bridge at 1.3. Cross small wooden bridge below waterfall and climb switchbacks at 2.8. Stay left uphill at 3.0 (06) where Montezuma Basin, Trail #23, goes right. Stay right at 3.2. Cross stream and climb up difficult rocky section at 3.5. Pass through field of large boulders and climb to Pearl Pass, reached at 6.0 miles (05).

Descend narrow shelf road down south side of pass. Road weaves through long stretch of rocky talus before crossing repaired bog at 9.2 miles. Stay left at 10.3 and 11.6 miles (04). Stay right at 13.4 miles (03). Cross creek at 13.7. Bear left after crossing creek again at 16.0. Stay right at 16.4 past camping and staging area at 16.4. Bear left on 738 at 16.6 miles (02). Follow well-defined Brush Creek Road. It becomes paved before reaching Highway 135 at 22.2 miles (01). Turn right for Crested Butte, left for Gunnison.

Services: Full services in Aspen and Crested Butte. Public toilet at Ashcroft Ghost Town. Nothing along trail.

Historical Highlights: The town of Ashcroft was born in 1880 and grew to a population of about 2,000. At that time, it had 20 saloons, a school, sawmills and two newspapers. Only five years later, the rich silver mines proved to be just shallow deposits and the town quickly died. In 1974, the town was placed on the National Register of Historic Places. The Aspen Historical Society has preserved the town for all to enjoy. A small fee is charged to keep things going.

Maps: Gunnison National Forest. Trails Illustrated, Aspen, Independence Pass #127 and Crested Butte, Pearl Pass #131. DeLorme Atlas & Gazetteer.

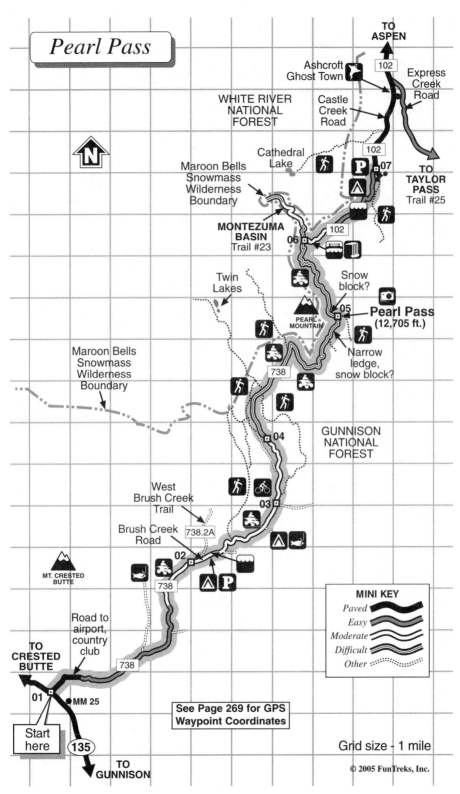

Pearl Pass

TO ASPEN

Ashcroft Ghost Town

Express Creek Road

`102`

WHITE RIVER NATIONAL FOREST

Castle Creek Road

`102`

Cathedral Lake

TO TAYLOR PASS
Trail #25

`07`

Maroon Bells Snowmass Wilderness Boundary

MONTEZUMA BASIN
Trail #23

`102`

`06`

Snow block?

Twin Lakes

Pearl Pass
(12,705 ft.)

`05`

PEARL MOUNTAIN

Maroon Bells Snowmass Wilderness Boundary

Narrow ledge, snow block?

`738`

`04`

GUNNISON NATIONAL FOREST

West Brush Creek Trail

`03`

Brush Creek Road

`738.2A`

`02`

`738`

MT. CRESTED BUTTE

`738`

Road to airport, country club

TO CRESTED BUTTE

`01`

MM 25

Start here

`135`

TO GUNNISON

See Page 269 for GPS Waypoint Coordinates

MINI KEY
Paved
Easy
Moderate
Difficult
Other

Grid size - 1 mile

© 2005 FunTreks, Inc.

109

Upper part of Express Creek Road.

Looking south from Taylor Pass.

Ashcroft Ghost Town.

Tough creek crossing for stock vehicles.

Trail follows creek for short distance.

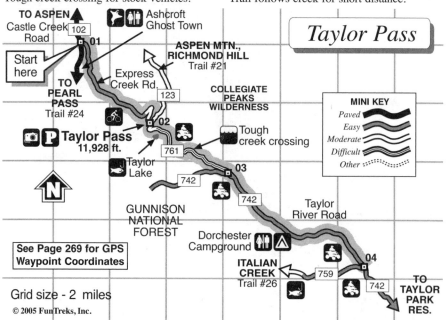

Taylor Pass

TO ASPEN
Castle Creek Road [102]
01

Start here

Ashcroft Ghost Town

ASPEN MTN., RICHMOND HILL
Trail #21

TO PEARL PASS
Trail #24

Express Creek Rd.
[123]

COLLEGIATE PEAKS WILDERNESS

Taylor Pass
11,928 ft.
02
[761]

Tough creek crossing

Taylor Lake

[742]
03
[742]

MINI KEY
Paved
Easy
Moderate
Difficult
Other

Taylor River Road

N

GUNNISON NATIONAL FOREST

Dorchester Campground

See Page 269 for GPS Waypoint Coordinates

ITALIAN CREEK
Trail #26

[759]

04
[742]

TO TAYLOR PARK RES.

Grid size - 2 miles

© 2005 FunTreks, Inc.

110

Taylor Pass 25

Location: Between Aspen and Taylor Park Reservoir.

Difficulty: Difficult. Many miles of bowling-ball size rocks. Stock, high-clearance vehicles can make it but undercarriage damage is possible. No major obstacles, but one creek crossing is fairly challenging. Rocky section is very slow going. Balance of trail is easy to moderate.

Features: Shortest way to Taylor Park Reservoir from Aspen. Nice views from Taylor Pass but not much after that. Ashcroft Ghost Town is near start. This trail is one third of popular loop that includes trails #24, #25 and #26. South end near Dorchester Campground is popular ATV and fishing area.

Time & Distance: Allow about 2 hours for the 9.1 miles between Castle Creek Road 102 and Taylor Creek Road 742. It's another 17 miles of fast gravel road to Taylor Park Reservoir once you reach 742.

To Get There: **From Aspen:** From the roundabout on Hwy. 82 west of Aspen, head south on paved Castle Creek Road, F.S. 102, about 11 miles and turn left on Express Creek Road just before Ashcroft Ghost Town. **From Crested Butte:** First drive Pearl Pass, Trail #24. Head north on Castle Creek Road about 2 miles and turn right on Express Creek Road. **From Taylor Park Reservoir:** Head northwest on Taylor River Road, F.S. 742 about 17 miles and turn right at signs for Taylor Pass. (See map of Area 3.)

Trail Description: Reset odometer at start (01). Climb Express Creek Road to Taylor Pass at 4.9 miles (02). Bear right and zigzag downhill to east end of Taylor Lake. Stay left at 5.6 where 761.1A goes right. The rocky road offers various choices, but all are bone-jarring. Drop steeply into creek at 7.4. Immediately bear right at bottom of creek, then left, staying in creek a short distance. Exit creek at 7.5 miles then cross it again. Continue downhill to Taylor River Road 742, reached at 9.1 miles (03). Turn left for Taylor Park Reservoir. Stay on good road going past Dorchester Campground. The turn for Italian Creek, F.S. 759, is on right at 14.9 miles (04). Continue straight on 742 approximately 12 miles to Taylor Park Reservoir.

Services: Full services in Aspen. Toilet at Dorchester Campground.

Maps: White River and Gunnison National Forests. Trails Illustrated, Aspen, Independence Pass #127 and Crested Butte, Pearl Pass #131. DeLorme Atlas & Gazetteer.

111

Fishing along north end of trail.

Much of route is easy and fun to drive.

Old log cabin privately owned.

Road shared by dirt bikes.

Upper Reno Divide optional.

Few signs along route.

Stock SUV successfully negotiates trail under dry conditions. Trail more difficult when wet.

112

Italian Creek, Reno Divide 26

Location: Between Crested Butte and Taylor Park.

Difficulty: Moderate. A narrow, remote road with steep climbs and potential mud bogs in wet weather. Moderate rating is based on dry conditions. Becomes difficult in rainy weather especially in early part of summer. A stock 4x4 with high clearance and low-range gearing can manage the trail when dry. Aggressive tire tread is very important. Do not drive this trail alone. Not recommended for novice drivers. Alternate trip via the Upper Reno Divide is difficult and dangerous.

Features: Both ends of the trail are popular recreation areas for hikers, bikers, fisherman, ATV and dirt bike riders. Many great places to camp along the trail. The connecting Reno Divide portion is less traveled and very remote. Combine this trail with Pearl and Taylor Passes for a great weekend adventure. Popular run for 4-wheel-drive clubs.

Time & Distance: A long trip of over 27 miles as described here. The southern half of the trail is easy and drive goes quickly. Allow 3 to 5 hours for the entire trip.

To Get There: **From Taylor Park Reservoir:** Take Taylor River Road, F.S. 742, north from reservoir about 12 miles and turn left on Italian Creek Road, F.S. 759. If you reach Dorchester Campground, you've gone too far. **From Crested Butte:** Head north on Castle Creek Road from Hwy. 135 about 7 miles south of Crested Butte. **From southern end of Taylor Pass Road, Trail #25:** Turn left on Taylor River Road 742 and go about 5.8 miles to Italian Creek Road 759 on right.

Trail Description: Reset odometer as you turn west on Italian Creek Road, F.S. 759 (01). Pass through popular dispersed camping and fishing area. At 2.7 miles, pass through fence indicating road ahead is 4-wheel drive. You gradually climb over a variety of terrain, most of it easy. Several lesser roads branch off that are open to ATVs and dirt bikes only. At 6.5 miles (02), make a hard right following signs to Cement Creek. Straight is private property. Bear left downhill at 7.2, avoiding private property again. Pass old cabin (see photo) and cross creek. At 7.6 miles, bear left at group of collapsed cabins. Watch out for mud holes that can be very deep at times. Turn left again at a T intersection at 7.7 miles. The road climbs steeply and can be difficult when wet. At 8.6 miles (03), bear right. Driver's choice at 8.7. Turn right at 9.0 miles. (The road to left climbs to top of American Flag

113

Mountain, a popular area for ATVs and dirt bikes.) The road weaves around, crossing several muddy spots. A very important fork is reached at 10.3 miles (04). Right goes over difficult Upper Reno Divide which includes a difficult rocky ledge and deep mud bogs. Directions here go left on the lower section. The lower section weaves through the woods on a narrow road that is steep and potentially muddy in places. The two roads merge back together at 14.4 miles (05). Pass through a cattle control gate and continue straight downhill on a better road. You'll begin to see more traffic and a number of excellent camp spots along the road.

Bear left when you reach Cement Creek Road, F.S. 740 at 18.2 miles (06). This scenic road winds through the trees and widens as it descends. Go by a parking and staging area at 20.4 and Cement Creek F.S. Campground at 23.6. The road becomes paved before reaching Hwy. 135 at 27.3 miles (07).

Return Trip: Crested Butte is about 7 miles to the right on Hwy. 135. Left goes to Gunnison.

Reverse directions from Crested Butte: *Reset odometer as you turn off Hwy. 135 about 7 miles south of Crested Butte* (07). Pass Cement Creek Campground at 3.7 miles. Parking on right at 6.9. Turn right uphill at 9.1 miles (06) following sign to Reno Divide. Reach ridge top at 12.9 miles (05) and pass through gate. Go straight downhill following sign for Italian Creek Road (see photo). Left goes over difficult Upper Reno Divide. Continue straight at 17.0 miles (04) where Upper Reno Divide joins on left. Bear left at 18.3 miles away from American Flag Mountain. Driver's choice at 18.6. Bear left at 18.7 miles (03). Turn right at 19.6 and 19.7 miles. Climb past an old log cabin and turn right at 20.1 miles away from private road. Make a hard left at 20.8 miles (02) where another private road goes right. Follow main road downhill over varied terrain, ignoring lesser side roads. Pass through fence onto easier road at 24.6 miles. Road winds through popular camping and fishing area before reaching Taylor River Road, F.S. 742, at 27.3 miles (01). Right on 742 goes to Taylor Park Reservoir in about 12 miles. Left goes to Taylor Pass Road, Trail #25.

Services: Full services in Crested Butte. Toilet at Cement Creek Campground.

Maps: Gunnison National Forest. Trails Illustrated Crested Butte, Pearl Pass #131. DeLorme Atlas & Gazetteer.

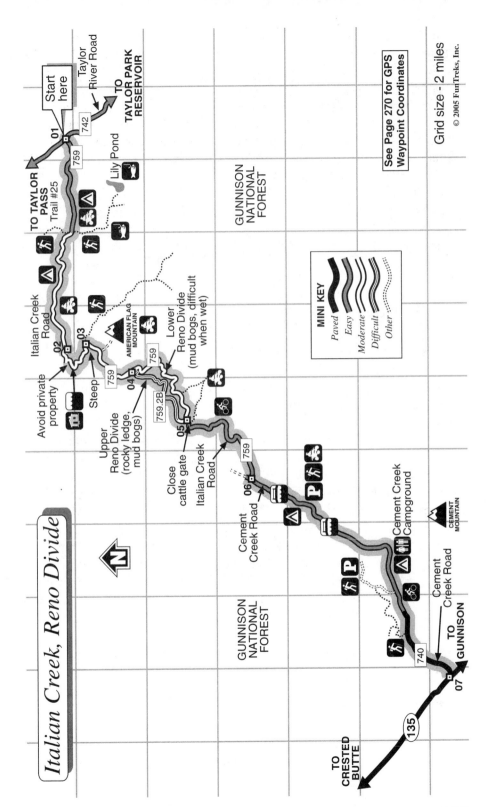

Italian Creek, Reno Divide

MINI KEY
Paved
Easy
Moderate
Difficult
Other

See Page 270 for GPS Waypoint Coordinates

Grid size - 2 miles

© 2005 FunTreks, Inc.

Start here

01

742

Taylor River Road

TO TAYLOR PARK RESERVOIR

759

Lily Pond

TO TAYLOR PASS
Trail #25

Italian Creek Road

02

03

759

Avoid private property

Steep

AMERICAN FLAG MOUNTAIN

Upper Reno Divide (rocky ledge, mud bogs)

759

04

759.2B

759

Lower Reno Divide (mud bogs, difficult when wet)

05

Close cattle gate

Italian Creek Road

759

06

Cement Creek Road

GUNNISON NATIONAL FOREST

P

P

Cement Creek Campground

CEMENT MOUNTAIN

Cement Creek Road

740

07

TO GUNNISON

135

TO CRESTED BUTTE

N

GUNNISON NATIONAL FOREST

27. Fourmile Area
28. Chinaman Gulch,
    Carnage Canyon
29. Mt. Princeton
30. Mt. Antero,
    Browns Lake
31. Baldwin Lakes,
    Boulder Mountain
32. Grizzly Lake
33. Iron Chest Mine
34. Pomeroy Lakes
35. Tincup Pass,
    St. Elmo
36. Hancock Pass,
    Alpine Tunnel
37. Tomichi Pass
38. Marshall Pass,
    Poncha Creek

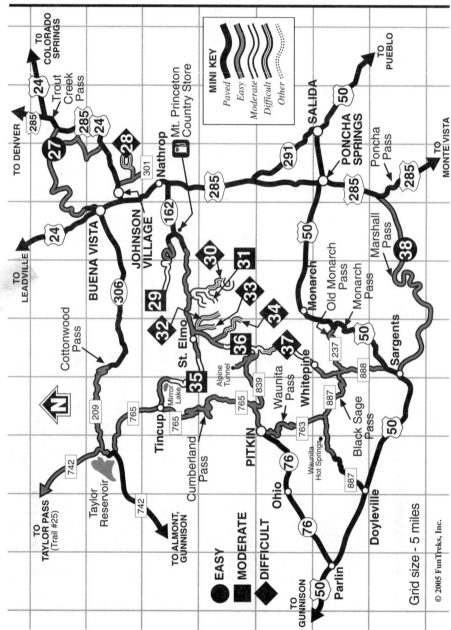

Grid size - 5 miles

© 2005 FunTreks, Inc.

116

Buena Vista, Salida, Sargents

The Buena Vista area is one of the most popular four-wheeling areas in Colorado because it offers a wide variety of beautiful trails within a two-hour drive of Denver and Colorado Springs. Colorado residents have learned that lower elevation trails in this area often get very little snow. Most of it seems to fall in the nearby mountains. For this reason, Chinaman Gulch, Trail #28, which is located on BLM land and seldom closed in the winter, has become very popular all year long. The narrow canyon is often protected from the wind and warmed by Colorado's persistent and penetrating sunshine. Carnage Canyon, an offshoot of Trail #28, is an extreme trail that has quickly developed a reputation as one of the toughest in the United States.

Readers of the first edition of this book will notice that several new trails have been added to Area 3. They include Chinaman Gulch/Carnage Canyon, described above, Baldwin Lakes/Boulder Mountain, Grizzly Lake, and Marshall Pass/Poncha Creek. In addition, some trails like Fourmile Area (formerly Sevenmile Road), Mt. Antero, and Pomeroy Lakes have been extended or expanded to include nearby trails.

Fourmile Area, Trail #27, easy. Old buildings at Goddard Ranch (private property).

Collegiate Peaks provide backdrop to variety of terrain.

Stay on road as it passes through private Goddard Ranch.

Motorhomes can reach first camp spots along F.S. 315.

Hike to mine above Wpt. 03.

Rafters on Arkansas River.

Very popular area for ATVs and dirt bikes.

Road is steep in a few places.

118

Fourmile Area ㉗

Location: The full name of this area is the Fourmile Travel Management Area. The northern portion, shown here, is east of Buena Vista and north of Hwy. 24/285. The southern half, known as Bassam Park, is south of Hwy. 24/285. It is better suited for hunting than touring.

Difficulty: Easy. Variety of conditions from graded roads to narrow, rutted and sandy roads. Steep in a few places. Suitable for all stock, high-clearance 4-wheel-drive SUVs.

Features: Outstanding dispersed camping with incredible views of the Collegiate Peaks. Northwest corner of area has spaghetti-like network of roads that are fun to explore. Great area for ATVs and dirt bikes. Vehicles must stay on existing roads at all times. Enjoy the Midland Mountain Bike Trail. Hike Davis Meadow in search of Natural Arch.

Seasonal gates close much of the area from December 1 to around April 30. Goddard Ranch is private property and is gated on each side during this same period.

Time & Distance: Allow 3 to 4 hours for the 25-mile circular route described here. If you drive the 18.5-mile northern portion only, start at Trout Creek Pass and allow 2 to 3 hours.

To Get There: From Hwy. 24/285, at a point 5.5 miles east of Hwy. 24, turn north on F.S. Road 315, marked with a blue sign. Alternate entry point, on F.S. 311 at Trout Creek Pass, is located between mile markers 225 and 226. Look for large San Isabel National Forest sign.

.

Trail Description: Reset odometer as you turn north on F.S. 315 (01). Follow wide, sandy road uphill past Midland Bike Trailhead. Near a curve at 1.8 miles, a small road goes left to great dispersed camping. More camping is available on left as you continue on 315. Bear right at 2.6 miles (02) on F.S. 376. Stay right at 3.5 where 376B goes left, then bear left at 3.6 miles where 305 goes right. There is an interesting mine on the hillside to the left at 4.9 miles (03). You must take a short hike uphill to see it. Don't get too close.

After a rocky section, you'll go over a cattle guard and pass a mine next to the road at 5.6. Drop downhill, passing through fences for Chubb Park. This is state land where camping is allowed in designated sites only. Turn left at 6.7 miles (04) on wider F.S. 309. Reenter Chubb Park and continue to F.S. 311 at 9.4 miles (05). Alternate entry point is 2.9 miles east (11).

Reset odometer and turn left on F.S. 311 at Waypoint 05 or continue straight if you've used the alternate entrance from Trout Creek Pass (11). The road winds uphill and crosses a ridge, then drops down and crosses Goddard Ranch. Great pictures here of old ranch buildings with mountain backdrop. The ranch is private property so take pictures from the road. Don't forget this section is closed December 1 through April 30. Bear left at 4.1 and right at 4.2 where ATV Trail #1414 goes left. The road drops steeply downhill and crosses the North Fork of Sevenmile Creek, then climbs steeply up the other side. At 4.9 miles (06), make a right on F.S. 373. Stay left at 5.5, then at 5.8, continue straight past a scenic camp spot on the left.

A triangular intersection is reached at 6.4 miles (07). *Reset your odometer here*. Right dead ends at a hiking trail for Davis Meadow. I've been told this steep trail gets you close to the Natural Arch. (See map for GPS coordinates.) To continue on trail, turn left at triangular intersection (07). Continue straight where road goes left to a campsite at 1.4. At 2.3 miles, continue straight on 375A that follows a sandy wash. Stay right at 2.9 miles. A road to the left dead ends at a camp spot under some trees. The road passes beaver ponds and crosses a small culvert bridge over Fourmile Creek.

Larger F.S. 375 is reached at 3.9 miles (08). Turn left and continue through an area with good campsites. Continue straight at 5.4 miles (09) where 376 joins on left. This fun road, known as the Lenhardy Cutoff, takes you back to the Shields Gulch where you started, but it is easy to get lost in a maze of side roads for ATVs and dirt bikes. As you continue downhill on the main road, you'll pass a parking and staging area. An information board here has a dispenser with maps of the Fourmile Area. If empty, contact the San Isabel National Forest of BLM and ask for a map of the Fourmile Travel Management Area.

At 6.5 miles (10), turn left on larger F.S. 371 that parallels railroad tracks and the Arkansas River. On summer weekends, the river is often filled with rafters. Follow 371 south into Buena Vista where it becomes North Colorado Avenue. Turn right when you reach Main Street at 9.0 miles. A traffic light marks Hwy. 24 at 9.2 miles.

Return Trip: Left on Hwy. 24 takes you back to Johnson Village and start of trail. Left also goes to Nathrop, Poncha Springs and Salida on Hwy. 285. Right on Hwy. 24 goes to Independence Pass, Leadville and Area 4 trails.

Services: Full services in Buena Vista. Johnson Village has several gas stations and restaurants. I did not see any toilets along the trail.

Maps: Map of the Fourmile Travel Management Area. San Isabel National Forest. Trails Illustrated, Buena Vista, Collegiate Peaks #129. DeLorme Atlas & Gazetteer.

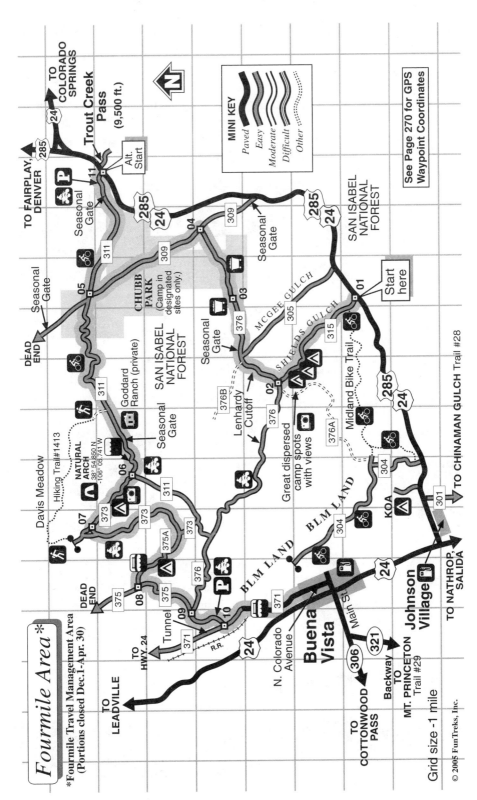

Fourmile Area*

*Fourmile Travel Management Area
(Portions closed Dec.1-Apr. 30)

MINI KEY

Paved
Easy
Moderate
Difficult
Other

See Page 270 for GPS
Waypoint Coordinates

N

TO COLORADO SPRINGS
24
285
TO FAIRPLAY, DENVER

Trout Creek Pass
(9,500 ft.)

Alt. Start
11
P
Seasonal Gate

285
24
04
309

Seasonal Gate

311
05
Seasonal Gate

CHUBB PARK
(Camp in designated sites only.)

309
03
376

285
24
SAN ISABEL NATIONAL FOREST

Start here
01

MCGEE GULCH

305
SHIELDS GULCH

315

Midland Bike Trail
02
376

376B
Lenhardy Cutoff
376

Goddard Ranch (private)

SAN ISABEL NATIONAL FOREST

311
Seasonal Gate

DEAD END

Davis Meadow

Hiking Trail #1413

NATURAL ARCH
38° 54.850 N
-106° 05.741 W

06
311

373
373
375A
373
375
376

07
373

DEAD END
375
08
375
371
09
Tunnel
371
371
R.R.
10
P

BLM LAND

BLM LAND
304
304
301

376A
Great dispersed camp spots with views

KOA

TO CHINAMAN GULCH Trail #28

24
Main St.
Buena Vista

N. Colorado Avenue

24
TO LEADVILLE

TO HWY. 24

306
321
Johnson Village

TO COTTONWOOD PASS

Backway TO
MT. PRINCETON Trail #29

TO NATHROP, SALIDA

Grid size -1 mile

© 2005 FunTreks, Inc.

121

Author's club—the Colorado Four Wheelers—gathers in Chinaman Gulch.

Tough climb begins after 0.3 miles.

Final descent is rocky, steep and scenic.

Attempting the toughest part of the *Waterfall*.

Watch for dirt bikes and ATVs.

Entry to Carnage Canyon.

More of Carnage Canyon.

Chinaman Gulch, Carnage Cyn. 28

Location: Southeast of Buena Vista and Johnson Village.

Difficulty: **Chinaman Gulch:** Difficult: The rockiest part of the trail is within the first half mile. Chinaman Gulch is narrow and sandy with isolated rock obstacles. Two obstacles in the gulch can be completely bypassed, while a third has a moderate approach on one side. A narrow trail climbs tightly through the trees out of the gulch, then descends a rocky ridge back to the start of loop. The trail is better suited for modified vehicles with lockers and skid plates. **Carnage Canyon:** An extreme trail for radically modified vehicles. Minimum 35-inch tires with lockers both ends. Even with this equipment, you'll need to winch much of the time. Mechanical failure and body damage are a common occurrence.

Features: This area is primarily used by four-wheelers, ATVs and dirt bikes. Hikers and mountain bikers find other places more appealing. The trail is open all year and receives comparatively small amounts of snow. Consequently, it is a popular winter destination. Carnage Canyon is a nationally recognized extreme trail. Out-of-state license plates are often seen in the parking area.

     The organized four-wheeling communtity has worked hard with the BLM to keep this area open for 4-wheeling. It is critical that users stay on established routes at all times. Users of Carnage Canyon are expected to clean up any type of fluid spills, immediately. Make sure someone in your group carries a spill kit. Rock-stacking is heavily frowned upon. If you must stack rocks to get over an obstacle, remove them when you are done.

Time & Distance: You will have covered 7.3 miles by the time you return to the start of Chinaman Gulch. Allow a couple of hours of driving time plus additional time for optional obstacles. The trail is a popular daytrip for 4WD clubs from Denver and Colorado Springs. Carnage Canyon is less than a mile long. I've seen a few people drive this trail in less than an hour, but first-time users can expect to take 3 or 4 hours. Spending all day on the trail is not uncommon. Most of the additional time is spent waiting for axle repairs. In the summer, the tight canyon gets very hot while waiting.

To Get There: Take Hwy. 285 southwest from Denver or Hwy. 24 west from Colorado Springs. As you approach Johnson Village south of Buena Vista, watch for County Road 301 on the left 0.3 miles before the Arkansas River Bridge. Turn south on 301 and go 1.6 miles on wide graded road. Several roads go left. The correct road is marked with a large BLM sign for

Chinaman Gulch and Carnage Canyon. Open and close the gate and head east another 0.4 miles. Pass through another gate before reaching open area for parking marked by large sign for the Fourmile Travel Management Area. More parking is available straight ahead for Carnage Canyon.

Trail Description: **Chinaman Gulch:** *Reset odometer at parking area* (01). Head north (left) along fenceline. At 0.2 miles (02), road curves right across a clearing and heads uphill in opposite direction. Ignore road to left. Vehicles with poor articulation and no lockers will struggle starting at 0.3 miles. The road splits and comes back together in a couple of places. Make a sharp left at 1.0 miles (03). (Road to right is exit route for Carnage Canyon.) The trail gets easier but remains steep and narrow in places. Bear right when you drop into a sandy wash at 1.7 miles (04). (The road to the left is closed and the road ahead is where you'll come out later.) Follow sandy wash east as it gradually narrows. The optional *Rockpile* is on the right at 2.0 miles. It is a fun challenge, but easy to get around.

You begin to encounter some rocks in the wash before reaching the *Waterfall* at 2.6 miles (05). The farther left you attack the obstacle, the more difficult it is. Those attempting the extremely difficult far left side can expect rollovers and broken axles. The far right side is fairly easy. After the *Waterfall*, the wash narrows with tight trees and climbs out of Chinaman Gulch to the right. Stay left at a high point at 3.6 miles (06) where 1423 goes right. Optional *Little Double Whammy* is on the right just after this intersection. The trail drops downhill to the left over varied terrain. It is narrow in spots with several tight switchbacks and rocky ledges. Turn left at 5.5 miles (07) and drop down steep, tippy spot before returning to start of loop at 5.6 miles (04). Redrive incoming route and return to start at 7.3 miles (01).

Trail Description: **Carnage Canyon:** Continue straight (east) after passing through second gate (01). Carnage Canyon starts just ahead at big sign and rock obstacle. Trail eases up a short distance then begins series of brutal challenges. After completing the final winch hill before first mile is reached, bear left and connect to Chinaman Gulch Trail (03). Once on Chinaman Gulch, turn left to return to start or right to complete Chinaman Gulch.

Return Trip: Return the way you came.

Services: Full services in Buena Vista. Gas and food at Johnson Village. Great KOA Campground across Hwy. 24 just east of 301. No toilets on trail.

Maps: Map of the Fourmile Travel Management Area.

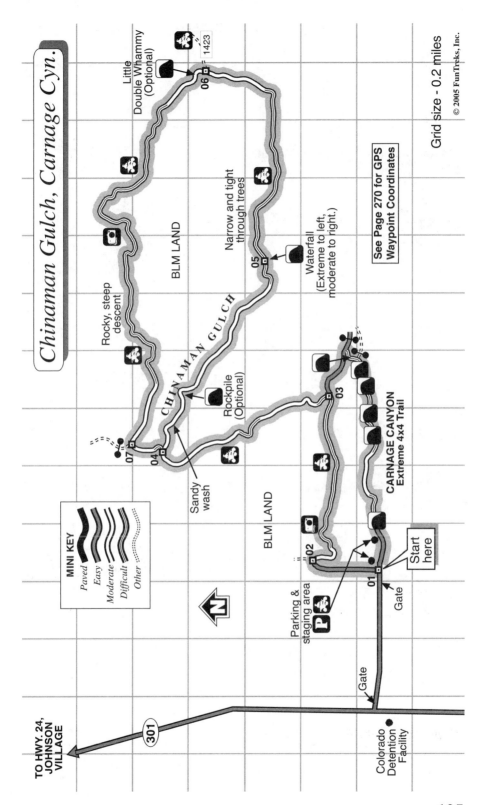

Chinaman Gulch, Carnage Cyn.

Little
Double Whammy
(Optional)

1423

06

BLM LAND

Rocky, steep
descent

Narrow and tight
through trees

05

Waterfall
(Extreme to left,
moderate to right.)

CHINAMAN GULCH

Rockpile
(Optional)

07

04

03

CARNAGE CANYON
Extreme 4x4 Trail

Sandy
wash

BLM LAND

02

Parking &
staging area

P

Start
here

01

Gate

Gate

Colorado
Detention
Facility

301

TO HWY. 24,
JOHNSON
VILLAGE

MINI KEY

Paved
Easy
Moderate
Difficult
Other

N

See Page 270 for GPS
Waypoint Coordinates

Grid size - 0.2 miles

© 2005 FunTreks, Inc.

125

Trail starts here. Mt. Princeton top center.

Lower road is wide but steep in places.

Passing is tight along this section of route.

Waypoint 02 begins moderate portion.

I hiked from here. Snow remained on June 14.

Bristlecone Park USFS Chalet open to public.

I was able to get around this snow.

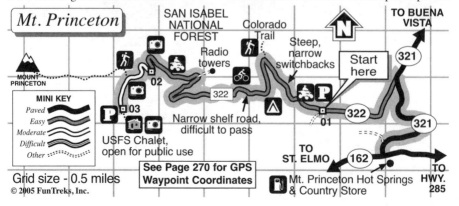

Mt. Princeton

SAN ISABEL
NATIONAL
FOREST

Colorado
Trail

TO BUENA
VISTA

N

Radio
towers

Steep,
narrow
switchbacks

Start
here

321

MOUNT
PRINCETON

02

322

01

322

321

MINI KEY

P

03

Paved
Easy
Moderate
Difficult
Other

USFS Chalet,
open for public use

Narrow shelf road,
difficult to pass

TO
ST. ELMO

162

Grid size - 0.5 miles

© 2005 FunTreks, Inc.

See Page 270 for GPS
Waypoint Coordinates

Mt. Princeton Hot Springs
& Country Store

TO
HWY.
285

Mt. Princeton 29

Location: Southwest of Buena Vista. West of Nathrop.

Difficulty: Moderate. Most of the road is easy except near top. Narrow shelf road may be intimidating to some. Most stock SUVs can do it. Low range is required for steep climbs. Snow may block trail in June and early July.

Features: A popular tourist road because of its easy access. A relatively short drive to outstanding views. Road does not go all the way to top. Enjoy famous Mt. Princeton Hot Springs. A few small camp spots along route. ATVs and dirt bikes are allowed, but area can get congested.

Time & Distance: About 5.5 miles to the end of the trail above 12,000 ft. Allow 2-3 hours for round trip—longer on busy weekends.

To Get There: From Johnson Village, head south on Hwy. 285 about 6 miles. Just past Nathrop, turn right on C.R. 162 and go 4.4 miles west to Mt. Princeton Hot Springs. Turn right uphill on C.R. 321. Stay on paved road 1.2 miles to C.R. 322. Bear left on dirt portion of 322, less than a mile to Mt. Princeton entrance.

Trail Description: Reset odometer at Mt.Princeton entrance (01). Pass through parking area and stay right uphill on F.S. 322 along fence. Road soon narrows with steep sections. Stay left at switchback at 1.1 miles where Colorado Hiking Trail goes right. The road comes out of the trees along a narrow shelf road where it is tricky to pass. Uphill vehicles have right-of-way, but use common sense. Stay left at 3.2 where road goes right to radio towers. At 4.2 miles (02), steeper road becomes more chewed up. Passenger cars often park here. One last switchback follows before shelf road crosses face of mountain. Hiking may be necessary in early season if snow blocks road. Steep climb to right leads to small parking area at 5.4 miles (03). Follow short hiking trail to Bristlecone Park USFS Chalet. The public is allowed to stay in the lodge but you are expected to leave it better than you find it. To reach top of Mt. Princeton, you must take a strenuous hike.

Return Trip: Return the way you came or take paved C.R. 321 directly north into Buena Vista. When you reach Main Street, turn right for Hwy. 24.

Services: Full services in Buena Vista. Gas/store at Mt. Princeton Hot Spgs.

Maps: San Isabel National Forest. Trails Illustrated Salida, St. Elmo, Shavano Peak #130. DeLorme Atlas and Gazetteer.

Crossing Baldwin Creek (Waypoint 02).

SUVs should stop here about half mile from top.

Just a few of the many switchbacks on Mt. Antero.

Last half mile is dangerous.

Brrrr! Fresh snow at summit on July 29.

Quiet and remote Browns Lake.

Mt. Antero,
Browns Lake

Alpine Res.

TO HWY. 285

01 162

TO
ST. ELMO

Start
here

277

MINI KEY
Paved
Easy
Moderate
Difficult
Other

BOULDER
MOUNTAIN

02

277

278

MT. ANTERO
(14,269 ft)

04

278A

BALDWIN
LAKES
Trail #31

03

278B

278

MT.
WHITE

SAN ISABEL
NATIONAL
FOREST

05 Browns
Lake

See Page 270 for GPS
Waypoint Coordinates

© 2005 FunTreks, Inc.

Grid size - 1 mile

128

Mt. Antero, Browns Lake ◆30◆

Location: Southwest of Buena Vista. West of Nathrop.

Difficulty: Difficult. Extremely narrow shelf road with tight switchbacks. Small SUVs with low-range gearing and high clearance can drive all but last half mile to top of Mt. Antero. Experienced drivers only. Snow melts late.

Features: Incredibly high drive to above 14,000 feet. Quiet camping at remote Browns Lake. Popular hiking area. Great ATV experience. Forest Service campgounds and private resorts along C.R. 162.

Time & Distance: 7.3 miles to top of Mt. Antero. Allow 3 to 4 hours for the round trip. Add another 2 hours for 7-mile round trip to Browns Lake.

To Get There: From Johnson Village, head south on Hwy. 285 about 6 miles. Just past Nathrop, turn west on C.R. 162 and go 12.3 miles to sign for Mt. Antero.

Trail Description: *Reset odometer as you turn left off 162* (01). Follow rocky F.S. 277 uphill. Turn left at 2.7 miles (02) and cross Baldwin Creek. Above trees, road narrows with very tight switchbacks. Timid drivers beware. Road levels out and forks at 6.2 miles (03). Turn left on 278A for Mt. Antero. Stay left at 6.3 where 278B goes right to Mt. White. Only hard-core vehicles with lockers should proceed past wide spot at 6.7 miles. Trail is mix of large boulders and soft soil. Stock SUVs should park and hike to top. Summit is reached at 7.3 miles (04).

　　To reach Browns Lake: *Reset odometer where road forks at 6.2 miles* (03). Turn right on 278. At 1.0 miles bear left downhill and descend rocky switchbacks. Good camp spot on left at 1.8 miles. Stay left at 2.1 where road goes right across creek to camp spot. Road weaves tightly through trees then opens up. Rocky, steep road follows before reaching Browns Lake at 3.5 miles (05). Note waterfalls on right 0.2 miles before lake.

Return Trip: Return the way you came. Remember to stay in low gear and use your brakes as little as possible on steep sections.

Services: Full services in Buena Vista and Salida. Gas and supplies at Mt. Princeton Country Store at Mt. Princeton Hot Springs Resort.

Maps: San Isabel National Forest. Trails Illustrated Salida, St. Elmo #130. DeLorme Atlas and Gazetteer.

Continue straight here. Mt. Antero to left.

Trail above Baldwin Lakes.

Rough talus slopes on way to Baldwin Lakes.

Mine at end of Baldwin Lakes Trail (keep out).

Going up narrow Boulder Mtn.

Near end of Boulder Mountain.

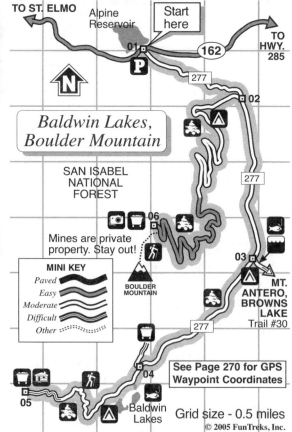

TO ST. ELMO

Alpine Reservoir

Start here

01

P

162

TO HWY. 285

277

02

Baldwin Lakes, Boulder Mountain

SAN ISABEL NATIONAL FOREST

277

N

06

Mines are private property. Stay out!

BOULDER MOUNTAIN

03

MT. ANTERO, BROWNS LAKE
Trail #30

277

MINI KEY

Paved
Easy
Moderate
Difficult
Other

04

05

Baldwin Lakes

See Page 270 for GPS Waypoint Coordinates

Grid size - 0.5 miles

© 2005 FunTreks, Inc.

130

Baldwin Lakes, Boulder Mtn.

Location: Southwest of Buena Vista. West of Nathrop.

Difficulty: Moderate: Rocky, narrow road suitable for aggressive, high-clearance SUVs. Oversize vehicles should not attempt Boulder Mountain. Marginally difficult above Baldwin Lakes. Snow melts late.

Features: Scenic, remote, lesser-traveled backroads. Camp and fish at Baldwin Lakes. Great for ATVs, especially narrower Boulder Mountain. Staging at several wide spots along C.R. 162 near start.

Time & Distance: Mine above Baldwin Lakes is 6.0 miles one way. Round trip takes 3 to 4 hours. Side trip to Boulder Mountain is 5 miles one way. Round trip takes 2 to 3 hours.

To Get There: From Johnson Village, head south on Hwy. 285 about 6 miles. Just past Nathrop, turn west on C.R. 162 and go 12.3 miles. Turn left at sign for Baldwin Lakes.

Trail Description: Reset odometer as you turn left off 162 (01). Follow rocky road uphill. Continue straight at 1.1 where lesser road goes right. Continue straight again at 1.2 miles (02) where road goes right to Boulder Mountain (described below). At 2.7 miles (03), continue straight uphill where road goes left across creek to Mt. Antero. Ignore smaller side roads. Stay right at 3.6 and begin crossing rocky talus slopes. Stay left at 4.2 miles (04) where lesser road goes right to mine. Climb past lakes, then bear right at 4.9 at small parking spot for hiking trail to upper lake. Rough, rocky road winds uphill to mine building at 6.0 miles (05). (Mines are dangerous, stay back.)

Side trip to Boulder Mountain: *Reset odometer and turn right at 1.2 miles* (02). Follow narrow road through tight trees. Road joins on left at cabin ruin at 0.9. Road follows valley, then turns sharply right up series of very narrow switchbacks. Watch for falling rocks. After 3 miles, road flattens out and gets easier. Gentle switchbacks follow, then easy talus slopes. Trail ends around corner at small mine hut about 5.0 miles (06).

Return Trip: Return the way you came.

Services: Full services in Buena Vista and Salida. Gas and supplies at Mt. Princeton Country Store at Mt. Princeton Hot Springs Resort.

Maps: San Isabel National Forest. Trails Illustrated Salida, St. Elmo #130. DeLorme Atlas & Gazetteer.

View upon arrival at Grizzly Lake.

Dispersed camping at north end of lake.

Author with dog Chevy. PHOTO BY TOM CROAK

Going down toughest spot. PHOTO BY TOM CROAK

Toughest spot is at the beginning.

132

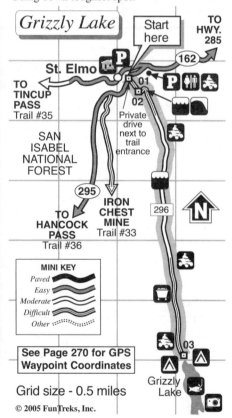

Grizzly Lake

Start here

TO HWY. 285

162

St. Elmo

P

01

P

02

TO TINCUP PASS
Trail #35

Private drive next to trail entrance

SAN ISABEL NATIONAL FOREST

295

296

N

TO HANCOCK PASS
Trail #36

IRON CHEST MINE
Trail #33

MINI KEY

Paved
Easy
Moderate
Difficult
Other

03

Grizzly Lake

See Page 270 for GPS Waypoint Coordinates

Grid size - 0.5 miles

© 2005 FunTreks, Inc.

Grizzly Lake ◆32◆

Location: Southwest of Buena Vista. West of Nathrop near St. Elmo.

Difficulty: Difficult. The toughest part of this trail is at the beginning where a difficult rock obstacle follows a stream crossing. The remainder of the trail is mostly moderate with a few marginally difficult muddy and rocky places. Not recommended for stock vehicles.

Features: Take your camera. The lake, with surrounding mountains, is pure Colorado beauty. Early fishing is best before the wind kicks up. Take insect repellent. Camp spots, near the lake, are limited in number. Tough trail for ATVs because of the initial obstacle.

Time & Distance: Allow 1 to 1-1/2 hours in a properly equipped vehicle. Lake is 2.7 miles from start.

To Get There: From Johnson Village, head south on Hwy. 285 about 6 miles. Just past Nathrop, turn right on C.R. 162. Go west 15.4 miles to parking/ staging area (with toilet) on left. Immediately after parking area, bear left on C.R. 295 where road forks right to St. Elmo. Watch for small road on left after 0.2 miles. A private drive next to trail entrance usually has KEEP OUT sign and chain across drive. Enter trail immediately left of sign.

Trail Description: Reset odometer as you turn left off 295 (01). Within 0.1 miles (02), turn left across creek and climb rock obstacle. Driver's choice follows as rocky trail turns right uphill. Soon trail levels out and gets easier. Stay right at 0.9 miles. Cross creek again at 1.1 miles and go by ruins of a cabin. Pass large, roofless cabin at 1.4. Cross possible muddy area, then rocky talus slopes. Bear left at 2.6 and lake soon appears. Road forks at 2.7 miles (03) at lake. Camping spots either way. Turn right to a high spot to get best pictures of lake.

Return Trip: Return the way you came.

Services: Full services in Buena Vista and Salida. Gas and supplies at the Mt. Princeton Hot Springs Country Store. Modern vault toilet at parking area 0.2 miles before start of trail. Small general store and ATV rental in St. Elmo. Forest Service campground northeast of St. Elmo.

Maps: San Isabel National Forest. Trails Illustrated Salida, St. Elmo #130. DeLorme Atlas & Gazetteer.

Upper end of boulder field.   Great scenery as you climb above timberline.

Lower end of boulder field.   Narrow shelf road can be blocked by snow.

Hike from start to see historic Ghost House.

Tram house at Iron Chest Mine (keep out).

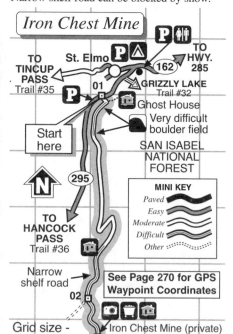

Iron Chest Mine

TO TINCUP PASS
Trail #35

St. Elmo

TO HWY. 285

162

01

GRIZZLY LAKE
Trail #32

Ghost House

Very difficult boulder field

Start here

SAN ISABEL NATIONAL FOREST

N

295

TO HANCOCK PASS
Trail #36

MINI KEY
Paved
Easy
Moderate
Difficult
Other

Narrow shelf road

See Page 270 for GPS Waypoint Coordinates

02

Grid size - 0.5 miles

Iron Chest Mine (private)

03   © 2005 FunTreks, Inc.

134

Iron Chest Mine ◆33◆

Location: Southwest of Buena Vista. West of Nathrop near St. Elmo.

Difficulty: Difficult. Iron Chest has always been known for its difficult boulder field. When the boulders were pushed aside to allow maintenance at the mine, many hard-core enthusiasts were disappointed. I'm happy to report that the boulders have returned and the trail is now harder than ever. I barely got through with 33-inch tires and two lockers. Extremely difficult for ATVs.

Features: Classic hard-core trail with historic structures at Iron Chest Mine. Ghost House at start of trail requires short hike. (Mines private, stay out.)

Time & Distance: Total of 2.9 miles, one way. Allow 3 to 4 hours for round trip. Most of that time is spent getting through the boulder field.

To Get There: From Johnson Village, head south on Hwy. 285 about 6 miles. Just past Nathrop, turn right on C.R. 162. Go west 15.4 miles to parking/staging area (with toilet) on left. Immediately after parking area, bear left on C.R. 295 where road forks right to St. Elmo. Watch for small road and parking area on left after 0.4 miles. (Don't confuse with Grizzly at 0.2 miles.)

Trail Description: *Reset odometer as you turn left off 295* (01). Road goes left, then immediately turns right and starts into boulder field. (Gate on left marks the start of hiking trail to Ghost House.) After 0.3 miles, boulder field ends and a narrow road weaves tightly through the trees. After a cabin at 1.7, cross very narrow shelf road. Snow lingers late here. If blocked, be prepared to back up. Stay left at 2.3 miles (02) where lesser road goes right. Rocky trail winds uphill to mine at 2.9 miles (03). Return the way you came.

Historical Highlights: The buildings at Iron Chest Mine are over 100 years old and are in relatively good condition given the 12,000-ft. altitude. A giant pulley lies on the ground in front of a large tram house with tram towers going down the mountain. Just over the high ridge above the mine is the Mary Murphy Mine, which can be reached via Pomeroy Lakes, Trail #34. Take a short 250-yard hike to the interesting Ghost House near start of trail. The cabin was built in 1886. Flattened tin cans were used as roof shingles.

Services: Full services in Buena Vista and Salida. Gas and supplies at Mt. Princeton Country Store. Small general store and ATV rental in St. Elmo.

Maps: San Isabel N.F. Trails Illustrated #130. DeLorme Atlas & Gazetteer.

Mary Murphy Mill (keep out).

Snow remains in mid June near top of trail.

Great trail for ATVs.

End of trail at (Lower) Pomeroy Lake.

Side trip to mine is very narrow.

Mary Murphy Mine at 12,000 ft.

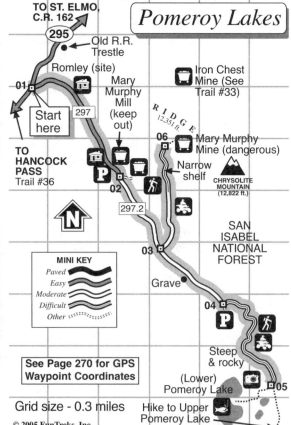

Pomeroy Lakes

TO ST. ELMO, C.R. 162

295

Old R.R. Trestle

Romley (site)

01

Start here

297

TO HANCOCK PASS
Trail #36

Mary Murphy Mill (keep out)

02

297.2

03

MINI KEY
Paved
Easy
Moderate
Difficult
Other

Grave

See Page 270 for GPS Waypoint Coordinates

Grid size - 0.3 miles

© 2005 FunTreks, Inc.

Iron Chest Mine (See Trail #33)

RIDGE 12,351 ft.

06

Mary Murphy Mine (dangerous)

Narrow shelf

CHRYSOLITE MOUNTAIN (12,822 ft.)

SAN ISABEL NATIONAL FOREST

04

Steep & rocky

(Lower) Pomeroy Lake

05

Hike to Upper Pomeroy Lake

Pomeroy Lakes ◆34◆

Location: Southwest of Buena Vista. West of Nathrop near St. Elmo.

Difficulty: Difficult. Steep and rocky below lakes. Very narrow shelf road climbs to Mary Murphy Mine. Mary Murphy Mill can be reached over easy terrain. Difficult portions of trail are not suitable for stock vehicles.

Features: Several historic mine buildings remain intact (private, keep out). Get close to remote fishing lakes. Great trail for ATVs and dirt bikes.

Time & Distance: Lower Pomeroy Lake is 2.7 miles. Add 0.6 miles for side trip to Mary Murphy Mine. Allow 2 to 3 hours to see everything.

To Get There: From Johnson Village, head south on Hwy. 285 about 6 miles. Just past Nathrop, turn right on C.R. 162. Go west 15.4 miles to parking/staging area (with toilet) on left. Immediately after parking area, bear left on C.R. 295. Go another 2.8 miles. Turn left at sign for Mary Murphy Mine after point where road dips to right to bypass old trestle.

Trail Description: *Reset odometer as you turn left off 295* (01). Rocky road climbs past scenic cabin to Mary Murphy Mill Complex at 0.7 miles. Bear right on 297.2 at 0.8 miles (02). Stay left at 1.0 where private road goes right. Bear right at 1.3 miles (03) where road goes left to Mary Murphy Mine. (Side trip described below.) Interesting grave on right at 1.6 followed by road that joins on left. Turn sharply left up steep, rocky road at 1.9 miles (04). Trail ends at 2.7 miles (05) near Lower Pomeroy Lake. Return the way you came.
  Side trip to Mary Murphy Mine: Turn left at 1.3 miles (03). Road gets very narrow after 0.3 miles. There is room to turn around at top near mine at 0.6 miles (06). View mine from distance. Return the way you came.

Historical Highlights: Mary Murphy Mine was a top producing mine that supported the town of Romley. The area flourished between 1870 and the early 1900s. The main part of Romley was located in a meadow below C.R. 295. Romley was also known as "Red Town," because all buildings in town were painted red with white trim. The railroad removed its tracks in 1926, but it was not until 1982 that the town was torn down by its owners.

Services: Full services in Buena Vista and Salida. Gas and supplies at Mt. Princeton Country Store. Small general store and ATV rental in St. Elmo.

Maps: San Isabel N.F. Trails Illustrated #130. DeLorme Atlas & Gazetteer.

Business end of St. Elmo. General store at right.   Camping along 267.

Stock SUV begins the journey.   ATVs start down south side of pass toward St. Elmo.

South side approaching pass.

View from Mirror Lake to Tincup Pass (low point on horizon).

No gas at Tincup Store.

Church in center of Tincup.   View of Tincup from F.S. 765, entering on south side.

138

Tincup Pass, St. Elmo 35

Location: Southwest of Buena Vista and west of Nathrop. Between St. Elmo and Tincup.

Difficulty: Moderate. Rocky at the top with one short section of narrow shelf road at 12,000 feet that often remains snow covered into early July. After the snow clears, this trail is suitable for any high-clearance, 4-wheel-drive SUV with low-range gearing. St. Elmo can be reached by car. The optional "Old Tincup" route has one difficult rocky section.

Features: A beautiful high-elevation route starting and ending at historic, quaint mountain towns. St. Elmo is one of the most popular ghost towns in Colorado. All of the buildings are privately owned and a few are occupied by active businesses. Tincup is a small residential community with many century-old buildings. A tiny steepled white church in the center of town punctuates the photogenic setting. Good area for ATVs.

Time & Distance: Total length from St. Elmo to Tincup is 13 miles. "Old Tincup" route saves 0.4 miles. Allow about 2 hours one way.

To Get There: From Johnson Village, head south on Hwy. 285 about 6 miles. Just past Nathrop, turn right on C.R. 162. Go west 15.4 miles to parking/staging area (with toilet) on left. Immediately after parking area, bear right following sign to St. Elmo. In center of town, turn right following sign to Tincup Pass. Cross wooden bridge and turn left. Trail starts uphill to right on F.S./C.R. 267 at large brown & white forest sign.

Trail Description: Reset odometer at start (01). Wide road climbs steadily uphill and gets progressively rougher. Plenty of places to park, unload and camp along the way. Hiking trail on left at 3.8. Popular camp spot on right at 5.0. Road switchbacks uphill and crosses narrow shelf road before reaching pass at 6.1 miles (02).

Roughest part of trail drops down other side of pass. "Old Tincup" goes right at 6.7 miles (03). Stay left on main trail as it circles downhill through a potentially muddy area. Stay left again at 7.6 miles (04) where "Old Tincup" joins on right. A rocky road splits various ways as it goes around the east side of Mirror Lake. The road closest to the lake is sometimes under water. Parking area for lake is reached at 9.5 miles (05). Follow better road downhill past Mirror Lake Campground and hiking trailhead. The center of Tincup at F.S. 765 is reached at 13.0 miles (06).

139

Return Trip: Right on 765 goes north to Taylor Reservoir. From there, you can take Cottonwood Pass Road back to Buena Vista. Left goes over Cumberland Pass to Pitkin. Left also goes to the Alpine Tunnel and Hancock Pass, Trail #36.

Reverse Directions: *Reset odometer in Tincup at intersection of 765 and 267* (06). Head east on 267. After about 3 miles, you'll pass a parking area for a hiking trail followed by Mirror Lake Campground. Parking lot for Mirror Lake is reached at 3.5 miles (05).

    Reset odometer and continue straight around east side of lake. Cross creek and head south uphill on rocky road. Make a hard right at 1.9 miles (04) where "Old Tincup" goes left. Circle around and climb through area that is sometimes muddy. Stay right at 2.8 miles (03) where "Old Tincup" joins on left. Continue uphill on rockiest part of trail to Tincup Pass at 3.4 miles (02). Follow wide, rocky road downhill to St. Elmo, reached at 9.5 miles (01).

    Turn right across wooden bridge into St. Elmo, then turn left through town on C.R. 162. Follow 162 east about 16 miles to Hwy. 285 at Nathrop. Left on 285 goes to Buena Vista and Johnson Village, right goes to Salida and Poncha Springs.

Historical Highlights: St. Elmo, Romley, and Iron City are the three main towns that served the prosperous Chalk Creek Mining District. St. Elmo was settled in 1878 and grew to a population of about 2,000. Like so many mining towns, the most prosperous businesses were saloons, dance halls and bawdy houses. In 1881, St. Elmo became an important station for the Denver, South Park and Pacific Railroad. During the construction of the Alpine Tunnel, St. Elmo was a bustling supply center. At that time, St. Elmo had multiple merchandise stores, hotels, restaurants and a weekly newspaper. By 1910, with mines failing and the Alpine Tunnel closed, St. Elmo lost its favor. When the last mine, Mary Murphy, closed down in 1920, St. Elmo was finished.

    Contrary to popular belief, Tincup is not a ghost town. Most of the old cabins in town have been restored to their original condition and are occupied. Still, one gets the impression the town is 150 years old.

Services: Full services in Buena Vista and Salida. Gas and supplies at Mt. Princeton Country Store on C.R. 162. Small general store and Jeep/ATV rental in St. Elmo. Tincup has one small log cabin restaurant and a tiny general store. I did not see a gas station in Tincup. See map for location of toilets at each end of the trail.

Maps: San Isabel and Gunnison National Forests. Trails Illustrated Maps #129 and #130. DeLorme Atlas & Gazetteer.

140

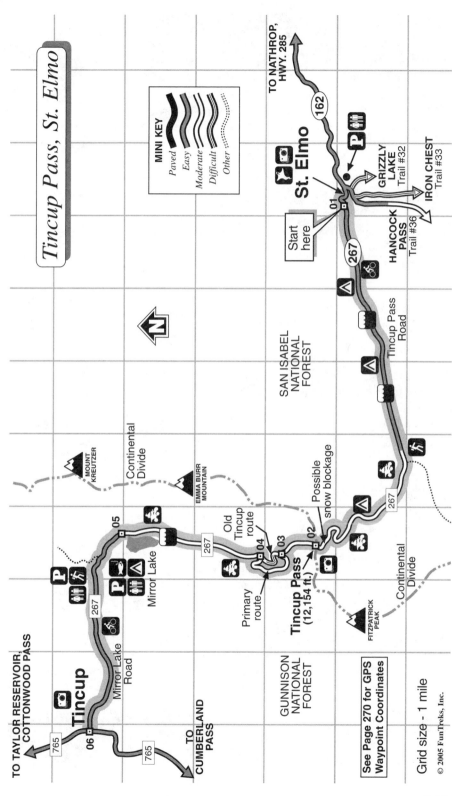

Tincup Pass, St. Elmo

MINI KEY
Paved
Easy
Moderate
Difficult
Other

St. Elmo

Start here

GRIZZLY LAKE
Trail #32

IRON CHEST
Trail #33

HANCOCK PASS
Trail #36

01

267

TO NATHROP, HWY. 285

162

SAN ISABEL NATIONAL FOREST

Tincup Pass Road

267

N

Continental Divide

MOUNT KREUTZER

EMMA BURR MOUNTAIN

Possible snow blockage

Old Tincup route

05

267

Mirror Lake

P

P

Tincup

06

765

TO TAYLOR RESERVOIR, COTTONWOOD PASS

Mirror Lake Road

TO CUMBERLAND PASS

765

04

03

02

Primary route

Tincup Pass (12,154 ft.)

FITZPATRICK PEAK

Continental Divide

GUNNISON NATIONAL FOREST

See Page 270 for GPS Waypoint Coordinates

Grid size - 1 mile

© 2005 FunTreks, Inc.

141

Parking/staging area on C.R. 162 just before start of trail.

Allie Belle Mine on C.R. 295.

North side climb is steep and rocky.

South side descent from Hancock Pass.

View of Hancock Pass from Tomichi.

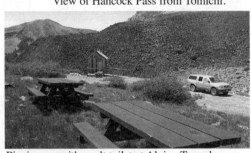
Picnic area with vault toilet at Alpine Tunnel.

Alpine Tunnel Road 839.

Restored railroad depot at Alpine Tunnel.

Hancock Pass, Alpine Tunnel 36

Location: Southwest of Buena Vista and south of St. Elmo.

Difficulty: Moderate. There are several fairly rocky sections but this trail is passable by stock, high-clearance vehicles with low-range gearing. Skid plates are helpful. The drive should not be attempted if snow is on the trail. Alpine Tunnel Road 839 is an easy graded gravel road.

Features: This trail offers just the right amount of challenge for aggressive, stock SUVs. There are outstanding views on the upper section. Two side trips are recommended: The first is to Hancock Lake, which requires passing through a fairly rocky section. The second is to the Alpine Tunnel over a well-maintained and easy ledge road. This road has signs along the way to explain the history of the area. ATVs can unload at a small parking area near Hancock Townsite.

Time & Distance: It is about 9.5 miles from St. Elmo to the end of Hancock where it runs into 839. The side trip to Hancock Lake and back adds 2.8 miles and the round trip to the Alpine Tunnel adds another 4.5 miles. Allow half a day including the side trips plus return time. If you return via Tincup Pass, Trail #35, or Cottonwood Pass, allow all day.

To Get There: From Johnson Village, head south on Hwy. 285 about 6 miles. Just past Nathrop, turn right on C.R. 162. Go west 15.4 miles to parking/staging area (with toilet) on left. Immediately after parking area, bear left on C.R. 295.

Trail Description: Reset odometer as you turn left on 295 (01). At the beginning, the road is fairly straight because you are following the original railroad bed that once led to the north side of the Alpine Tunnel. This is apparent at 2.7 miles where there is a detour around an old deteriorated railroad bridge. After the detour, there are signs to the Mary Murphy Mine to the left. Continue straight and at 5.4 miles (02) you reach the historic remains of the old town of Hancock. Please obey all signs and respect the property.

Immediately, as you leave Hancock, take the left fork marked as 295.2. At 5.6 miles (03), you come to a clearing surrounded by large trees. As you enter the clearing, look to your right and you will see F.S. 299. This is the road to Hancock Pass.

Side Trip to Hancock Lake: Before heading up to the pass, I recommend you continue straight on 295.2 to Hancock Lake for some great wheeling and beautiful scenery. As you continue on 295.2 there is another fork at 6.5 miles. Bear left. From this point, the trail gets a little rockier. The lake is another 0.6 miles ahead. You have to walk to the lake to see it.

Continuation of trail to Hancock Pass: After visiting the lake, return to the clearing at Waypoint 03, *reset your odometer* and turn left on 299. A rocky road climbs through the forest and at 1.5 miles, turns right up a steep, rocky ledge road. The pass is reached at 2.2 miles (04). As you go over the pass, you enter Gunnison National Forest and the road changes to 266. The road is steep and bumpy but not as rocky. You can stop at 3.1 miles to enjoy lunch and great views of Tomichi Pass, Trail #37.

You intersect with Tomichi Pass Road at 3.2 miles (05). Continue straight on what is now F.S. 888. A narrow road drops downhill and intersects with 839 at 3.9 miles (06). Turn right to see the Alpine Tunnel, reached at 6.2 miles (07).

Return Trip: The quickest way out is to return the way you came. However, if you have plenty of time, you have other interesting options as follows: Go back up Hancock and take Tomichi Pass, Trail #37. Or, follow 839 downhill to 765 where you can go left to Pitkin or right to Tincup. At Tincup, you can turn right and return via Tincup Pass, Trail #35. You can also head north past Tincup and connect to Cottonwood Pass Road back to Buena Vista. This last option is the most time consuming.

Services: Full services in Buena Vista and Salida. Gas and supplies at Mt. Princeton Country Store on C.R. 162. Small general store and Jeep/ATV rental in St. Elmo. Pitkin has several great country stores and gas. Tincup has one small restaurant and general store, but no gas. Modern vault toilet at parking area before start of trail and at the Alpine Tunnel.

Historical Highlights: Hancock Road and the Alpine Tunnel Road were built along the original railroad bed that passed through the Alpine Tunnel in the 1880s. Notice the black soot that still clings to the side of the road at various points along the way. Structures along the road serviced the railroad. At one time you could drive to the north side of the tunnel, but the road is now closed and you must hike or bike.

For many years, the 4x4 road over Williams Pass was permanently closed. But, in recent years, the Forest Service decided to open the road one month out of the year. As long as it lasts, you can now drive this road in the month of August. I drove the road and would rate it difficult because of one long stretch of wet, slippery boulders.

Maps: San Isabel and Gunnison National Forests. Trails Illustrated Map Salida, St. Elmo #130. DeLorme Atlas & Gazetteer.

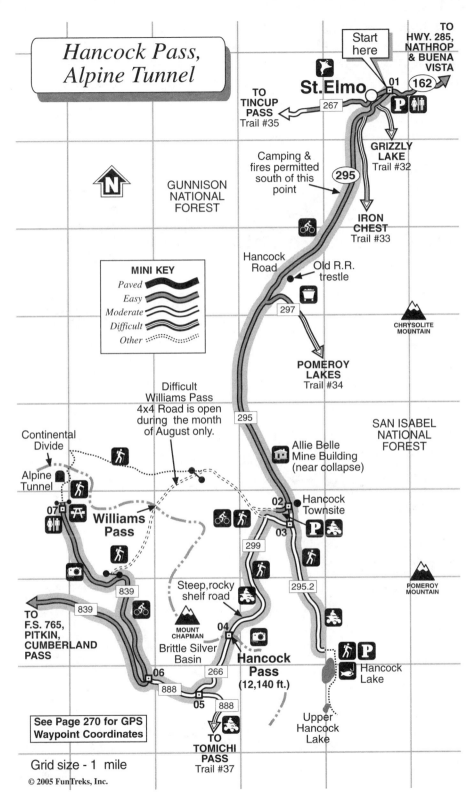

Hancock Pass, Alpine Tunnel

TO HWY. 285, NATHROP & BUENA VISTA

Start here

St.Elmo

01

162

TO TINCUP PASS Trail #35

267

GRIZZLY LAKE Trail #32

Camping & fires permitted south of this point

295

IRON CHEST Trail #33

Hancock Road

Old R.R. trestle

297

GUNNISON NATIONAL FOREST

N

CHRYSOLITE MOUNTAIN

POMEROY LAKES Trail #34

MINI KEY
Paved
Easy
Moderate
Difficult
Other

295

Difficult Williams Pass 4x4 Road is open during the month of August only.

SAN ISABEL NATIONAL FOREST

Continental Divide

Allie Belle Mine Building (near collapse)

Alpine Tunnel

07

Williams Pass

02 Hancock Townsite

03

P

299

295.2

POMEROY MOUNTAIN

839

839

Steep, rocky shelf road

TO F.S. 765, PITKIN, CUMBERLAND PASS

MOUNT CHAPMAN

04

Brittle Silver Basin

Hancock Pass (12,140 ft.)

P

Hancock Lake

06

266

05

888

888

Upper Hancock Lake

See Page 270 for GPS Waypoint Coordinates

TO TOMICHI PASS Trail #37

Grid size - 1 mile

© 2005 FunTreks, Inc.

145

Mine, cabin, and boiler at Brittle Silver Basin.

Deteriorating log bridge that crosses bog.

North side ascent. Wait until clear.

Looking north from Tomichi Pass. Hancock top left.

Water crossing on south-side descent.

Not much left at Tomichi Cemetery.

Turn at this sign when driving south to north.

146

Location: Southwest of Buena Vista between St. Elmo and Sargents.

Difficulty: Difficult. This rating is based on the narrowness of the trail rather than the road surface. Passing is extremely difficult on the north side. You may have to back up a considerable distance if you meet another vehicle. There are no hard-core obstacles, but several places are moderately rocky. Do not drive this trail if it is snow covered. Snow sometimes remains on the trail in late July. Be careful crossing deteriorating log bridge at bog. Trail is suitable for stock, high-clearance SUVs with low-range gearing. Not recommended for novice drivers or anyone afraid of heights.

Features: If you are ready to try a difficult trail that doesn't involve serious rock crawling, this is your opportunity. Views going up are spectacular but the driver won't be able to enjoy them until he reaches the pass. Don't start up the trail if someone is coming down even though uphill drivers have the right of way. The area is remote, so make sure you go with another vehicle. ATVs and dirt bikes will feel at home on the narrow trail.

Time & Distance: The route described here is 11.9 miles and takes about 2 hours. When you factor in getting to start of trail and the long trip home, allow a full day.

To Get There: Most people will first drive Hancock Pass, Trail #36, and turn left when they reach F.S. 888. You can also reach 888 from the Alpine Tunnel Road 839. (See map of Area 3.)

Trail Description: Reset odometer at start where 266 and 888 intersect (01). Head east on 888 following sign to Tomichi Pass. Trail is rocky with tight brush and intermittent standing water. Trail curves to right and goes by mine with cabin and boiler, then begins to climb. At 0.9 miles, you must cross a deteriorating log bridge over a bog. Hopefully, the bridge will be repaired at some future date; otherwise, the trail may eventually become impassable. After the bog, the trail starts its steep, narrow climb across the northwest face of Central Mountain. Look ahead to make sure no one is coming down. A curve in the road blocks view of upper part of trail, so watch for wide spots in case you have to back up to get around another vehicle. The pass, at 1.2 miles (02), has plenty of room to park.

A wide, more gradual 4x4 road descends the other side of the pass. It is a beautiful drive as it descends through the trees with water crossings and seasonal wildflowers. Stock vehicles will have to take their time to get through several rocky places. Tomichi Cemetery is reached at 4.3 miles (03). Stay right. The road becomes less defined as it drops downhill to the right across an open rocky area. When you get to the bottom of the hill at 4.6 miles (04), turn left on a better road.

Follow embedded-rock road downhill past private cabins. Dispersed camp spot on right at 6.2. The road gradually improves and crosses a bridge before passing through rustic town of Whitepine. Stay right at 7.1 where road goes left to large mining area. Pass Whitepine Cemetery and Snowblind F.S. Campground. Continue straight at 10.4 miles (05) where 887 goes right to Black Sage Pass. At 11.9 miles (06), you must choose an exit route. See below.

Return Trip: If you are heading towards Gunnison, continue straight on 888 for about 5 miles. The road soon becomes paved and runs into Hwy. 50 just east of Sargents. If you are heading to Salida or Buena Vista, turn left on Old Monarch Pass Road 237. This is a beautiful, fast drive as it winds uphill through dense forest more than 10 miles. After crossing Old Monarch Pass, the road drops downhill to Hwy. 50 about one mile below Monarch Pass.

Reverse Directions: Head north from Sargents on C.R. 888 or connect to 888 via Old Monarch Pass Road 237. *Reset odometer at the intersection of 888 and 237* (06) and head north. Continue straight where 887 goes left at 1.5 miles (05). Watch for big metal sign for Tomichi Pass at 7.3 miles (04). Just past sign, turn right uphill and climb rocky road. Stay left as roads branch right until you reach Tomichi Cemetery at 7.6 miles (03). Bear left at cemetery and climb 4x4 road to Tomichi Pass at 10.7 miles (02). Check for vehicles coming up before you descend narrow shelf road to connect with Hancock Pass Road, Trail #36, at 11.9 miles (01). Right goes over Hancock Pass to St. Elmo and connects to Hwy 285 via C.R. 162. Left goes to Alpine Tunnel, Cumberland Pass and Pitkin.

Services: Gas at Sargents, Pitkin and the Mt. Princeton Country Store along C.R. 162 west of Nathrop. Full services in Buena Vista, Salida and Gunnison.

Historical Highlights: The town of Tomichi (near site of cemetery) had a population of 1500 during the boom years of the 1880s. The silver crash of 1893 brought an end to the town. In 1896 a few prospectors returned, but most were killed in 1899 when a snowslide destroyed the town. Remnants of building foundations can be found with patient examination of the area.

Maps: Gunnison National Forest. Trails Illustrated Salida, St. Elmo #130. DeLorme Atlas & Gazetteer.

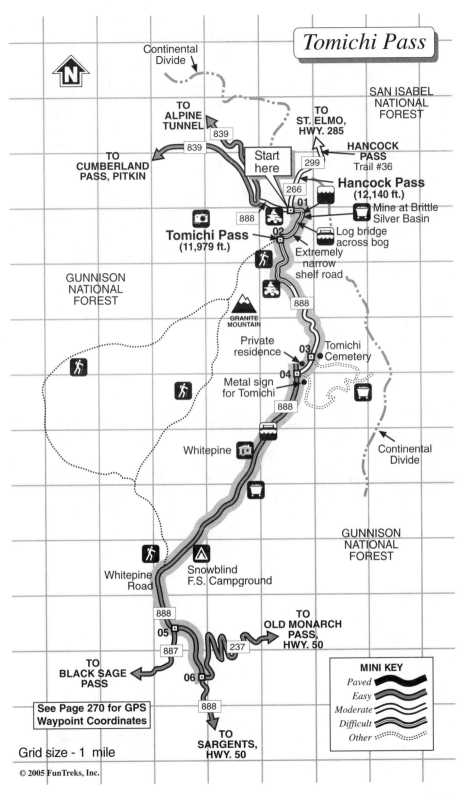

Tomichi Pass

Continental Divide

N

SAN ISABEL NATIONAL FOREST

TO ALPINE TUNNEL

839

839

TO ST. ELMO, HWY. 285

HANCOCK PASS
Trail #36

TO CUMBERLAND PASS, PITKIN

Start here

299

266

01

Hancock Pass
(12,140 ft.)

Mine at Brittle Silver Basin

888

Tomichi Pass
(11,979 ft.)

02

Log bridge across bog

Extremely narrow shelf road

GUNNISON NATIONAL FOREST

GRANITE MOUNTAIN

888

Private residence

03

Tomichi Cemetery

Metal sign for Tomichi

04

888

Whitepine

Continental Divide

GUNNISON NATIONAL FOREST

Whitepine Road

Snowblind F.S. Campground

888

TO OLD MONARCH PASS, HWY. 50

05

887

237

TO BLACK SAGE PASS

06

888

See Page 270 for GPS Waypoint Coordinates

MINI KEY
Paved
Easy
Moderate
Difficult
Other

Grid size - 1 mile

TO SARGENTS, HWY. 50

© 2005 FunTreks, Inc.

Start here at Hwy. 285 & C.R. 200.

F.S. 203 runs along Poncha Creek.

Road climbs through dense aspen forest. Great fall color.

Looking west from Marshall Pass. Several OHV routes depart from pass. Look for signs.

Aspens chewed down by beavers.

Store at Sargents has gas, food and restrooms.

Marshall Pass, Poncha Ck.

Location: Southwest of Poncha Springs; east of Sargents.

Difficulty: Easy. Marshall Pass can be reached from either side via well-graded, two-wheel-drive roads F.S. 243 and F.S. 200. The route shown here bypasses 200 and takes you up the east side along parallel Poncha Creek Road, F.S. 203. This 4-wheel-drive road is less traveled with fewer tourists. Suitable for any four-wheel-drive SUV. Road closed Nov. 15 to May 30.

Features: A popular camping and fishing area with several Forest Service campgrounds around O'Haver Lake. Poncha Creek Road offers a better backcountry experience with stream fishing and dispersed camping next to the water. A parking lot near Shirley Townsite and Marshall Pass provide convenient staging for ATVs and dirt bikes. Unlicensed vehicles are not allowed on major county roads entering and leaving the area.

Time & Distance: Total trip from Hwy. 285 to Hwy. 50 is 27.3 miles. Allow 3 to 4 hours. The four-wheel-drive portion of the trip is 10.5 miles.

To Get There: Take Hwy. 285 south from Poncha Springs about 5 miles. Turn right on well-marked C.R. 200 following signs to Marshall Pass.

Trail Description: Reset odometer as you turn off 285 (01). Head west on C.R. 200 and enter San Isabel National Forest. Continue straight at 2.3 miles at information board for Shirley Townsite. (Right is the most direct route to O'Haver Lake and easiest way to Marshall Pass via C.R. 200.) Make a right at 2.4 miles next to parking lot. Note places for RVs to camp on left. Cross one-lane bridge and turn left at 3.1 miles (02) on F.S. 203. (Right goes back to C.R. 200.) Lesser 203 stays fairly flat as it passes many great camp spots along Poncha Creek. Lesser roads branch off to other camp spots. Note many beaver ponds along route and fallen aspen trees chewed down by beavers.

     Starvation Creek Hiking Trailhead is on left at 5.6 miles (03). Road gets rougher and begins to climb more. Continue straight at 7.4 where road goes left downhill to nice spot in trees next to creek. Road winds through thick aspen forest and climbs more steeply. You may need low range as you climb above 10,000 feet into thinning pine forest. Stay right at 9.9 miles where 203A goes left. You reach a flat area near Marshall Pass at 10.5 miles. Staying completely to the right connects to C.R. 200 and takes you back to where you started. To reach Marshall Pass, continue west a few feet, then bear right downhill and connect to C.R. 200 at 10.6 miles (04). Marshall Pass has a parking area and views to the west. Note signs for OHV routes.

Reset odometer at pass (04), cross cattle guard into Gunnison N.F. and follow C.R. 243 downhill. County Roads 243 and 200 follow the historic railroad grade of the Denver and Rio Grande Railroad. The widening road twists back and forth and passes more beaver ponds as the valley widens. Stay left on 243 at 11.3 miles (05) where a large road joins on right. Follow super wide gravel road into Sargents on Hwy. 50 at 16.7 miles (06).

Return Trip: Left on Hwy. 50 goes west to Gunnison. Right goes uphill to Monarch Pass and on to Poncha Springs, Salida or Buena Vista. To reach Tomichi Pass, Trail #37, turn right on Hwy. 50 and go uphill about 1.2 miles, then turn left on County Road 888 following sign to Whitepine.

Reverse Directions: Reset odometer at Sargents on Hwy. 50 (06). Head southeast on wide C.R. 243. Turn right at 5.4 miles (05) and note seasonal gate. (Road closed Nov. 15 through May 30.) Road follows old railroad grade uphill to Marshall Pass at 16.7 miles (04).

Reset odometer after cattle guard (04), turn right off main road on lesser F.S. 203. Go east 0.1 miles and connect to a road that continues east downhill. Road is marked 203A which is confusing. However, 203 and 203A are the same road for a short distance before 203A goes right at 0.7 miles. At this point, stay left downhill through pine forest into aspen forest. Continue straight at 3.2 miles where road goes right to great camp spot.

Pass Starvation Creek Hiking Trailhead at 5.0 miles (03). Road gradually levels out and passes through popular dispersed camping area. Turn right on larger road at 7.5 miles (02). Cross one-lane bridge and pass more good camp spots along Poncha Creek. Turn left when you reach parking lot at 8.2. Continue straight on wide C.R. 200 until you reach Hwy. 285 at 10.6 miles (01). Turn left on 285 to reach Hwy. 50 in about 5 miles. At Hwy. 50, left goes to Poncha Springs and Buena Vista; right goes to Salida.

Services: Full services in Salida. Gas and food at Poncha Springs and Sargents. Modern vault toilet at parking lot near Shirley Townsite. Nothing along trail. Sargents has an auto repair shop and an RV park.

Historical Highlights: In the 1920s, the town of Shirley was a transfer point for silver, zinc, lead and copper ores that arrived via aerial tram from the Rawley Mine in Bonanza located over the mountains to the south. From there, the ore was loaded onto rail cars of the Denver and Rio Grande Western Railroad and hauled over Marshall Pass to smelters in Salida and Leadville. Shirley died in 1930 when the Rawley Mine shut down.

Maps: San Isabel and Gunnison N. F. DeLorme Atlas & Gazetteer.

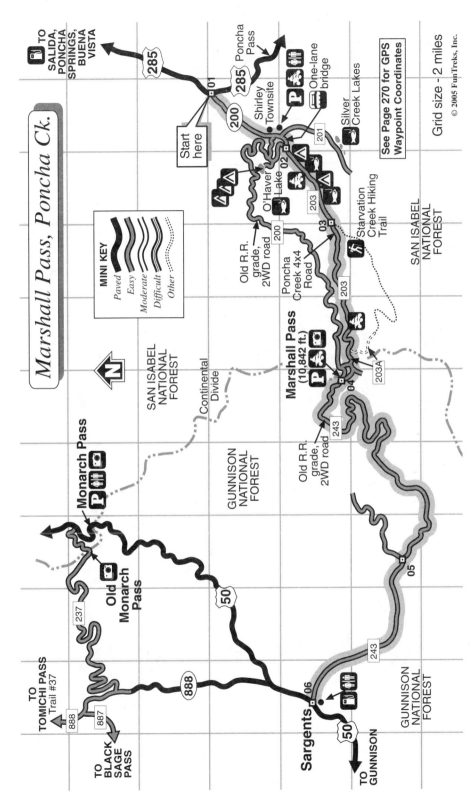

Marshall Pass, Poncha Ck.

MINI KEY

- Paved
- Easy
- Moderate
- Difficult
- Other

N

TO SALIDA, PONCHA SPRINGS, BUENA VISTA

285

285 Poncha Pass

200

Shirley Townsite

One-lane bridge

Start here

01

P

201

Silver Creek Lakes

See Page 270 for GPS Waypoint Coordinates

Grid size - 2 miles

© 2005 FunTreks, Inc.

O'Haver Lake **02**

203

Old R.R. grade, 2WD road

200

Poncha Creek 4x4 Road

03

Starvation Creek Hiking Trail

203

SAN ISABEL NATIONAL FOREST

203A

SAN ISABEL NATIONAL FOREST

Continental Divide

Marshall Pass (10,842 ft.)

P

04

Old R.R. grade, 2WD road

243

GUNNISON NATIONAL FOREST

Monarch Pass

P

Old Monarch Pass

237

50

888

TO TOMICHI PASS Trail #37

888

887

TO BLACK SAGE PASS

05

243

GUNNISON NATIONAL FOREST

06

Sargents

50

TO GUNNISON

153

AREA 4

Vail, Leadville, Fairplay

39. Mill Creek Road
40. Shrine Pass
41. Lime Creek, Benson Cabin
42. McCallister Gulch
43. Wearyman Creek
44. Holy Cross

45. Hagerman Pass
46. Wheeler Lake
47. Mt. Bross, Kite Lake
48. Mosquito Pass
49. Weston Pass

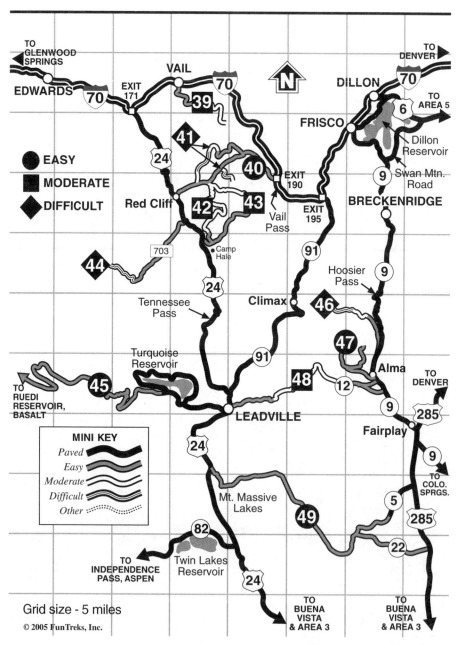

● EASY
■ MODERATE
◆ DIFFICULT

MINI KEY
Paved
Easy
Moderate
Difficult
Other

Grid size - 5 miles

© 2005 FunTreks, Inc.

154

Vail, Leadville, Fairplay

Like many trails in Colorado, those in Area 4 were originally built as mining roads during the boom years of the 1880s and 1890s. Some trails, like Mosquito Pass, were abandoned within a short time of their construction and replaced by fast-developing railroads. Much of Hagerman Pass Road follows an old railroad grade left from the first standard gauge railroad built across the Continental Divide. It is hard to imagine that today's little-used Weston Pass was once a busy stagecoach route hauling thousands of people and tons of supplies into Leadville, which, in 1877, was the world's richest silver mining camp. Today, Leadville is home to the National Mining Museum, a must stop for anyone passing through town.

Mill Creek Road is a new trail added to Area 4. This road takes you through the center of the Vail Ski Area, then climbs to the top of Red Peak, where you'll find incredible views of Interstate 70, the Gore Range and Vail's steep back bowls. Also added are Lime Creek and Benson Cabin (Trail #41), two challenging side trips off easy Shrine Pass Road. If you make these trips soon after the roads open, you'll find abundant wildflowers and a prominent white cross from lingering snow on Mount Holy Cross.

North London Mine on Mosquito Pass, Trail #48, moderate. (Private property, keep out).

155

Trail starts here. Turn right at Vista Baun Lift.

Lower part of Mill Creek Road is easy.

Gore Range as seen from upper portion of trail.

Upper section of trail can get very muddy.

One of many chair lifts along the route.

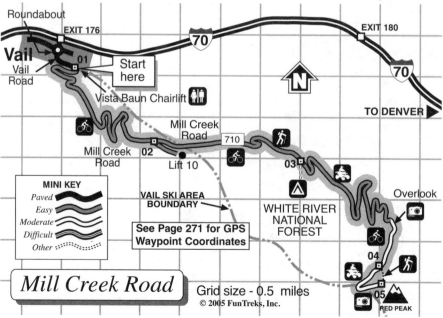

MINI KEY

Paved
Easy
Moderate
Difficult
Other

VAIL SKI AREA
BOUNDARY

See Page 271 for GPS
Waypoint Coordinates

Mill Creek Road

Grid size - 0.5 miles

© 2005 FunTreks, Inc.

156

Location: Immediately southeast of Vail.

Difficulty: Moderate. This rating applies to the last few miles where the road becomes narrow, rutted and, at times, muddy. Most of the trail is easy, especially the lower section that passes through the ski area. Suitable for most stock SUVs.

Features: The road climbs through the heart of Vail Ski Area then continues into White River National Forest to top of Red Peak. On the way up, a stunning overlook offers views to the north of Vail Valley, Interstate 70 and the Gore Range. From the summit of Red Peak, look down into Vail's back bowls with distant views of Mount Holy Cross. In late July, I found incredible wildflowers all along the route at higher elevations. Marvelous fall color. Very popular hiking and mountain biking area. ATVs are allowed all along road, but roads above ski area are best.

Time & Distance: Total of 10 miles one way. Allow 3 hours for round trip.

To Get There: Get off Interstate 70 at exit 176. Head south through the roundabout on south side of freeway onto Vail Road. Within 1/2 mile, the road curves to the left and enters a parking area behind the Lodge Tower. Continue east under chair lift to intersection by Vista Baun Lift. Turn right uphill on Mill Creek Road, F.S. 710.

Trail Description: Reset odometer at start (01). Follow road uphill in westerly direction then turn left at 0.2 miles. Watch for fast-moving construction trucks. Follow wide dirt road uphill through heart of ski area. Bear slightly left on single-lane road at 3.2 miles (02). (Main road goes right to Lift #10.) Stay left uphill at 5.4 miles (03) where lesser road goes downhill to primitive camp spot. Continue straight at 6.9 miles. Road soon becomes narrow and rutted. Mud holes may be present during rainy periods. Stop at overlook on left at 8.9 miles. Watch kids and pets because of dangerous cliff. Road worsens as you continue uphill. Bear right at 9.4 miles (04). Left is hiking trail to top of Red Peak. Road turns sharply left at 9.8 as it briefly passes in and out of ski area. Road ends at summit of Red Peak at 10.1 miles (05).

Services: Full services in Vail. Nothing along trail.

Maps: White River National Forest. Trails Illustrated, Vail, Frisco, Dillon #108. DeLorme Atlas & Gazetteer.

157

Large parking area at Shrine Pass. Hikers and mountain bikers often start here.

Observation deck/chapel.

View of Mt. Holy Cross on July 18 using 8X zoom lens.

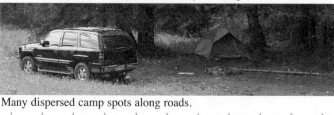

Many dispersed camp spots along roads.

Scenic, easy drive.

Shrine Pass

WHITE RIVER
NAT. FOREST

See Page 271 for GPS
Waypoint Coordinates

Shrine
Pass

MINI KEY
Paved
Easy
Moderate
Difficult
Other

LIME
CREEK
Trail #41

03

Observation
Deck

02

709

709

04

06

05

BENSON CABIN
Trail #41

Start
here

EXIT
190

01

24 07

Red Cliff

WEARYMAN CREEK
Trail #43

Rest Area

70

24

McCALLISTER GULCH
Trail #42

N

Grid size - 1 mile

© 2005 FunTreks, Inc.

Shrine Pass 40

Location: Between Vail Pass on Interstate 70 and Red Cliff.

Difficulty: Easy. Suitable for passenger cars to the observation deck. Road gets narrower and rougher as you descend towards Red Cliff. This portion can get muddy and 4-wheel drive may be necessary.

Features: Views of Mt. Holy Cross from the west side of Shrine Pass. Short walk to observation deck/outdoor chapel (handicap accessible). Popular area for mountain biking and hiking. Snow lingers at Shrine Pass (11,089 ft.) often well into July. Gates at each end of Shrine Pass Road may open before entire road is clear of snow. Early in the season you may not be able to reach Red Cliff. West end of Shrine Pass Road best for ATVs.

Time & Distance: Just under 12 miles from Interstate 70 to Hwy. 24 above Red Cliff. One way trip takes about an hour.

To Get There: Get off Interstate 70 at exit 190 between Copper Mountain and Vail. There is a large rest area here. Continue straight (west) on Shrine Pass Road where paved road turns left for the rest area.

Trail Description: *Reset odometer at start* (01). Follow wide gravel road west then north. Large parking lot on left at 2.3 miles (02) marks location of Shrine Pass. Road descends gradually to smaller parking area on left at 3.7 miles (03). Park here and take short walk to observation deck. At 3.8 miles, you'll go by the exit point for Lime Creek, Trail #41. The first time you can see Mt. Holy Cross from Shrine Pass Road occurs at 4.2 miles. Stay right at 4.6 miles where F.S. 713 goes left. Benson's Cabin, Trail #41, is on left at 7.0 miles (04). Small wooden bridge on left at 8.7 miles (05) goes to McCallister Gulch, Trail #42, and Wearyman Creek, Trail #43. Brown information board on right at 9.3 (06) miles marks start of Lime Creek Road. You reach a T intersection in Red Cliff at 11.2 miles (07). Turn right for Hwy. 24.

Return Trip: Return the way you came or from Red Cliff take 24 north to Interstate 70 or south to Leadville.

Services: Full services at Vail and Copper Mountain. Toilets at rest area on I-70, Shrine Pass and observation deck parking area.

Maps: White River National Forest. Trails Illustrated Vail, Frisco, Dillon #108. DeLorme Atlas & Gazetteer.

Difficult spot on Lime Creek Road.

Lime Creek tippy in places.

Remains of Benson Cabin.

Mt. Holy Cross from top of Benson Cabin.

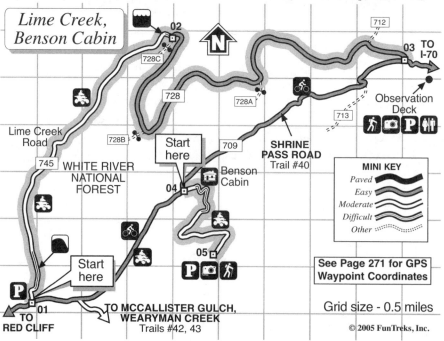

Lime Creek,
Benson Cabin

02

712

N

728C

03 TO
I-70

728

728A

Observation
Deck

713

Lime Creek
Road

728B

Start
here

709

SHRINE
PASS ROAD
Trail #40

MINI KEY

745

WHITE RIVER
NATIONAL
FOREST

04

Benson
Cabin

Paved
Easy
Moderate
Difficult
Other

05

See Page 271 for GPS
Waypoint Coordinates

Start
here

P

01

TO
RED CLIFF

TO MCCALLISTER GULCH,
WEARYMAN CREEK
Trails #42, 43

Grid size - 0.5 miles

© 2005 FunTreks, Inc.

Lime Creek, Benson Cabin ◆41▸

Location: Between Vail Pass on Interstate 70 and Red Cliff.

Difficulty: Difficult. Lime Creek is narrow and overgrown in spots with two short, rocky climbs and a few tippy spots. Just one rocky, steep spot on Benson Cabin gives the trail its difficult rating. Both trails can be done in a high-clearance, aggressive SUV. Tree branches may brush against vehicle.

Features: Both trails offer solitude, wildflowers and real adventure. For drivers seeking more challenge than easy Shrine Pass Road, Trail #40. Benson Cabin has a hiking trail at the end with great views of Mt. Holy Cross. Okay to ride ATVs on Shrine Pass Road between trailheads.

Time & Distance: Lime Creek measures 9.2 miles and takes less than 2 hours. Benson Cabin is 1.9 miles one way. Round trip takes about an hour.

To Get There: Get off Interstate 70 at exit 190 between Copper Mountain and Vail. There is a large rest area here. Follow Shrine Pass Road west 7.0 miles to Benson Cabin on the left. Continue another 2.3 miles to Lime Creek on the right. Lime Creek is about 2 miles from Red Cliff.

Trail Description:
   Lime Creek: *Reset odometer at start* (01). Head north through jungle-like terrain. Difficult rocky climb at 0.4 miles. Trail is narrow and tippy in places but gradually gets easier as you climb. Trail swings right at 3.7 miles and crosses Lime Creek. One rocky climb remains before reaching easier F.S. 728 at 3.8 miles (02). At top of hill, turn left. Follow easy winding road, bearing right at 8.6 miles where 712 joins on left. Shrine Pass Road is reached at 9.2 miles (03).
   Benson Cabin: *Reset odometer at start* (04). Stay right of Benson Cabin following rough road uphill until it ends at small, tight parking spot at 1.9 miles (05). Follow hiking trail short distance to view Mt. Holy Cross.

Return Trip: East on Shrine Pass Road goes back to Interstate 70. West goes to Red Cliff.

Services: Full services at Vail and Copper Mountain. Toilets at rest area on I-70, Shrine Pass and observation deck parking area.

Maps: White River National Forest. Trails Illustrated Vail, Frisco, Dillon #108. DeLorme Atlas & Gazetteer.

View of Camp Hale from rock outcrop on Hornsilver Mountain.

Steep, rocky climb is difficult in wet weather.

Top of Resolution Mountain above 11,900 feet.

Easy stretch across Hornsilver Mtn.

162

Location: Trail starts at Camp Hale between Leadville and Vail.

Difficulty: Moderate. Steep in places, with ruts that require careful tire placement to maintain traction. When wet, this trail is difficult in spots, especially near the top. Snow can linger on the trail well into July. Best conditions will be found mid-summer through fall. When dry, trail is suitable for stock SUVs with high ground clearance and low-range gearing. Steepness at top on south side may be intimidating to novice drivers.

Features: Trail begins at historic Camp Hale and climbs to 11,900-ft. Resolution Mountain. Panoramic views of Gore Range and Sawatch Mountains including Mt. Holy Cross. Fee camping at Camp Hale Memorial Campground at the south end of Camp Hale or dispersed camping at many other places in the valley. Great area for ATVs and dirt bikes. Combine this trail with Wearyman Creek, Trail #43, which loops back to the starting point of McCallister Gulch.

Time & Distance: The trip is 12.7 miles as described here. Allow 2-1/2 to 3 hours. Add another 2 hours if you return via Wearyman Creek.

To Get There: **From Leadville:** Take Hwy. 24 north from Leadville about 17 miles to the north end of Camp Hale. Turn right 0.4 miles north of mile marker 159. **From Vail:** Head west on Interstate 70 to Exit 171. Head south on Hwy. 24, continuing south past the turnoff for Red Cliff. Turn left into Camp Hale 0.6 miles south of mile marker 158. **From Shrine Pass Road:** See *Reverse Directions* next page.

Trail Description: Reset odometer as you turn off Hwy. 24 into Camp Hale (01). Within short distance, bear right following sign for F.S. 702. Follow wide gravel road south and bear left across small earthen bridge at 0.5 miles. Turn left at T intersection where 714 goes right. Immediately turn left again onto F.S. 708 at 1.1 miles (02). (Right takes you uphill to Ptarmigan Pass. This is where you'll come out if you drive Wearyman Creek.) Road narrows as it passes through a forested area. This is one of the best places for ATV and dirt bike riders to unload and camp.

Bear right at 1.9 miles along Eagle River. Turn right again at 2.4 miles (03) onto single lane road that climbs across face of hillside. Bear right at private residence and begin long climb into forest. Road is narrow and steep in places. The worst section is at 5.5 miles where the road is very steep and chewed up. Don't attempt this section if muddy. You soon exit the trees with views on the right. At 6.0 miles (04), a narrow, steep road goes right to the top of Resolution Mountain. The road is rutted but most 4-wheel-drive SUVs can do it. This side trip adds 0.5 miles to trip total.

Reset odometer (04) and continue north on 708. If the weather is clear, at 1.2 miles, you should be able to see Mt. Holy Cross directly ahead on the horizon. At 1.9 miles, walk to a rock outcrop on the left for great view of Camp Hale below (see photo). Stay right on the main trail at 2.4 miles. Continue straight at 3.3 and 4.4. When you reach bottom at 5.5 miles (05), turn left and cross Wearyman Creek several times. This way goes out to Shrine Pass Road reached at 6.2 miles (06). Straight at Waypoint 05 continues on Wearyman Creek, Trail #43.

Return Trip: At Shrine Pass Road, turn left to reach Red Cliff and Hwy. 24 or right to reach Interstate 70 at Exit 190.

Reverse Directions: To find northern end of McCallister Gulch, see directions for Shrine Pass Road, Trail #40. Look for wooden bridge 8.7 miles from Interstate 70. *Reset odometer* (06) and cross wooden bridge as trail winds through tight brush and crosses creek several times. When you reach T intersection at 0.7 miles (05), turn right. (Left goes up Wearyman Creek.) Stay right at 1.8 miles and left at 2.9 and 3.8 miles. Trail opens up and climbs more gently across ridge of Hornsilver Mountain. At 6.2 miles (04), a rough, steep road goes left to the top of Resolution Mountain.

After visiting mountain top (or not), *reset odometer* and continue south on 708. Drop into trees at 0.4 and descend steep, rough hill. Follow narrow road down the mountain through the forest. After going by a residence, follow ledge road across open hillside until you reach a better road at 3.6 miles (03). Turn left, then turn left again at 4.1. When you reach F.S. 702 at 5.0 miles (02), turn right. After crossing river, stay right on 702 to Hwy. 24 at 6.0 miles (01).

Services: Full services in Leadville and Vail. Gas in Minturn, which is north on Hwy. 24 before I-70. Camp Hale Memorial Campground has vault toilets. Nothing along trail.

Historical Highlights: Camp Hale was established in 1942 as a winter training post for the army. At its peak, the camp housed about 16,000 soldiers, 14,000 of whom were members of the famous 10th Mountain Division. In addition to barracks, the post included mess halls, a hospital, chapel, fire station, post exchange, stockade, ski shop, bakery and an ice-making plant.

Maps: White River National Forest. Trails Illustrated Maps #108 and #109. DeLorme Atlas & Gazetteer.

164

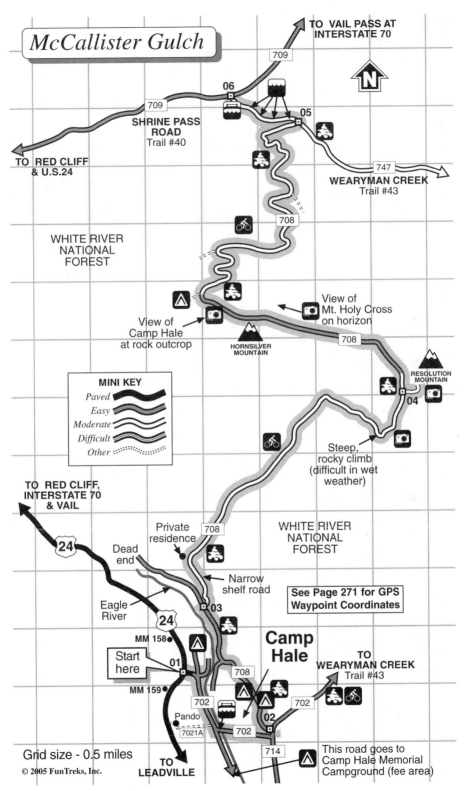

McCallister Gulch

TO VAIL PASS AT INTERSTATE 70

709

N

709

SHRINE PASS ROAD
Trail #40

TO RED CLIFF & U.S.24

06

05

747

WEARYMAN CREEK
Trail #43

708

WHITE RIVER NATIONAL FOREST

708

View of Camp Hale at rock outcrop

View of Mt. Holy Cross on horizon

HORNSILVER MOUNTAIN

RESOLUTION MOUNTAIN

04

MINI KEY
Paved
Easy
Moderate
Difficult
Other

TO RED CLIFF, INTERSTATE 70 & VAIL

24

Steep, rocky climb (difficult in wet weather)

Private residence

708

Dead end

Eagle River

24

WHITE RIVER NATIONAL FOREST

Narrow shelf road

See Page 271 for GPS Waypoint Coordinates

MM 158

03

Start here

01

708

Camp Hale

TO WEARYMAN CREEK
Trail #43

MM 159

702

Pando

7021A

702

02

702

714

Grid size - 0.5 miles

© 2005 FunTreks, Inc.

TO LEADVILLE

This road goes to Camp Hale Memorial Campground (fee area)

165

Cross Wearyman Creek several times.

Descending south side of Ptarmigan Pass is easy.

Wearyman Road.

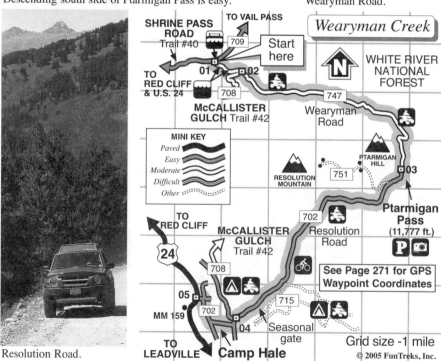

Resolution Road.

SHRINE PASS ROAD
Trail #40
709
TO VAIL PASS
Start here
01
02
TO RED CLIFF & U.S. 24
708
McCALLISTER GULCH Trail #42
747
Wearyman Road

Wearyman Creek

N

WHITE RIVER NATIONAL FOREST

MINI KEY
Paved
Easy
Moderate
Difficult
Other

RESOLUTION MOUNTAIN
751
PTARMIGAN HILL
03

702
Resolution Road

Ptarmigan Pass
(11,777 ft.)
P

TO RED CLIFF
24
McCALLISTER GULCH
Trail #42
708

See Page 271 for GPS Waypoint Coordinates

05
MM 159
702
715
04
Seasonal gate

TO LEADVILLE
Camp Hale

Grid size -1 mile

© 2005 FunTreks, Inc.

166

Wearyman Creek 43

Location: North of Leadville between Shrine Pass Road, Trail #40, and Camp Hale. South of Vail.

Difficulty: Moderate. First part of trail is somewhat overgrown with tight brush in a few places. Water crossings are shallow except during times of heavy runoff. Northern half of trail is quite narrow as it climbs toward Ptarmigan Pass, and this portion is not recommended for oversize vehicles. South side is a wide gravel road.

Features: Little-used, scenic backcountry ascent to Ptarmigan Pass. Combine with McCallister Gulch, Trail #42, to form a great loop trail. Fun trail for ATVs and dirt bikes.

Time & Distance: Allow about 2 hours for the 12.2 miles described here.

To Get There: Follow directions for Shrine Pass Road, Trail #40. Wearyman Creek starts 8.7 miles south of Interstate 70 at small wooden bridge on left. This point is about 2.5 miles east of Red Cliff.

Trail Description: Reset odometer at start (01). Cross small wooden bridge heading south. The trail winds in and out of Wearyman Creek. Do not attempt this trail during spring runoff because the creek can be deep and fast moving. At 0.7 miles (02), McCallister Gulch, Trail #42, goes to right. Bear left for Wearyman Creek. The road gets quite narrow and passing can be inconvenient. The climb is constant as the road twists in roller coaster fashion up the steep valley walls. Ptarmigan Pass is reached at 5.7 miles (03). The pass is wide and flat. Resolution Road on the south side of the pass is a two-lane, graded road all the way. Bear left at 6.2 miles where 751 goes to the right. At 9.8 miles, go straight where F.S. 715 goes left to popular camping area. Pass through seasonal closure gate at 10.9. Stay left briefly at 11.2 miles (04) then bear right, staying on 702. Turn right after crossing Eagle River at 11.7 to reach Hwy. 24 at 12.2 miles (05).

Return Trip: At Hwy. 24, turn left for Leadville or right for I-70.

Services: Full services in Leadville and Vail. Nothing along trail.

Maps: White River National Forest. Trails Illustrated #108 and #109. DeLorme Atlas & Gazetteer.

French Creek. Wet tires make this obstacle doubly difficult.

Looking down on Hunky Dory Lake. Must hike to this spot.

Rusty mining equipment.

Park near Holy Cross City and walk to cabins.

Dangerous tippy spot before Cleveland Rock.

Cleveland Rock is harder than it looks.

Location: North of Camp Hale between Leadville and Red cliff.

Difficulty: Difficult. One of the most difficult hard-core trails in the state, offering non-stop challenges to the serious four-wheeler. The toughest obstacle, Cleveland Rock, occurs just above Holy Cross City. Here, body damage is likely even for modified vehicles. Rollovers are not uncommon. Minimum 33-inch tires and differential lockers are basic necessities for the entire trail. Expect to pay exorbitant towing charges if you get in trouble—a good reason to go with a group as most people do.

Features: One of the most popular hard-core trails in the state of Colorado replete with stunning scenery, historical points of interest and fun obstacles. The trail is surrounded by Holy Cross Wilderness, which offers remote hiking to many high-mountain lakes. See rusting mining equipment below Holy Cross City. Take your fishing pole and hike to beautiful Cleveland Lake when trail ends at wilderness boundary. The trail can get very busy, especially on weekends. French Creek is one of the worst spots for backups. It is not unusual to spend an hour waiting for vehicles to clear the area.

This trail is extremely difficult for ATVs, but in recent years, more riders are attempting it. Make sure you travel with a group. Staging is available at Gold Park Forest Service Campground, at the main trailhead and at the secondary trailhead by the exit route.

Time & Distance: It is 3.8 miles to Holy Cross City and approximately 0.4 miles to the end of trail at wilderness boundary. If no problems occur and no traffic gets in your way, you might drive this trail, both ways, in half a day. However, it is more likely that you'll spend a full day.

To Get There: Head west from Hwy. 24 on Homestake Road, F.S. 703. The road heads south between mile markers 156 and 157 a few miles north of Camp Hale and about 20 miles north of Leadville. Follow sign to Blodgett Campground. The wide gravel road usually has stretches of brutal washboard. It follows along Homestake Creek where you can camp and fish. The start of Holy Cross Trail is on the right after 7.4 miles. Watch for signs after Gold Park Campground.

Trail Description: Reset odometer at start (01). Carefully review warning information at trailhead. A narrow, rocky road heads up the hillside. The first 1.3 miles is one way. This stretch has several obstacles that pale in comparison to what follows. If you have trouble with this section, you

169

should bail out at the exit route.

After crossing a short section of corduroy road, you reach the exit route on the left at 1.3 miles (02). Another warning sign precedes a large obstacle at 1.5 miles. At 2.5 miles, you pass through a tippy, rocky section. A tree once leaned across the road at this point making this spot very difficult. Many 4-wheelers were saddened when they learned someone toppled the tree. At 2.6 miles, you encounter a very rocky section. Look it over carefully before attempting to get through.

You reach French Creek at 2.8 miles (03). The challenge is getting across a wall of large boulders with wet tires. Frequently, vehicles back up at this point, especially in the afternoon when downhill traffic meets uphill traffic. Don't hesitate to ask for assistance when people are waiting. If you can't get up the first time, take a tow strap or winch yourself up.

Several rough spots remain after French Creek, including one section where a large tree root tries to roll you over. You'll pass a mine site before reaching a fork at 3.8 miles (04). A right turn here takes you to Holy Cross City. From there you can head left uphill to Cleveland Rock. Bear right when road joins on left (05).

You can also reach Cleveland Rock by continuing straight at Waypoint 04 then turning right at the next intersection. A tippy spot before Cleveland Rock is very dangerous. If you make it up Cleveland Rock, another tough spot follows immediately. After that, there are no more major obstacles and the trail soon ends at wilderness boundary (06). Hike beyond the boundary to Cleveland Lake.

Return Trip: Return the way you came. When you reach the exit route passed earlier (02), *reset your odometer,* turn right and head downhill on an easy gravel road. Stay left at 0.8 miles where 727.1B goes right. Pass through parking area for Fancy Creek Hiking Trail and turn left at 1.8 miles (07). Follow Missouri Creek Road 704 as it winds downhill. Turn left at 4.0 miles (08) on Homestake Road and return to start of trail at 4.4 miles. Straight goes back to Hwy. 24.

Historical Highlights: Holy Cross City once had a population of about 300 people, a school and a hotel. Look around and you should be able to count about 17 foundations along with a dwindling number of cabins. The town survived only a few short years during the 1880s.

Services: Full services in Leadville. Primary services in Red Cliff and Minturn. Toilets at Gold Park C.G. and Fancy Creek Hiking Trailhead.

Maps: White River National Forest. Trails Illustrated Holy Cross, Ruedi Reservoir #126. DeLorme Atlas & Gazetteer.

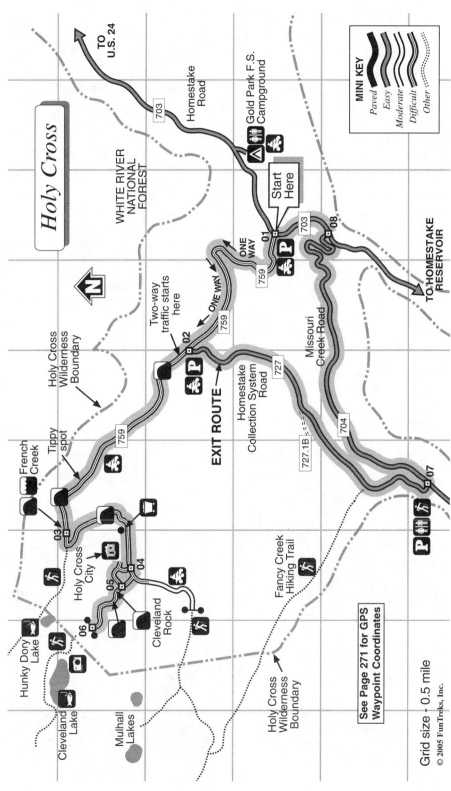

Holy Cross

WHITE RIVER NATIONAL FOREST

TO U.S. 24

Homestake Road

703

Gold Park F.S. Campground

Start Here

703

01

759

P

08

TO HOMESTAKE RESERVOIR

N

Two-way traffic starts here

ONE WAY

ONE WAY

ONE WAY

759

02

P

759

EXIT ROUTE

Homestake Collection System Road

727

Missouri Creek Road

704

727.1B

07

P

Holy Cross Wilderness Boundary

French Creek

Tippy spot

759

03

Holy Cross City

04

05

06

Cleveland Rock

Fancy Creek Hiking Trail

Hunky Dory Lake

Cleveland Lake

Mulhall Lakes

Holy Cross Wilderness Boundary

MINI KEY
Paved
Easy
Moderate
Difficult
Other

See Page 271 for GPS Waypoint Coordinates

Grid size - 0.5 mile

© 2005 FunTreks, Inc.

171

Looking down on Turquoise Reservoir from point close to Hagerman Pass.

East side approach to Hagerman Pass.

ATVs and dirt bikes allowed.

West side of pass above Ivanhoe Lake. F.S. Road 105 seen at right of picture.

Seasonal wildflowers galore.

Fishing on Fryingpan River on way to Basalt.

Location: West of Leadville and southwest of Turquoise Reservoir.

Difficulty: Easy. Some embedded rock on each side of the pass but most of the road is wide and graded. Do not attempt to haul a boat trailer over the pass from either side.

Features: With three outstanding wilderness areas as a backdrop, Turquoise Reservoir serves as a focal point for a vast number of recreational activities. Many great hiking trails, including the Colorado Trail, crisscross the area. In addition, there are two historically significant railroad tunnels (See *Historical Highlights* section). If you visit this area around Memorial Day, you may have an opportunity to drive through deep snow tunnels at the summit. Fun ATV area. Plenty of seasonal wildflowers on the west side.

Time & Distance: The trail is described here from Turquoise Reservoir to F.S. 527. This 11.8-mile stretch can be driven in about an hour one way. You could easily spend an entire day hiking or exploring a vast number of side roads on the west side of the pass. Add another 43.5 miles if you continue all the way to Hwy. 82 at Basalt. This portion adds about 2 hours to the trip. In summer, you can visit Aspen and return to Leadville via Independence Pass.

To Get There: Take 6th Street west from Leadville and bear right on paved County Road 4. Continue another 3.5 miles until the road forks south of Turquoise Reservoir. Bear left over the dam and around the south side of the lake. After another 3.5 miles, turn left up F.S. 105, a wide gravel road.

Trail Description: Set your odometer to zero at start of 105 (01). The first few miles remain smooth and then it gets a little bumpier with more frequent narrow sections. The main road is obvious, so route-finding is not a problem. At 3.6 miles (02) the road turns sharply right. At this point you pass the sealed entrance to the Carlton Tunnel. You can park and camp in the large lot across from tunnel. As you climb higher, there are several places to pull over, offering fantastic views of Turquoise Reservoir. You pass a large sign on the left explaining some of the history of the Colorado Midland Railway. A popular hiking trail here leads to the Hagerman Tunnel. More parking is available on the right.

After 5 miles, the road swings left back into the mountain. It is rocky and narrow in places but represents no threat when dry. At 7.9 miles (03) you reach the summit at 11,925 feet. As you start down the west side, a wide vista opens up, exposing the upper Fryingpan Valley and Ivanhoe Lake. As you continue down into the valley, road conditions improve quickly. At 11.1 miles, you diagonally cross a water diversion ditch. At 11.8 miles (04) you reach the intersection of F.S. 527. Going left takes you to Ivanhoe Lake. This road follows the original railroad bed to the west entrance of the Carlton Tunnel. The road continues past the tunnel to Lily Pad Lake and another hiking trail into the Hunter-Fryingpan Wilderness.

Return Trip: Return the way you came or see next paragraph.

Directions to Ruedi Reservoir and Basalt: You can make an all-day trip out of this by continuing on to Basalt. The long but beautiful drive offers plenty of recreational opportunities at Ruedi Reservoir and along the Fryingpan River. This area is a fisherman's paradise. More than 32 miles of this 43.5-mile trip is paved.

    Reset odometer where F.S. 527 goes left to Ivanhoe Lake (04). Bear right on larger F.S. 105. (Avoid the lesser road that goes uphill.) The road descends gradually along an old railroad grade. Continue straight at 7.4 miles where a road from Diemer and Sellar Lakes joins on right. Stay on the main road as unmarked roads branch off. Bear right downhill when you reach paved Fryingpan Road (C.R. 4) at 10.7 miles. The road winds above Ruedi Reservoir and crosses dam at 29 miles. Many great campgrounds and fishing spots along the way. You reach Basalt at 42.7 miles. The town is on Two Rivers Road that parallels Hwy. 82. Left connects to Hwy. 82 in the direction of Aspen. Right connects to Hwy. 82 in the direction of Glenwood Springs.

Services: Full services in Leadville and Basalt.

Historical Highlights: The Hagerman Tunnel was completed in 1886 and connected Colorado Springs to Aspen. The railroad was the first standard gauge railroad to cross the Continental Divide. Due to high maintenance costs, the Busk-Ivanhoe Tunnel was built at a lower altitude seven years later. It too proved to be impractical and was later bought by mining magnate Albert Carlton. He renamed the tunnel after himself and converted it to automobile use. It served as such between 1924 and 1937. A third tunnel at yet a lower altitude was built in the 1960s by the Corps of Engineers to divert water from the Fryingpan Wilderness to the Turquoise Reservoir. Known as the Charles H. Boustead Tunnel, it is four miles long and runs perpendicular to the other tunnels.

Maps: San Isabel and White River National Forests. Trails Illustrated Holy Cross, Ruedi Reservoir #126, DeLorme Atlas & Gazetteer.

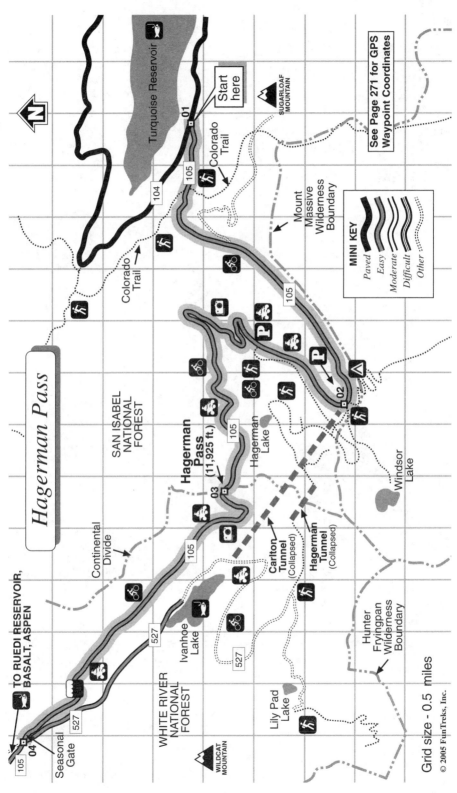

Hagerman Pass

N

See Page 271 for GPS Waypoint Coordinates

Turquoise Reservoir

Start here

01

SUGARLOAF MOUNTAIN

Colorado Trail

105

104

Colorado Trail

SAN ISABEL NATIONAL FOREST

Mount Massive Wilderness Boundary

MINI KEY
Paved
Easy
Moderate
Difficult
Other

105

105

P

P

02

Hagerman Pass
(11,925 ft.)

105

Hagerman Lake

03

Windsor Lake

105

Continental Divide

Carlton Tunnel
(Collapsed)

Hagerman Tunnel
(Collapsed)

TO RUEDI RESERVOIR, BASALT, ASPEN

527

Ivanhoe Lake

527

WHITE RIVER NATIONAL FOREST

Hunter Fryingpan Wilderness Boundary

527

Seasonal Gate

105

04

WILDCAT MOUNTAIN

Lily Pad Lake

Grid size - 0.5 miles

© 2005 FunTreks, Inc.

175

Magnolia Mill. (Stay out of buildings.)

One of the toughest spots on trail.

Trail floods during spring runoff.

Narrow trail with tight brush makes passing difficult.

Wheeler Lake. Stay in established parking area around lake.

Waterfall by lake.

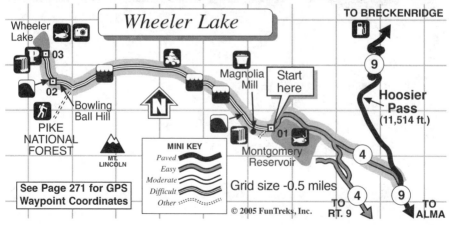

Wheeler Lake

TO BRECKENRIDGE

Wheeler Lake

03

02

Bowling Ball Hill

PIKE NATIONAL FOREST

MT. LINCOLN

Magnolia Mill

Start here

01

Montgomery Reservoir

9

Hoosier Pass (11,514 ft.)

4

4

9

TO RT. 9

TO ALMA

MINI KEY
Paved
Easy
Moderate
Difficult
Other

Grid size -0.5 miles

© 2005 FunTreks, Inc.

See Page 271 for GPS Waypoint Coordinates

Location: West of Route 9 between Breckenridge and Fairplay.

Difficulty: Difficult. Several large rock obstacles. Very narrow in spots with tight brush that could scratch paint, especially if you have to pull over to pass. Water rushes down the trail during early season snow melt. Not recommended for stock vehicles although I went through with a group of upgraded Land Rovers. They managed the trail with no problems.

Features: Climbs beautiful valley to high mountain lake with waterfall. Pass directly under Magnolia Mill. Gorgeous seasonal wildflowers. Fun during early-season runoff. Take a fishing pole. ATVs allowed. Absolutely stay on main trail at all times. Abuses threaten trail closure. Report violators.

Time & Distance: Just 3.4 miles but slow. Gets quite busy on weekends. Allow 3 to 4 hours for the round trip—even longer on holiday weekends.

To Get There: **From Breckenridge:** Head south on Route 9 and turn right on wide dirt road about a mile south of Hoosier Pass. Go another mile or more to Montgomery Reservoir. Follow road around northwest side of reservoir until road narrows and turns uphill to right. **From Fairplay:** Head north on Rt. 9 past Alma about 2 miles. Turn left on County Road 4. Stay left at 1.9 miles, then bear right uphill at 2.7. Continue straight on F.S. 408 at 3.2 miles around northwest side of reservoir until road narrows and turns right uphill.

Trail Description: Reset odometer where road narrows and turns right uphill on northwest side of reservoir (01). Bear right up a couple of rocky switchbacks and pass under Magnolia Mill. Note waterfall behind mill. Trail gets rockier with large rock obstacle at 0.7. Left side is easier. Narrow, rocky trail follows with tight brush. Cross potentially deep mud hole at 2.3. Stay right uphill after 2.8 miles and climb Bowling-Ball Hill. At 3.0 miles (02), turn right uphill at rock ledge. (This spot used to be much harder.) Stop at parking area below Wheeler Lake at 3.4 miles (03). Stay on firm ground.

Return Trip: Return the way you came.

Services: Food in Alma. Full services in Breckenridge and Fairplay.

Maps: Pike National Forest. Trails Illustrated Breckenridge, Tennesee Pass #109. DeLorme Atlas & Gazetteer.

Hiking trails depart from Kite Lake Campground.

Thousand-year-old trees.

Looking down on Alma from Windy Ridge.

Short hike to pine forest.

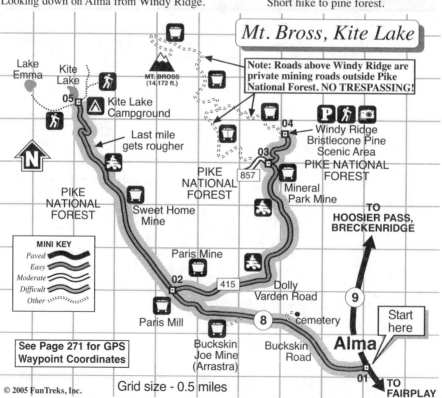

Mt. Bross, Kite Lake

Note: Roads above Windy Ridge are private mining roads outside Pike National Forest. NO TRESPASSING!

Lake Emma

Kite Lake

MT. BROSS (14,172 ft.)

05

Kite Lake Campground

Last mile gets rougher

N

Windy Ridge Bristlecone Pine Scenic Area

04

PIKE NATIONAL FOREST

PIKE NATIONAL FOREST

857

03

Mineral Park Mine

PIKE NATIONAL FOREST

Sweet Home Mine

Paris Mine

02

415

Dolly Varden Road

Paris Mill

8

cemetery

Buckskin Road

Buckskin Joe Mine (Arrastra)

Alma

9

TO HOOSIER PASS, BRECKENRIDGE

Start here

01

TO FAIRPLAY

MINI KEY
Paved
Easy
Moderate
Difficult
Other

See Page 271 for GPS Waypoint Coordinates

© 2005 FunTreks, Inc.

Grid size - 0.5 miles

Mt. Bross, Kite Lake 47

Location: Northwest of Fairplay and Alma. South of Breckenridge.

Difficulty: Easy. Lower portion of road, when dry, is suitable for passenger cars. Upper sections are steep and rough. High clearance is recommended.

Features: Pass through historic mining area on way to Windy Ridge Bristlecone Pine Scenic Area, which features 1000-year-old trees and great views. Three hiking trails depart from Kite Lake Campground to 14,000-ft. Mt. Bross, Mt. Lincoln and Mt. Democrat.

IMPORTANT: Mines and nearby structures are dangerous and should be viewed from a distance. Mines in this area are on private land. Don't trespass. Roads above Windy Ridge are private mining roads and are closed to the public. STAY OUT—STAY ALIVE.

Time & Distance: Windy Ridge is 6.4 miles from Alma. Kite Lake is 5.5 miles from Alma. Allow 2 to 4 hours to see area described.

To Get There: Take Hwy. 9 south from Breckenridge or north from Fairplay to small town of Alma. Turn west on Buckskin Road (County Road 8).

Trail Description: Reset your odometer at Hwy. 9 in Alma (01). Head west 2.8 miles on Buckskin Road to intersection just after Paris Mill (02).

    For Windy Ridge: *Reset odometer* (02) and make sharp right on Dolly Varden Road, F.S. 415. After 2.9 miles, bear left uphill at Mineral Park Mine. Stay right at 3.1 miles (03) where tougher F.S. 857 goes left. Windy Ridge Bristlecone Pine Scenic Area is reached at 3.6 miles (04). After visiting area, turn around and return to intersection near Paris Mill (02).

    For Kite Lake: *Reset odometer* (02) and continue north on Buckskin Road. Road gets rougher after Sweet Home Mine, especially as you get close to Kite Lake, which is reached at approximately 2.7 miles (05).

Return Trip: Return the way you came.

Services: A few stores and restaurants in Alma but no gas. Full services in Fairplay and Breckenridge.

Maps: Pike National Forest. Trails Illustrated Breckenridge, Tennessee Pass #109. DeLorme Atlas & Gazetteer. (For explanation of numbered wagon-wheel posts along route, obtain flyer from N.F. Ranger Station in Fairplay.)

Lower west side. Road at right goes to Birdseye Gulch. Trail marker at Mosquito Pass.

Approaching the summit on west side.

North London Mine (stay out).

Snow remains on east side in late July.

Lower east side. North London Mill behind trees.

North London Mill (stay out).

180

Mosquito Pass 48

Location: Between Leadville and Alma.

Difficulty: Moderate. The upper portion of the trail is narrow and rocky on both sides of pass but suitable for aggressive, high-clearance, stock sport utility vehicles. Road is closed when blocked by snow, which can occur well into late summer. Check with the Bureau of Land Management or the Pike National Forest for road conditions.

Features: This is the highest pass road in Colorado open to travel. Views from the 13,185 ft. summit are impressive on a clear day. Legal side roads can be difficult, especially Birdseye Gulch, which includes a nasty mud bog. Great area to explore on an ATV. Seasonal wildflowers. View mines from a distance—they are dangerous and private.

Time & Distance: Trail measures 13.6 miles as described here. Allow 2 to 3 hours one way.

To Get There: **From Leadville:** From Hwy. 24 in downtown Leadville, head east on 7th Street. Go by Matchless Mine and continue after pavement ends. Continue straight at 1.8 miles, then bear left at 2.7 miles. Bear left at 4.1 miles at unofficial parking area. Take left fork next to gated road that goes into private Diamond Mine. **From Alma:** From Hwy. 9 south of Alma, head west on either County Road 10 or 12. This description starts where the two roads merge before Park City. (See reverse directions.)

Trail Description: **From Leadville:** *Reset odometer at start* (01). Start uphill as road splits in various directions. I took shortest way straight uphill to right. Follow the road uphill as it climbs east towards the pass. Stay right where a lesser road goes north at 1.6 miles (02) towards Birdseye Gulch. Soon the road begins climbing narrower switchbacks. At 2.2 miles, bear right at a tight switchback where a lesser road goes straight. Continue straight at 2.7 where switchback goes right. Pass is reached at 3.2 miles (03).

As you start down the other side, you'll encounter several rocky spots, perhaps the hardest of the trip. Snow also lingers in the shadows at certain points and may block a portion of the road. Stay left at 4.2 miles where F.S. 41 goes right and is closed ahead. Stay left, pass through cut in the rock and start down other side of ridge at 4.8 miles. Intimidating rocky road descends to North London Mine—great spot for pictures. Note tram towers that go down to North London Mill. Continue past mine as road gets wider and easier. After sign for Mosquito Pass, turn right at 6.1 miles (04) where lesser road 856 goes left. Continue straight at 6.6 miles (05). (Road that joins on right is private road to North London Mill.)

Reset odometer and continue east (05). Stay left at 0.7 where lesser road goes right. Continue straight at 1.9 miles (06) where wide gravel road 419 joins on right. Continue straight at 3.3 where road goes left to London Mine. Slow down as you pass through residential area called Park City at 3.9. Driver's choice at 4.2 miles (07). Bear right on C.R. 12 if you are headed for Fairplay. Bear left on C.R.10 if you are headed for Alma or Breckenridge.

Reverse Directions from Alma side: *Reset odometer where County Roads 10 and 12 merge west of Alma* (07). Head west past Park City. Continue straight at 0.9 where road goes right to London Mine. Stay right at 2.3 miles (06) where 419 goes left. At 4.2 miles (05), a private road goes left to North London Mill.

Reset odometer and continue right towards Mosquito Pass (05). Bear left uphill at 0.5 miles (04) where 856 goes straight. Pass sign for Mosquito Pass and follow good road up switchbacks. Go past North London Mine and begin climb on narrower, rocky road. Pass over ridge through cut in rocks. Stay right uphill at 2.4 where F.S. 41 goes left. Toughest part of trail follows as you cross a couple of rocky spots. Snow tends to collect in the shadows through this area. Pass is reached at 3.4 miles (03).

Start down west side of pass on narrow shelf road. Stay right at 3.9 where road goes left uphill. Make hard left at tight switchback at 4.4 miles. Stay left at 5.0 miles (02) where lesser road goes right to Birdseye Gulch. At 6.5 miles, road drops downhill to left and exits trail next to gated entrance to Diamond Mine. Stay right and follow better road west into Leadville in another 4.4 miles.

Services: Full services at Leadville and Fairplay. Food in Alma. No toilets along trail.

Historical Highlights: This short-lived trail was actively used in the 1870s as the quickest way to reach western mining activities. Like so many of these high pass roads, travelers eventually found it easier to take longer but lower routes like Weston Pass. In the late 1870s, Leadville was the most famous silver mining camp in the world and by the 1890s, it was the second largest city in Colorado. Today, Leadville is home to the National Mining Museum.

Maps: San Isabel and Pike National Forest. Trails Illustrated Breckenridge, Tennesee Pass #109. DeLorme Atlas & Gazetteer. (For flyer of numbered wagon-wheel posts along route, contact Fairplay or Leadville Ranger Station.)

182

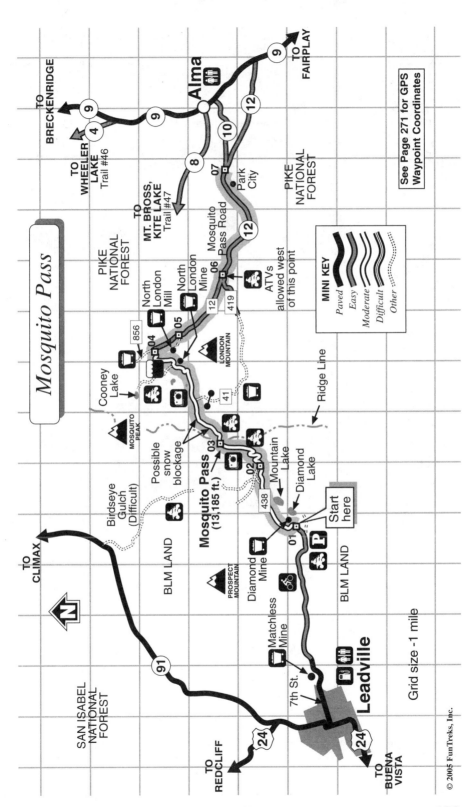

Mosquito Pass

See Page 271 for GPS Waypoint Coordinates

TO FAIRPLAY

TO BRECKENRIDGE

TO WHEELER LAKE Trail #46

TO MT. BROSS, KITE LAKE Trail #47

Alma

Park City

PIKE NATIONAL FOREST

Mosquito Pass Road

North London Mill

North London Mine

ATVs allowed west of this point

MINI KEY
Paved
Easy
Moderate
Difficult
Other

Cooney Lake

MOSQUITO PEAK

LONDON MOUNTAIN

Ridge Line

Possible snow blockage

Mosquito Pass (13,185 ft.)

Birdseye Gulch (Difficult)

Mountain Lake

Diamond Lake

Start here

BLM LAND

PROSPECT MOUNTAIN

Diamond Mine

BLM LAND

TO CLIMAX

N

SAN ISABEL NATIONAL FOREST

Matchless Mine

7th St.

Leadville

TO REDCLIFF

TO BUENA VISTA

Grid size -1 mile

© 2005 FunTreks, Inc.

183

Many secluded camp spots like this along the road next to the river.

Climbing towards Weston Pass.

Cabin next to mine near pass.

Variety of road conditions.

Views of Sawatch Mountains descending west side.

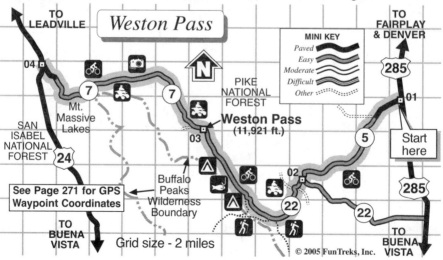

TO
LEADVILLE

Weston Pass

TO
FAIRPLAY
& DENVER

MINI KEY
Paved
Easy
Moderate
Difficult
Other

285

N

04

7

Mt.
Massive
Lakes

7

PIKE
NATIONAL
FOREST

Weston Pass
(11,921 ft.)

01

SAN
ISABEL
NATIONAL
FOREST

24

03

5

Start
here

See Page 271 for GPS
Waypoint Coordinates

Buffalo
Peaks
Wilderness
Boundary

02

22

285

22

TO
BUENA
VISTA

Grid size - 2 miles

22

© 2005 FunTreks, Inc.

TO
BUENA
VISTA

Weston Pass 49

Location: South of Fairplay and Leadville between Hwys. 285 and 24.

Difficulty: Easy. Suitable for passenger cars in good weather on the east side. High clearance is needed on the west side.

Features: Pleasant drive over relatively low 11,921-ft. pass. Forest campground and many great dispersed camp spots along South Fork of South Platte River and Big Union Creek. Good fishing. Several hiking trails lead to the nearby Buffalo Peaks Wilderness. Wildflowers. ATVs permitted.

Time & Distance: Allow 1-1/2 to 2 hours for this 26.8-mile trip.

To Get There: **From Fairplay:** Take Hwy. 285 south 4.7 miles and turn right on C.R. 5 between mile markers 178 and 179. **From Leadville:** Take Hwy. 24 south about 7 miles and turn left on C.R. 7 to Mt. Massive Lakes.

Trail Description: **From Fairplay:** *Reset odometer when you turn off Hwy. 285* (01). Head west on C.R. 5 following sign to Weston Pass. Stay right at 7.0 miles (02) where C.R. 22 joins on left. Stay left at 7.6. Go by Weston Pass campground after 11 miles. Stay left at 15.7. You'll pass many great camp spots by river before reaching Weston Pass at 15.9 miles (03). West side descent is not maintained so road is narrower and rougher. Stay right at 20.1. More camp spots and views of Mt. Massive ahead. Exit forest and follow well-defined road through developed area. Hwy. 24 is reached at 26.8 miles (04). Right goes into Leadville in about 7 miles.

Reverse Directions: **From Leadville:** *Reset odometer as you turn off Hwy. 24* (04). Follow C.R. 7 through Mt. Massive Lakes. Bear right at 2.6 miles. Road enters forest with many camp spots along Big Union Creek. Weston Pass is reached at 10.9 miles (03). Continue straight at 11.1 where road goes left. Many great camp spots along South Platte River. Weston Pass Campground is on right at 15.8. Continue straight at 19.2 where good road joins on left. Driver's choice at 20.8 miles (02). Right on C.R. 22 is best way to Buena Vista and Colorado Springs. Left on C.R. 5 is best way to Fairplay and Denver. C.R. 5 reaches Hwy. 285 at 26.8 miles (01).

Services: Full services in Fairplay and Leadville.

Maps: Pike and San Isabel National Forests. Trails Illustrated Leadville, Fairplay #110. DeLorme Atlas & Gazetteer. (For flyer of numbered wagon-wheel posts along route, contact Fairplay or Leadville N.F. Ranger Station.)

50. Spring Creek
51. Saxon Mountain
52. Argentine Pass,
    McClellan Mtn.
53. Peru Creek
54. Santa Fe Peak
55. Deer Creek,
    Saints John
56. North/Middle
    Fork Swan River
57. Radical Hill
58. Webster Pass,
    Handcart Gulch
59. Red Cone
60. Georgia Pass
61. Boreas Pass
62. Slaughterhouse
    Gulch

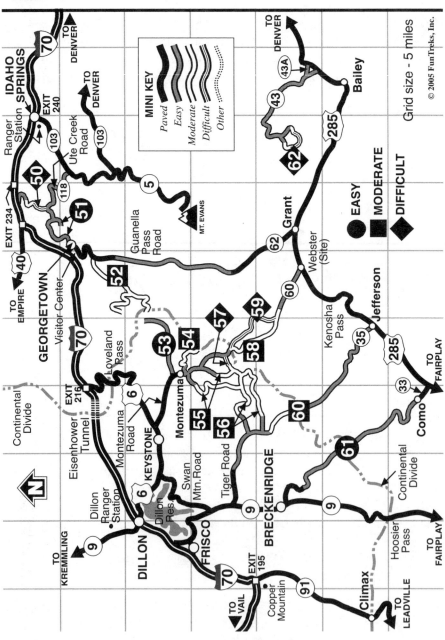

MINI KEY
Paved
Easy
Moderate
Difficult
Other

● EASY
■ MODERATE
◆ DIFFICULT

Grid size - 5 miles

© 2005 FunTreks, Inc.

Breckenridge, Bailey, Idaho Springs, Montezuma

A total of ten new trails have been added to Area 5. In some cases, two trails are combined under one heading to form a convenient loop. Loyal readers familiar with this area have been quick to point out that my first edition missed some great trails in Area 5. One customer, a 20-year resident of Breckenridge, took a week off and gave me a personal tour of the area.

Combined loop trails include: Deer Creek and Saints John, Trail #55, and the North and Middle Forks of the Swan River, Trail #56. Argentine Pass and McClellan Mountain, Trail #52, are also combined, but they each dead end. McClellan Mountain takes you past unforgettable Santiago Mine and Ghost Town. All six trails offer moderate high-elevation terrain suitable for aggressive stock SUVs. Individual new trails include Peru Creek, Santa Fe Peak, Radical Hill and Slaughterhouse Gulch. Peru Creek is one of the most enjoyable easy trails in Colorado. Moderate Santa Fe Peak provides a 12,000-ft. birdseye view of the entire area. Radical Hill and Slaughterhouse Gulch round out the selection by offering difficult terrain within a short drive of Denver. I also learned that mountain goats like to hang around at the top of Deer Creek and Radical Hill. I got some great pictures on my last visit. (See pages 202 and 210.)

Santa Fe Peak, Trail #54, moderate. (In distance: Red Cone top left, Webster Pass top center.)

187

Turn right at this metal sign.

First tough spot at 1.9 miles.

No easy way through the Rock Garden.

View from lower part of trail.

Spring Creek

Start here

To Downieville
Exit 234

70

TO DENVER

To Empire & Rt.40

shelf rd.

01 02

03

Alvarado Road

Very rocky

Ore loading chute

Metal Sign

ARAPAHO NATIONAL FOREST

N

MINI KEY
Paved
Easy
Moderate
Difficult
Other

Rock Garden

04

Grid size - 0.5 miles

TO GEORGETOWN VIA SAXON MTN.
Trail #51

712.2J

See Page 271 for GPS Waypoint Coordinates

712.2

712.2

05

06

710.1

SAXON MTN.
Trail #51

CASCADE CK. ROAD

TO UTE CREEK ROAD

Molly Bawn Mine/Cabin

© 2005 FunTreks, Inc.

Ore loading chute next to trail.

188

Spring Creek ◆50◆

Location: Southwest of Downieville.

Difficulty: Difficult. Steep climbs, narrow shelf roads, and boulder fields.

Features: A fun hard-core trail within a short drive of Denver. Much private land nearby—stay on main road at all times. Avoid shortcuts. ATVs okay.

Time & Distance: About 5.5 miles to point where the trail intersects with F.S. 712.2 at the top of the mountain. Allow about 2 hours one way. Add an hour or two more to get back down off the mountain.

To Get There: Get off Interstate 70 at Downieville exit 234 west of Idaho Springs. Go west on the access road. It starts on the north side and passes under the freeway. At 1.1 miles from the exit, turn left on Alvarado Road. Cross the bridge and immediately pull over to the left.

Trail Description: Reset odometer at start (01). Head east on wide gravel road, ignoring private roads on left and right. Bear right at switchback at 0.2 miles (02). Take main switchback to left at 0.3. Continue uphill at 0.6. Stay left on main trail at 1.2 until you reach multiple forks at 1.3 miles (03). Make a hard right at Spring Creek metal sign. Road swings left after sign and becomes narrow shelf road. First tough spot at 1.9. Stay left at 2.1 and go past ore loading chute. Continue to follow main trail as it winds relentlessly uphill. Shortcuts at some switchbacks are all illegal. Road levels off and goes downhill a short distance before reaching the difficult Rock Garden at 4.7 miles (04). This long boulder field winds tightly through trees with few bypasses. Worst is over at 5.2 miles. Stay right of large mud holes as trail comes out of trees and climbs to better road (712.2) at 5.5 miles (05).

Return Trip: Three choices: 1.) Return the way you came. 2.) Turn right and go 0.6 miles to Saxon Mountain, Trail #51 (06). Right goes downhill to Georgetown. 3.) Turn left and follow a nightmare of confusing roads down the back side of the mountain to Hwy. 103. (Note: New construction is planned for the area around the Lamartine Townsite and roads will change in this area. You should still be able to get down Cascade Creek Road if you know the way. Instructions are not included in this book.)

Services: Full services in Georgetown and Idaho Springs.

Maps: Arapaho N. F. Trails Illustrated #104. DeLorme Atlas & Gazetteer.

Dizzying sequence of switchbacks.

Loose boulders can block road at any time.

One of several log cabins along route.

Narrow in places. Stay off if snow covered.

Picnic tables and fire rings at top.

Georgetown Visitor Center.

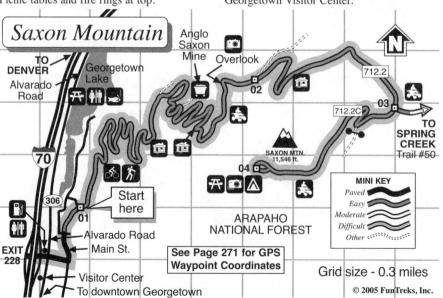

Saxon Mountain

TO DENVER

Georgetown Lake

Alvarado Road

Anglo Saxon Mine

Overlook

02

712.2

712.2C

03

TO SPRING CREEK
Trail #50

SAXON MTN.
11,546 ft.

04

ARAPAHO NATIONAL FOREST

Start here

01

I-70

306

Alvarado Road
Main St.

EXIT 228

Visitor Center
To downtown Georgetown

See Page 271 for GPS Waypoint Coordinates

MINI KEY
Paved
Easy
Moderate
Difficult
Other

Grid size - 0.3 miles

© 2005 FunTreks, Inc.

190

Saxon Mountain 51

Location: Northeast of Georgetown.

Difficulty: Easy. A steep shelf road with many switchbacks. The road is wide most of the way but very narrow in a few places. Rock falls are a common occurrence with the possibility that a large boulder could block the road at any time. Use extra caution after rainy periods. The road is rocky and bone jarring but suitable for stock, high-clearance SUVs under normal conditions. Stay off road if snow covered.

Features: Great views of Georgetown, I-70 corridor and Mt. Evans from different points along the route. Endless switchbacks are impressive. Old log cabins scattered along the route. Extensive mining history explained on information boards at the top of Saxon Mountain. Don't miss historic Georgetown and great visitor center. ATVs are allowed on road but no staging at start. Drive part way up until you find wide spot to unload.

Time & Distance: Allow an hour for the 7-mile drive to top. Easy to spend 3 or 4 hours on the mountain. Other roads to explore in the area.

To Get There: Get off Interstate 70 at Georgetown exit 228. Head due east past Alvarado Road about 0.1 miles to Main Street and turn left. Main Street becomes dirt and ends at entrance to Saxon Mountain Road at 0.5 miles.

Trail Description: Reset odometer at start of Saxon Mountain Road (01). Road climbs north past a few private driveways then begins series of switchbacks up mountain. Tiny log cabin on right at 1.8. Narrow spot with loose boulders at 2.0. Stay right at 2.1 where lesser road goes left downhill. Cabins on right at 3.6. Wide spot at 4.1 serves as unofficial overlook. Good spot for pictures. Stay right at 4.3 miles (02) where large road goes left. Pass roofless cabin before reaching turn for Spring Creek, Trail #50, at 5.8 miles (03). Continue straight uphill on 712.2C and climb another 1.2 miles on wide rocky road. After "OPEN LANDS Historic Georgetown" sign, road ends at loop at top of mountain at 7.0 miles (04). Explore area on foot.

Return Trip: Return the way you came or via difficult Spring Creek, Trail #50. Complex network of roads on south side descends to Hwy. 103.

Services: Full services in Georgetown. Picnic tables, fire rings at top.

Maps: Arapaho N. F. Trails Illustrated #104. DeLorme Atlas & Gazetteer.

191

6th Street in Georgetown.

Narrow trail that climbs to Argentine Pass.

Remains at Waldorf.

Looking down on Peru Creek, Trail #53, from Argentine Pass.

Looking down on Santiago Mine and Ghost Town. (Private, stay on road.)

Take photos from road. Do not enter buildings.

Stop here at top of McClellan Mountain.

Argentine Pass, McClellan Mtn. 52

Location: Southwest of Georgetown.

Difficulty: Moderate. Rocky at the start and very narrow at the top of Argentine Pass. Much of the lower route is easy. Snow can block trail well into summer. Follow an old railroad bed as it climbs gradually to the top of McClellan Mountain, but watch out at the end, where the road appears to go over a cliff. Suitable for most high-clearance, 4x4 SUVs. Oversize vehicles should not attempt Argentine Pass, but should be able to drive much of McClellan Mountain.

Features: Incredible views from 13,132-ft. Argentine Pass and top of McClellan Mountain. Don't miss Santiago Mine and Ghost Town. (Caution: Mine is on private property. Stay on road and well away from buildings.) Many legal side roads for Jeeps and ATVs to explore. Great fall color and seasonal wildflowers. Numerous tourist attractions in quaint Georgetown. Stop at visitor center near freeway exit to learn more.

Time & Distance: Waldorf is 6.2 miles from start. Add an additional 2.3 miles to reach Argentine Pass. McClellan Mountain is 4.7 miles from Waldorf. Allow 4 to 6 hours for the entire trip.

To Get There: Get off Interstate 70 at Georgetown, Exit 228. At 4-way stop east of freeway, turn right following signs to Guanella Pass. Bear left when the road forks, then left again at 6th Street. As you pass through the heart of Georgetown, turn right (south) on Rose Street, which becomes Guanella Pass Road as it leaves town. Follow steep, winding road just 2.7 miles and watch for tiny sign for Waldorf on right. This point is located on a tight switchback with a small area to park.

Trail Description: Reset odometer at start (01) and head uphill on fairly rocky road 248.1. Bear right at 0.2 miles. Cross small creek over culvert, then, at 0.4, follow switchback to right where shortcut goes left through trees. Bear left continuing to climb at 0.5. Stay right at 0.9 miles where 248.1B joins on left. Stay left on main road at 1.2 where lesser road goes right. Stay right at 3.6 miles (02) where good road goes left. Climb shelf road by power lines before important fork at 6.2 miles (03). Left goes to Argentine Pass; right goes to McClellan Mountain.

    For Argentine Pass: *Reset odometer* (03), bearing left a short distance to flat area of mine tailings. This is the site of Waldorf and not much remains except a small building with equipment. Continue southwest across

193

the flat area to narrower road. (Do not take the steeper road that goes northwest.) Bear right at 0.3 following sign for 248.1V. Bear left at 0.5 by intermittent lake. Make a hard right at 1.0 miles where 248.1U goes left. Climb narrow shelf road to Argentine Pass at 2.3 miles (04). Years ago, the road continued down the back side of the mountain, but today it is just a hiking trail. The beautiful valley below is Peru Creek, Trail #53.

For McClellan Mountain: *Reset odometer* and turn north on 248.1 (03). Continue straight at 0.6 where lesser road joins on left. At 0.7 miles (05), F.S. 248.1N joins on left. (This is the turn for the Santiago Mine described below.) Continue straight for McClellan Mountain. Continue straight again at 1.0, then bear left up switchback at 1.3. Bear right up switchback at 1.9. The last place for snow to melt is at 2.4 miles, so trail could be blocked here early in the summer. Make a sharp left uphill at 3.3 miles. This turn is easy to miss because the road continues straight. Make a hard right at 4.5. This is one of the few places where you can see the Santiago Mine below. At 4.7 miles, another tight switchback goes to the left. You can turn here to reach the top (06) or park and walk. If you drive the last few feet, be careful. The road seems to continue over edge of the mountain. The spectacular view below is Stevens Gulch. Turn around at this point.

To reach Santiago Mine & Ghost Town: *Reset odometer* and turn west on 248.1N at Waypoint 05. Bear left downhill at 0.2. Mine is reached at 0.6 miles (07). All buildings are privately owned. Stay on main road and take pictures from a distance.

Return Trip: Retrace your steps back to the start.

Services: Full services in Georgetown. Nothing along trail. Make sure you stop at the beautiful new visitor center in Georgetown to learn all about the many activities in the area. Guanella Pass Road is a very popular scenic tour suitable for passenger cars.

Historical Highlights: Not much remains of Waldorf. In the 1860s, it had the highest post office in the United States at 11,666 ft. The railroad that ran to Waldorf, in addition to carrying freight, also carried tourists. In 1905, the railroad was extended to the top of McClellan Mountain and was known as the *Stairway to the Stars*. At the top, tourists were given a tour of the *Ice Palace*, an old mining tunnel filled with ice formations. F.S. 248.1 follows the old railroad grade. If you wonder how the trains made the tight turns at the switchbacks, they didn't. They continued past the turn, then backed up, alternating forwards and backwards up the mountainside.

Maps: Arapaho National Forest. Trails Illustrated Idaho Springs, Georgetown, Loveland Pass #104. DeLorme Atlas & Gazetteer.

194

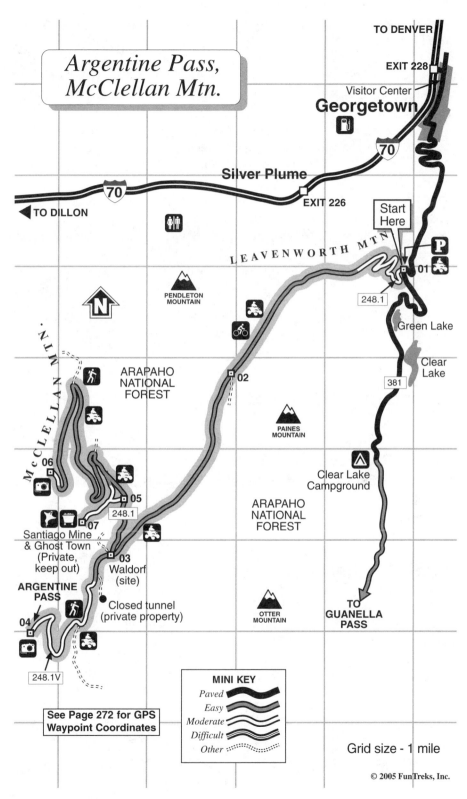

Argentine Pass, McClellan Mtn.

TO DENVER

EXIT 228

Visitor Center

Georgetown

🅸70

Silver Plume

🅸70

EXIT 226

◀ TO DILLON

Start Here

LEAVENWORTH MTN

🅿

01

248.1

Green Lake

Clear Lake

381

PENDLETON MOUNTAIN

N

ARAPAHO NATIONAL FOREST

PAINES MOUNTAIN

02

Clear Lake Campground

ARAPAHO NATIONAL FOREST

06

05

248.1

07

Santiago Mine & Ghost Town (Private, keep out)

03

Waldorf (site)

ARGENTINE PASS

04

Closed tunnel (private property)

OTTER MOUNTAIN

TO GUANELLA PASS

248.1V

See Page 272 for GPS Waypoint Coordinates

MINI KEY
Paved
Easy
Moderate
Difficult
Other

Grid size - 1 mile

© 2005 FunTreks, Inc.

Road follows Peru Creek.   ATV riders take a break at Shoe Basin Mine parking area.

Photogenic mine on hillside above Cinnamon Gulch (Waypoint 06).

Upper trail descent from Horseshoe Basin.   Beaver dam blocks road. Stop here.

Peru Creek (53)

Location: East of Keystone, northeast of Montezuma.

Difficulty: Easy. Although the trail is mostly easy, it is not boring. There is just enough variety to make the drive fun. Optional upper end of trail, at Horseshoe Basin, is narrower and rougher, but most high-clearance SUVs should have no problem. Optional side trip up Cinnamon Gulch is manageable to mine at Waypoint 6, but is very rocky above the mine.

Features: This trail is truly an outstanding SUV adventure. It offers stunning scenery, rich mining history with many well-preserved structures, bubbling brooks, abundant wildflowers, beaver ponds, shaded camp spots, hiking and mountain biking trails, and many legal side roads for ATVs and Jeeps. As you pass Cinnamon Gulch, you can't miss the picturesque mines on the hillside. The road to the mines looks intimidating, but it is only moderately challenging in good weather. The highest point of the trail at Horseshoe Basin is above 12,000 feet, so expect snow to linger here well into July. The lower part of the trail would be open earlier.

Time & Distance: The easy section to Shoe Basin Mine is 4.6 miles and takes less than an hour one way. Add another 1.7 miles to end of road at Horseshoe Basin. Allow about 3 hours to drive everything described here.

To Get There: Get off Route 6 just east of the Keystone Ski Area, following signs to Montezuma Road. There is an exit ramp for eastbound traffic but westbound traffic must turn left at Gondola Road and backtrack to Montezuma Road (See map detail next page.) Head south on Montezuma Road 4.5 miles along the Snake River. When the road curves left, immediately turn left into a fenced parking area.

Trail Description: *Reset odometer at start of trail at north end of parking area* (01). Head north on F.S. Road 260. (Some maps show this road as 214 but the road was definitely marked 260.) Stay left at 1.0 miles on better road and cross bridge. Continue straight at 2.0 miles where Warden Gulch goes right. Continue straight again at 2.1 miles (02) where Chihuahua Jeep Road goes left. Watch for nice camp spots along the creek as you continue. Stay left at 3.7 miles (03) where Cinnamon Gulch goes right. (This side trip is described on next page.) Pass a stone cabin before reaching Shoe Basin Mine at 4.6 miles (04). There is a large parking area at this point for hikers, bikers and ATVers. Many hikers park here to take the popular hiking trips to the top of Grays Peak and Argentine Pass.

197

Continue straight uphill to reach Horseshoe Basin. The road is a bit rougher but very doable in a high-clearance SUV. You can always turn around if the trail gets too rough. Go by the Argentine Pass Hiking Trail on the right at 5.0 miles. (The top of this trail is pictured on the photo page of Argentine Pass, Trail #52.) Continue uphill as lesser roads branch off. The road follows Peru Creek and is very scenic with cascading water surrounded by wildflowers much of the summer. Avoid several side roads that go to different mines. Stay left at 6.2 miles where 262C goes right to cabin and mine. The road is blocked by a beaver dam next to a lake at 6.3 miles (05). Please stop here and hike if you want to go farther.

Cinnamon Gulch side trip: *Reset odometer* (03) and head south towards mines on hillside. Drop downhill and cross creek. Bear left at 0.1 where road goes right to stamp mill. Bear right at 0.2 past the large, decaying Pennsylvania Mine complex. Climb rocky hill to another mine on left at 0.5 miles (06). To reach this photogenic mine structure, you must drive or walk on a rough road just a short distance to the left. The main road continues uphill and gets rougher. It is blocked at 1.1 miles.

Return Trip: Return the way you came.

Services: Full services in the town of Keystone. Nothing along trail.

Maps: White River National Forest. Trails Illustrated Idaho Springs, Georgetown, Loveland Pass #104. DeLorme Atlas & Gazetteer. *(Note: This area used to be in the Arapaho National Forest, but in 1998 the boundaries were changed east of the Continental Divide. Unfortunately, forest maps have not yet been reprinted. Until then, use the Dillon Ranger District map for the Arapaho National Forest.)*

Special Note: The road above Shoe Basin Mine is under consideration by the Forest Service for permanent closure to motor vehicles. Check with the Dillon Ranger District for latest status (see appendix).

The mines along Peru Creek have been under scrutiny lately for contaminating the creek which flows into the larger Snake River. Water from this river is used for snow making at the Keystone Ski Area. As more water is used for snowmaking, it increases the concentration of contaminates in the drinking water. The Pennsylvania and Shoe Basin Mines are at the top of the list of offenders because they are very close to Peru Creek. If the problem interferes with snow making, you can bet that corrective action will be taken to clean up the site. This could interfere with traffic flow along the trail at some future date. It is even possible that the entire trail could be temporarily closed. Again, contact Dillon Ranger District for latest status.

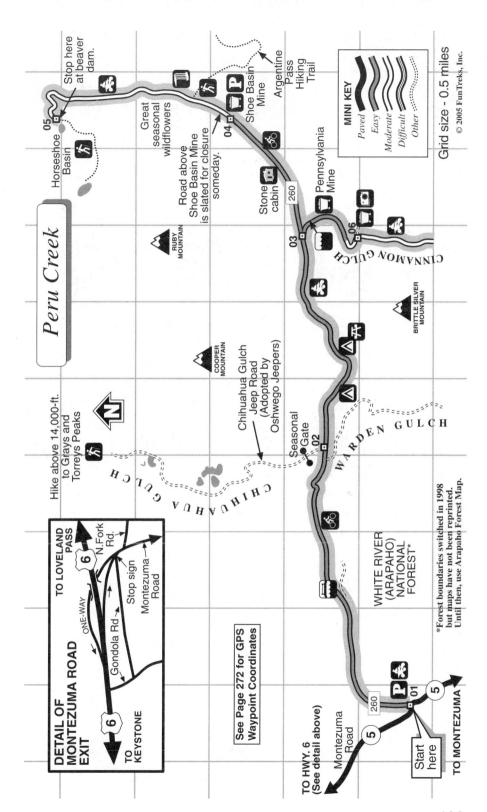

Peru Creek

Stop here at beaver dam.

Horseshoe Basin

05

Great seasonal wildflowers

Road above Shoe Basin Mine is slated for closure someday.

04

Shoe Basin Mine

Argentine Pass Hiking Trail

RUBY MOUNTAIN

Stone cabin

260

03

Pennsylvania Mine

06

CINNAMON GULCH

BRITTLE SILVER MOUNTAIN

COOPER MOUNTAIN

Hike above 14,000-ft. to Grays and Torreys Peaks

N

CHIHUAHUA GULCH

Chihuahua Gulch Jeep Road (Adopted by Oshwego Jeepers)

Seasonal Gate

02

WARDEN GULCH

WHITE RIVER (ARAPAHO) NATIONAL FOREST*

*Forest boundaries switched in 1998 but maps have not been reprinted. Until then, use Arapaho Forest Map.

TO HWY. 6 (See detail above)

Montezuma Road

260

01

5

5

Start here

TO MONTEZUMA

MINI KEY

Paved
Easy
Moderate
Difficult
Other

Grid size - 0.5 miles

© 2005 FunTreks, Inc.

DETAIL OF MONTEZUMA ROAD EXIT

TO LOVELAND PASS

N. Fork Rd.

6

ONE-WAY

Gondola Rd

Stop sign

Montezuma Road

6

TO KEYSTONE

See Page 272 for GPS Waypoint Coordinates

199

Looking down on the town of Montezuma from a short distance up the trail.

Getting off the peak as thunderstorm moves in. Trail is tippy in places.

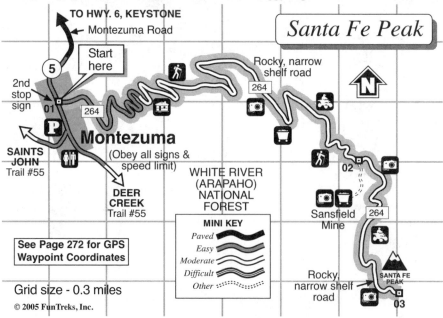

TO HWY. 6, KEYSTONE
← Montezuma Road

Santa Fe Peak

Start here

5

Rocky, narrow shelf road

264

N

2nd stop sign
01

264

P

SAINTS JOHN
Trail #55

Montezuma
(Obey all signs & speed limit)

WHITE RIVER (ARAPAHO) NATIONAL FOREST

02

Sansfield Mine

264

DEER CREEK
Trail #55

MINI KEY
Paved
Easy
Moderate
Difficult
Other

See Page 272 for GPS Waypoint Coordinates

SANTA FE PEAK

Rocky, narrow shelf road

03

Grid size - 0.3 miles

© 2005 FunTreks, Inc.

Santa Fe Peak 54

Location: East of Keystone and Montezuma.

Difficulty: Moderate: A tippy, narrow, ledge road that climbs steeply up many switchbacks to near the top of 13,180-ft. Santa Fe Peak. Mildly rocky in spots but suitable for stock, high-clearance, 4-wheel-drive SUVs. Low-range gearing a must. May be intimidating to novice drivers.

Features: Stunning panoramic views, including Grays Peak and Breckenridge Ski Area. High enough to look down on Webster Pass and Red Cone Peak. Great route for ATVs. Watch for hikers on road.

Time & Distance: This 10-mile round trip takes about 2 hours.

To Get There: Get off Route 6 just east of the Keystone Ski Area, following signs to Montezuma Road. There is an exit ramp for eastbound traffic but westbound traffic must turn left at Gondola Road and backtrack to Montezuma Road (See detail map of Trail #53.) Head south on Montezuma Road 5.2 miles where pavement ends. Continue into town of Montezuma on dirt road to second stop sign. When I drove this route, there was a bright purple house at this intersection. (Warning: When passing through town, go extremely slowly to minimize dust. Local residents do not take kindly to inconsiderate visitors.)

Trail Description: Reset odometer and turn left uphill on residential street at second stop sign (01). Easy road climbs through forest, then narrows above timberline. Pass mine at tight switchback at 3.0 miles. Road gets rougher as you climb to ridge with view of Peru Creek, Trail #53. The trail turns south and climbs more switchbacks. Bear left at 3.9 miles (02) staying on F.S. 264. Road to right dead ends at mine. Finally, the road levels off across a broad area near top of peak. If you've been uncomfortable with the trip so far, this is a good place to stop. I continued around the peak on a rockier shelf road and stopped at 5.0 miles (03). Below were incredible views of Webster Pass and Red Cone Peak (see photo page 187). From this point, you could see several other trails in Area 5. Return the way you came.

Services: In the summer, there is usually a portable toilet in the center of Montezuma. Full services in Keystone.

Maps: White River National Forest. Trails Illustrated Idaho Springs, Georgetown, Loveland Pass #104. DeLorme Atlas & Gazetteer.

This stock Grand Cherokee managed the entire trip.

Deer Creek Trail above timberline.

Popular trail for ATVs and dirt bikes.

Not an uncommon sight at top of Radical Hill.

Cabins at Wild Irishman Mine.

Steep climb up Glacier Mountain.

Great views near top of Glacier Mountain.

Deer Creek, Saints John 55

Location: Southeast of Keystone and south of Montezuma.

Difficulty: Moderate: This trail has a few sections that are borderline difficult, however, the trail is commonly traveled by stock, high-clearance SUVs. Low-range gearing is required. I do not recommend this trail for novice drivers.

Features: An incredibly fun trail to drive with some of Colorado's best scenery. You won't be able to stop taking pictures. A side trip provides the easiest access to the top of Radical Hill where there's a good chance to see mountain goats. I was able to get within 50 feet of a molting herd. Locals tell me this is a common occurrence. This whole area is very popular for dirt bikes and ATVs. You can unload at a large parking area just south of Waypoint 2. Unlicensed vehicles are not allowed on county roads so don't ride through town of Montezuma. Many riders also come up through Handcart Gulch, Trail #58, from Highway 285.

Time & Distance: The main loop measures 12.4 miles. Add 1.8 miles for side trip to Radical Hill and 1.0 miles for side trip to north end of Glacier Mountain. Allow 4 to 5 hours for everything.

To Get There: Get off Route 6 just east of the Keystone Ski Area following signs to Montezuma Road. There is an exit ramp for eastbound traffic but westbound traffic must turn left at Gondola Road and backtrack to Montezuma Road. (See detail of exit on map.) Head south on Montezuma Road 5.2 miles where pavement ends. Continue into town of Montezuma on dirt road to point where Saints John Road goes right (F.S. 275). In the summer, there is usually a portable toilet at this intersection. (Note: When passing through town, drive slowly to minimize dust, or risk the wrath of local residents.)

Trail Description: Reset odometer and bear left following Deer Creek Road (01). (You can drive loop either way, but it is described here in a clockwise direction.) Continue straight at 1.0 (02) where road goes left to Webster Pass, Trail #58. After the parking area on right at 1.2 miles, the road gradually narrows and gets rougher. Stay left at 1.8 and 2.5, then right at 2.6. At 3.1, stay left where a road to the right dead ends. Follow white arrow sign uphill to the left at 3.3 miles where a good size road goes right. The road climbs steadily uphill with many switchbacks taking you above timberline.

At 4.5 miles the main trail continues to the right. Left takes you uphill to the top of Radical Hill in about a mile. I highly recommend this side trip. The views are great and there's a good chance to see mountain goats at the top. When you come back down the hill, continue straight and you'll reconnect with the main trail just ahead (03).

Whether you take the side trip or not, *reset your odometer at Waypoint 03* when you reconnect with the main trail. Climb across the face of the mountain to an intersection at 0.5 miles (04). Left goes down the Middle Fork of the Swan River, Trail #56. Turn right on road marked 279. There's a steep hill to climb before reaching another fork at 1.3 miles (05). Left takes you down the North Fork of the Swan River, also Trail #56. Turn right downhill along a gorgeous ridge.

As you proceed, look left for a distant view of the Breckenridge Ski Area. The road descends before starting a steep climb up narrowing Glacier Ridge. It is a spectacular but intimidating sight. As you continue to climb, stay left at 3.2 miles (06) where a dead-end road goes right downhill. Great views from ridge top at 4.0 miles in vicinity of General Teller Mine. (Stay away from mine. Ground is unstable in this area.)

At 4.1 miles (07) a road goes right to an overlook in about half a mile. *Return to this point and reset odometer.* The road winds downhill on narrow, twisting switchbacks. You are now on Saints John Road. You'll go past the Wild Irishman Mine at 0.7 with log cabins below the road. Stay right downhill at 1.5 miles and pass through seasonal Forest Service gate followed by a small stream crossing. You'll see many beaver ponds along the left side of road. Pass by a private cabin at 2.3 miles, cross stream and follow S-curve to left. At 2.4 miles (08), pass through Saints John Townsite with remains of a large mill. Continue straight at 3.2 miles where a road comes out of Saints John Creek and joins on the left. Bear left downhill at 3.6. At 3.8 miles (01), you return to Montezuma Road where you started.

Return Trip: Turn left on Montezuma Road and head back to Hwy. 6 at the Keystone Ski Area. If you are heading west on Hwy. 6, Montezuma Road passes under bridge and merges effortlessly onto the highway. If you are heading east on Hwy. 6 toward Loveland Pass, turn left on Gondola Road and head west, then right to the highway. (See map detail at right.)

Services: In the summer, there is usually a portable toilet in the center of Montezuma at start of trail. The tiny parking area here is only big enough for 3 or 4 cars. It is not a staging area. Full services in Keystone.

Maps: White River National Forest. Trails Illustrated Idaho Springs, Georgetown, Loveland Pass #104. DeLorme Atlas & Gazetteer.

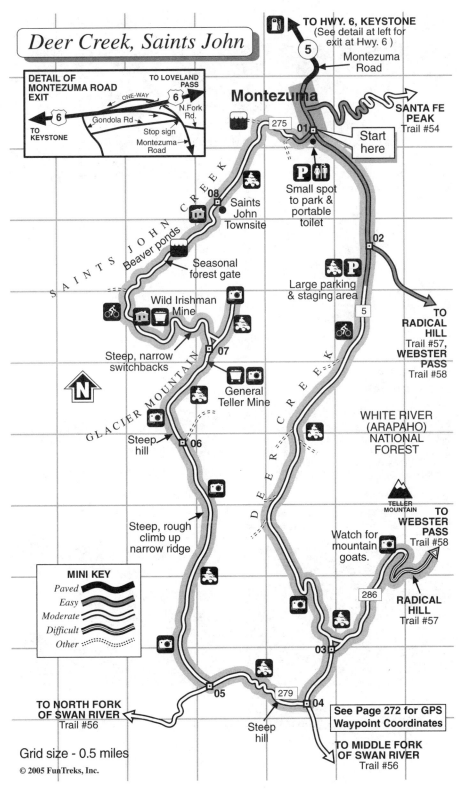

Deer Creek, Saints John

DETAIL OF MONTEZUMA ROAD EXIT

TO LOVELAND PASS

ONE-WAY

N. Fork Rd.

6

Gondola Rd

6

TO KEYSTONE

Stop sign

Montezuma Road

TO HWY. 6, KEYSTONE
(See detail at left for exit at Hwy. 6)

5

Montezuma Road

SANTA FE PEAK
Trail #54

Montezuma

275

01

Start here

SAINTS JOHN CREEK

08

Saints John Townsite

Beaver ponds

Seasonal forest gate

P

Small spot to park & portable toilet

Large parking & staging area

5

TO RADICAL HILL
Trail #57,
WEBSTER PASS
Trail #58

Wild Irishman Mine

Steep, narrow switchbacks

07

General Teller Mine

GLACIER MOUNTAIN

N

Steep hill

06

DEER CREEK

WHITE RIVER (ARAPAHO) NATIONAL FOREST

TELLER MOUNTAIN

TO WEBSTER PASS
Trail #58

Steep, rough climb up narrow ridge

Watch for mountain goats.

286

RADICAL HILL
Trail #57

MINI KEY

Paved
Easy
Moderate
Difficult
Other

03

05

279

04

See Page 272 for GPS Waypoint Coordinates

TO NORTH FORK OF SWAN RIVER
Trail #56

Steep hill

TO MIDDLE FORK OF SWAN RIVER
Trail #56

Grid size - 0.5 miles

© 2005 FunTreks, Inc.

Open area for dry camping near Waypoint 2.

Typical trail below timberline.

Very steep in places.

Cabin at top of Wise Mountain provides winter shelter.

Highest point of trail is above 12,500 feet.

Cabin at Swandyke Townsite.

Steep descent down Middle Fork route.

Location: Northeast of Breckenridge, southwest of Montezuma.

Difficulty: Moderate. The upper section of the Middle Fork half of loop is very narrow, rough and steep in places. Early season conditions, when snow lingers on the trail, can create difficult and potentially dangerous conditions. The trail is gated closed on the western end until conditions are passable. Every few years, the Forest Service comes through and knocks down the roughest places so conditions may be easier. When dry, trail is usually suitable for aggressive stock SUVs with high ground clearance and low-range gearing, but use careful judgment if conditions deteriorate. A side trip up "Number 10" Hill offers a difficult challenge.

Features: Several well-preserved cabins along route, including a habitable cabin with functioning stove at top of Wise Mountain. Breathtaking views above timberline. ATVs can use entire trail and dirt portion of Tiger Road.

Time & Distance: This 13.5-mile loop takes about 3 hours under ideal conditions. Add 5.8 miles for easy Tiger Road.

To Get There: From Hwy. 9 about 3 miles north of Breckenridge, head east on well-marked Tiger Road. Follow sign to the Breckenridge Golf Course. Continue east after the pavement ends on a well-graded gravel road. After 4.8 miles, you'll go past a treed area on the right where camping is allowed. This is a popular staging area for ATVs and dirt bikes. When dry, the area is also suitable for motorhomes. Continue another mile to start of North Fork Route on left before heavy wooden bridge.

Trail Description: Reset odometer as you turn left off Tiger Road (01). Follow easy road and turn left uphill at 0.6 miles (02) on F.S. 221. Right goes to a large open area suitable for camping. Bear right at 0.8 where a lesser road goes left. At 1.8 miles, the main road appears to go left, but you stay right on lesser road. Near a partial cabin at 2.3 miles (03), turn right on lesser road. You'll cross over the North Fork of the Swan River where the road follows a lesser tributary up Garibaldi Gulch. The road narrows and steepens with increasing rocky sections. You'll pass a small cabin then a mine before reaching T intersection at 3.7 miles (04). Turn right to visit cabin at the top of Wise Mountain. The cabin is stocked with a few supplies and is primarily used as a warming hut for winter activities. Please leave cabin as you find it. After visiting cabin, return to Waypoint 04 and go straight.

207

The trail continues across a high ridge and climbs steeply to a fork at 4.7 miles. Stay left. Right is illegal route. The main trail remains steep, then begins to level off as you climb higher. At 5.3 miles, along a rock outcrop, there are spectacular views to the right. You can see the Middle Fork descending through a beautiful valley. Stay right at 5.7 miles (05) where a road goes left down Saints John, Trail #55.

At 6.5 miles (06) *reset odometer* where a road goes left to Deer Creek, Trail #55, and Radical Hill, Trail #57. Turn right and begin the Middle Fork portion of the route. Driver's choice at 0.6 miles; I went right. Bear right at 0.7 miles (07) where a dead-end road goes left. The road gets very steep and narrow and snow often lingers through this area. Turn around if it doesn't look safe. Stay left at 1.2 and continue left as several roads branch right. Bear right at 1.7 on road marked F.S. 6. Cross the Middle Fork of the Swan River at 2.4 miles then turn left at 2.6. A well-preserved cabin marks the townsite of Swandyke at 2.9 miles. Stay left at 3.3, then right at 3.7 miles (08). (Left here goes up difficult "Number 10" Hill and across a tippy, sidehill road to Georgia Pass.)

Make a right downhill at 3.9, a left downhill at 4.3, then continue straight at 4.4 where a road joins on left. Stay right at 5.1 miles where a road goes left across a dilapidated wooden bridge. This road used to be a shortcut over to the South Fork Road, but it is now closed. The main road continues downhill through a popular camping area, then intersects with Tiger Road at 7.0 miles (09).

Return Trip: Continue straight on Tiger Road to return to Hwy. 9. You'll pass the start of trail after crossing a heavy wooden bridge. Left at Waypoint 09 goes up the South Fork of Swan River to Georgia Pass, Trail #60.

Services: Full services in Breckenridge; nothing along trail.

Historical Highlights: The piles of rock seen along Tiger Road were left over from dredge mining that took place between 1898 and 1942. Large barges created their own deep ponds as they sucked silt and rock from the bottom of the Swan and Blue Rivers. Parts of an old dredge barge can be seen in a pond along Tiger Road 2.5 miles east of Hwy. 9.

Swandyke was an active mining town between 1898 and 1910 with a population near 500. The town was a stage stop for passengers coming over Georgia Pass. Businesses included a saloon, barber shop, butcher shop and blacksmith shop.

Maps: White River National Forest. Most of this trail is shown on Trails Illustrated Map # 104.

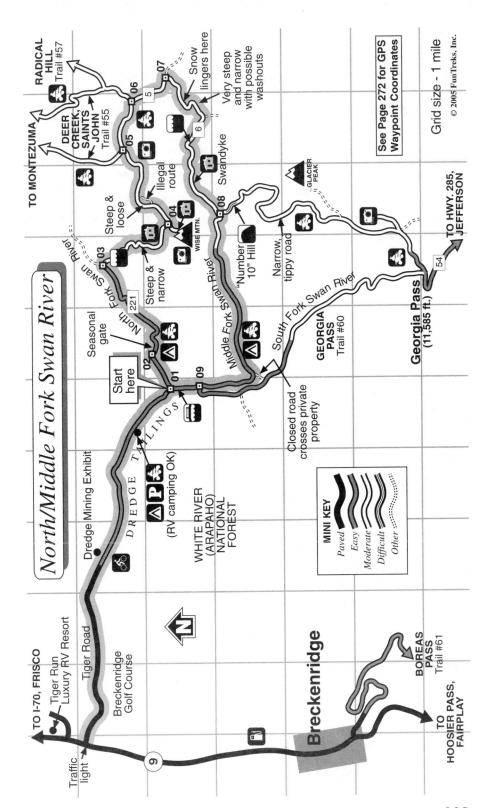

North/Middle Fork Swan River

RADICAL HILL Trail #57

TO MONTEZUMA

DEER CREEK, SAINTS JOHN Trail #55

Snow lingers here

Very steep and narrow with possible washouts

07

06

5

05

6

Swandyke

Illegal route

Steep & loose

04

08

WISE MTN.

"Number 10" Hill

Narrow, tippy road

GLACIER PEAK

03

Steep & narrow

221

North Fork Swan River

Seasonal gate

02

Start here

01

09

Middle Fork Swan River

South Fork Swan River

GEORGIA PASS Trail #60

Closed road crosses private property

Georgia Pass (11,585 ft.)

54

TO HWY. 285, JEFFERSON

See Page 272 for GPS Waypoint Coordinates

Grid size - 1 mile

© 2005 FunTreks, Inc.

DREDGE TAILINGS

Dredge Mining Exhibit

P

(RV camping OK)

WHITE RIVER (ARAPAHO) NATIONAL FOREST

MINI KEY
Paved
Easy
Moderate
Difficult
Other

N

TO I-70, FRISCO

Tiger Run Luxury RV Resort

Tiger Road

Breckenridge Golf Course

Traffic light

9

Breckenridge

BOREAS PASS Trail #61

TO HOOSIER PASS, FAIRPLAY

209

Crossing Snake River.

Lower section is rocky in places.

Tippy spots not for novice drivers.

Very narrow ledge road near the top.

Looking down from top of trail.

Watch for mountain goats.

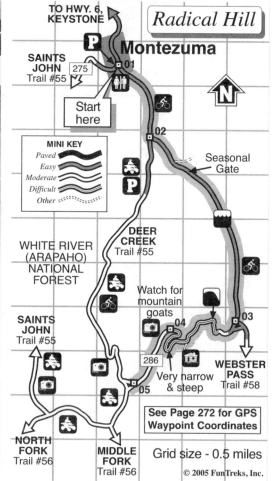

Radical Hill

TO HWY. 6, KEYSTONE

Montezuma

SAINTS JOHN Trail #55 — 275

Start here

MINI KEY
Paved
Easy
Moderate
Difficult
Other

Seasonal Gate

WHITE RIVER (ARAPAHO) NATIONAL FOREST

DEER CREEK Trail #55

Watch for mountain goats

SAINTS JOHN Trail #55

286

Very narrow & steep

WEBSTER PASS Trail #58

NORTH FORK Trail #56

MIDDLE FORK Trail #56

See Page 272 for GPS Waypoint Coordinates

Grid size - 0.5 miles

© 2005 FunTreks, Inc.

Radical Hill ◆57◆

Location: South of Montezuma, east of Breckenridge.

Difficulty: Difficult. Very tippy, narrow and steep with several mildly challenging rocky sections. A very aggressive stock SUV can make it with an experienced driver. Low range and skid plates highly recommended. Snow may block trail mid or late summer.

Features: A short, white-knuckle climb to an outstanding view above 12,600 feet. Watch for mountain goats. Popular for ATVs and dirt bikes.

Time & Distance: The steep section of Radical Hill is only 1.7 miles and takes less than an hour. Add 3.7 miles from Montezuma to the base of Radical Hill. Add another hour or two to get back down the mountain.

To Get There: Get off Route 6 just east of the Keystone Ski Area, following signs to Montezuma Road. There is an exit ramp for eastbound traffic but westbound traffic must turn left at Gondola Road and backtrack to Montezuma Road (See detail map of Trail #53.) Head south on Montezuma Road 5.2 miles where pavement ends. Continue into town of Montezuma on dirt road to fork for Saints John Road, F.S. 275, at portable toilet.

Trail Description: Reset odometer at start (01) *and continue south following sign for Deer Creek Road.* Turn left after 1.0 miles (02), following sign to Webster Pass. Continue straight at 1.4, then bear right at 1.5. After seasonal gate, trail swings right and crosses headwaters of the Snake River. Bear right at 3.7 miles (03) at sign for Deer Creek. *Reset odometer* and start up hill. Stay on trail at all times; do not go around tough spots. Stay right through rocky section with possible lingering snow at 0.8 miles. Stay right at 1.1 where lesser road goes left to tiny cabin. Narrow trail climbs very steeply. Top is reached at 1.7 miles (04). Head left (south) downhill to intersect with Deer Creek, Trail #55, at 2.5 miles (05).

Return Trip: Right down Deer Creek is shortest way back to Montezuma. My favorite way is to turn left and follow directions for Saints John, Trail #55. You can also go down several other routes shown on map.

Services: Portable toilet in Montezuma. Full services in Keystone.

Maps: White River National Forest. Trails Illustrated Idaho Springs, Georgetown, Loveland Pass #104. DeLorme Atlas & Gazetteer.

Narrow switchbacks descend from Webster Pass at right of picture.

Great fun for ATVs and dirt bikes.

Very narrow and tippy in a couple of places.

Drive carefully through this bog area.

Stay clear of this old miner's cabin.

Location: East of Breckenridge between Montezuma and Highway 285.

Difficulty: Moderate. Switchbacks that descend south from Webster Pass are not as narrow as in past years, but careful driving and caution are still the order of the day. The rockiest part of trail is near the bottom where the trail intersects with Red Cone, Trail #59. A bog area (see map) has been repaired with logs but can still be challenging when the logs move. Upper portion of trail is often blocked by snow well into August. When dry, this trail is suitable for stock, high-clearance, 4WD vehicles with low-range gearing.

Features: Outstanding scenery from 12,096-ft. Webster Pass. Exciting descent down narrow switchbacks through historical mining area. A very enjoyable drive for experienced drivers seeking real adventure. Very popular ATV and dirt bike area. Unlicensed vehicles are not allowed on county roads, which includes town of Montezuma. Camping and staging available at north end of County Road 60 five miles from Highway 285. Combine this trail with Red Cone, Trail #59, to form convenient loop.

Time & Distance: As described here, trail is 10 miles from Montezuma to lower junction of Webster Pass and Red Cone. This portion takes about 2 hours. Add another quick 5 miles to reach Hwy. 285 on County Road 60.

To Get There: Get off Route 6 just east of the Keystone Ski Area, following signs to Montezuma Road. There is an exit ramp for eastbound traffic but westbound traffic must turn left at Gondola Road and backtrack to Montezuma Road (See detail map of Trail #53.) Head south on Montezuma Road 5.2 miles where pavement ends. Continue into town of Montezuma on dirt road to fork for Saints John Road, F.S. 275, at portable toilet.

Trail Description: Reset odometer at start (01) *and continue south following sign for Deer Creek Road.* Turn left after 1.0 miles (02), following sign to Webster Pass. Continue straight at 1.4, then bear right at 1.5. After seasonal gate, trail swings right and crosses headwaters of the Snake River. Stay left at 3.7 miles (03). (Road to right, with sign for Deer Creek, goes up difficult Radical Hill, Trail #57.) You reach Webster Pass at 5.1 miles (04) after a series of gentle switchbacks. Look east from pass to see the steep, one-way road that descends from Red Cone Peak.

Reset odometer at Webster Pass (04) *and descend south down narrow ledge road. (Under no circumstances should you attempt to drive up the*

213

one-way road to Red Cone. This is illegal and could result in trail closure.) Follow narrow switchbacks down south side of Webster Pass, using extreme caution. Do not attempt if snow is blocking road. Narrowest point of trail is reached at 1.0 miles. Water crossing at 1.6 miles. Pass through repaired bog area at 2.4 miles. Watch for overturned logs that could expose sharp spikes. (Note: This section was a major work project for the Colorado Association of 4-Wheel-Drive Clubs. Fences, on each side of the trail, have been erected to protect the soft ground. Stay on trail at all times. Further damage to this area could result in trail closure.)

Continue straight past mine on left at 2.8 miles, then stay right around a dilapidated miner's cabin at 3.1. Stay right on F.S. 121 at 4.4 miles where 565.2 goes left on shortcut to Red Cone. The road drops downhill and gets rockier. At 4.9 miles (05), you reach the lower fork for Red Cone, Trail #59, which goes left. This will take you back to Webster Pass via the difficult one-way descent described earlier. If you continue right downhill, you'll encounter two Forest Service campgrounds and a parking/staging area. From there, County Road 60 goes to Highway 285 in another 5 miles.

Return Trip: Left on Hwy. 285 heads back to Denver.

Reverse Directions: To reach Webster Pass from Highway 285, follow directions for Red Cone, Trail #59. When you reach the fork for Webster and Red Cone (05), turn left and climb to top of Webster Pass (04). This requires steep climb up narrow switchbacks which are often blocked by snow. Bear left at pass down series of gentle switchbacks. Stay right where F.S. 286 goes left up Radical Hill (03) and follow well-defined road to Deer Creek Road (02). Turn right to reach Montezuma.

Services: Portable toilet in Montezuma during the summer. Two Forest Service campgrounds with pit toilets on south end of trail. Gas available in Keystone and at various places along Hwy. 285 coming from Denver.

Historical Highlights: In the late 1870s, the road up Handcart Gulch and over Webster Pass was an important mining road into Montezuma and Breckenridge. The road was built by William Emerson Webster and the Montezuma Silver Mining Company. The townsite of Webster and a cemetery are located northeast of the intersection of Hwys. 285 and Park County Road 60. Not much is left to see. Handcart Gulch got its name from handcarts used by miners to carry supplies up the valley. The road has remained open largely through the efforts of the state four-wheeling community.

Maps: White River and Pike National Forests. Upper portion of trail is shown on Trails Illustrated Map #104. DeLorme Atlas & Gazetteer.

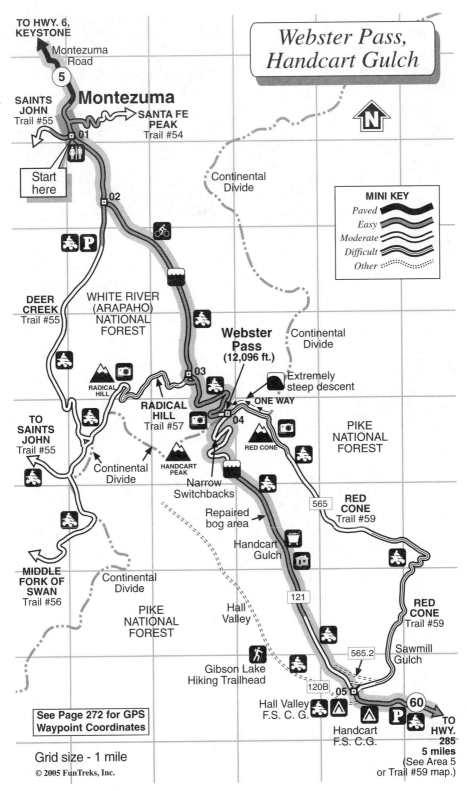

TO HWY. 6,
KEYSTONE

Montezuma
Road

(5)

SAINTS
JOHN
Trail #55

Montezuma

01

SANTA FE
PEAK
Trail #54

Start
here

02

DEER
CREEK
Trail #55

WHITE RIVER
(ARAPAHO)
NATIONAL
FOREST

Continental
Divide

MINI KEY

Paved
Easy
Moderate
Difficult
Other

Webster Pass,
Handcart Gulch

N

RADICAL
HILL

TO
SAINTS
JOHN
Trail #55

03

RADICAL
HILL
Trail #57

04

**Webster
Pass
(12,096 ft.)**

Extremely
steep descent

ONE WAY

RED CONE

Continental
Divide

Continental
Divide

PIKE
NATIONAL
FOREST

HANDCART
PEAK

Narrow
Switchbacks

MIDDLE
FORK OF
SWAN
Trail #56

Continental
Divide

PIKE
NATIONAL
FOREST

Repaired
bog area

Handcart
Gulch

565

RED
CONE
Trail #59

121

RED
CONE
Trail #59

Hall
Valley

565.2

Sawmill
Gulch

Gibson Lake
Hiking Trailhead

120B

05

Hall Valley
F.S. C. G.

60

TO
HWY.
285
5 miles
(See Area 5
or Trail #59 map.)

Handcart
F.S. C.G.

See Page 272 for GPS
Waypoint Coordinates

Grid size - 1 mile

© 2005 FunTreks, Inc.

215

First part of trip is rocky and steep.

Approaching Little Rascal Hill.

Point of no return begins at Waypoint 03.

Trail drops off ridge to Webster Pass at left.

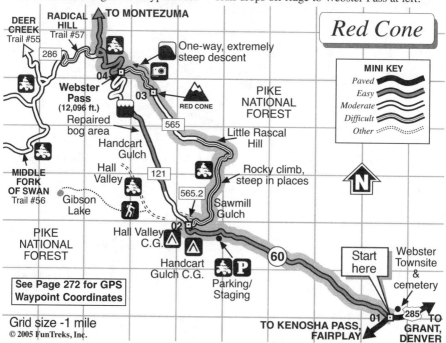

Red Cone

TO MONTEZUMA

DEER CREEK Trail #55

RADICAL HILL Trail #57

286

Webster Pass (12,096 ft.)

04

03

RED CONE

PIKE NATIONAL FOREST

One-way, extremely steep descent

Repaired bog area

Handcart Gulch

Hall Valley

565

121

565.2

Little Rascal Hill

Rocky climb, steep in places

MIDDLE FORK OF SWAN Trail #56

Gibson Lake

Sawmill Gulch

PIKE NATIONAL FOREST

Hall Valley C.G.

02

Handcart Gulch C.G.

Parking/ Staging

P

60

Start here

Webster Townsite & cemetery

285

01

See Page 272 for GPS Waypoint Coordinates

Grid size -1 mile
© 2005 FunTreks, Inc.

TO KENOSHA PASS, FAIRPLAY

TO GRANT, DENVER

MINI KEY
Paved
Easy
Moderate
Difficult
Other

N

216

Red Cone 59

Location: Northeast of Grant and Highway 285, south of Montezuma.

Difficulty: Difficult. South end of trail winds steeply uphill through the forest with intermittent rocky and muddy sections. North end descends steeply down a dangerous ridge line to Webster Pass. This section is one way downhill only. Those who attempt to drive up this section will damage trail and risk getting the trail closed. Do not descend this section if Webster Pass is snow covered or you will get boxed in with no place to go. Only the most aggressive stock SUVs with experienced drivers should attempt this trail.

Features: A real adventure with high views of a stunningly beautiful area. Return via Handcart Gulch, Trail #58, to complete a great loop route. Very popular area to explore on ATVs and dirt bikes.

Time & Distance: About 5 miles on County Road 60 to start of trail from Hwy. 285. Trail is another 6.3 miles to Webster Pass. Allow about 2 hours to Webster Pass. From there, Montezuma is another half hour or return to start via Handcart Gulch in about an hour.

To Get There: Take Hwy. 285 west from Denver. About 3.2 miles west of Grant, turn right on C.R. 60. Watch for house with red roof and cemetery.

Trail Description: Reset odometer at start (01). Follow signs to National Forest campgrounds. Parking/OHV staging on left at 4.4 miles. Bear right at 5.1 miles (02) where 120B goes left to Hall Valley. *Reset odometer again.* Sign says "Experienced Drivers Only" for F.S. 565. Stay right at 0.1 miles where 565.2 goes left to Webster Pass via Handcart Gulch. A steep, rocky and sometimes muddy road climbs through forest and above timberline after about 3 miles. Ascend steep, loose "Little Rascal Hill" at 3.3. You climb to the top of Red Cone at 5.7 miles (03) where one-way begins. Don't lock up brakes if you start to slide; allow front wheels to turn in order to maintain steering control. Steep descent ends at Webster Pass at 6.4 miles (04).

Return Trip: Right at Webster Pass goes downhill to Montezuma. Left goes down Handcart Gulch back to start. (See map for Trail #58.)

Services: Pit toilets at Forest Service campgrounds. Nothing along trail.

Maps: Pike National Forest. Trails Illustrated Map #104 shows only northern half of trail. DeLorme Atlas & Gazetteer.

Southern view from Georgia Pass.

Georgia Pass. Mt. Guyot in distance.

Part of "Number 10" Hill on alternate route.

Seasonal forest gate scheduled for removal.

North side of pass is rough and steep.

Dredge exhibit along Tiger Road.

Georgia Pass 60

Location: Between Breckenridge and Jefferson on Hwy. 285.

Difficulty: Moderate. This rating is based on a 2-mile stretch on the north side of the pass. The south side approach is easy. The entire route is very suitable for stock sport utility vehicles unless snow covered. The trail may be impassable in the spring because of one wet area on the upper north side.

Features: An interesting backcountry shortcut to Breckenridge from Denver. The route connects to many other great trails in Area 5. From Georgia Pass, hard-core enthusiasts can take an alternate route across Glacier Peak and descend down difficult "Number 10" Hill to the Middle Fork of the Swan River, Trail #56. ATVs and dirt bikes can unload at a wide parking area at Georgia Pass or at the east end of Tiger Road if coming from Breckenridge side.

Time & Distance: About 23 miles from Hwy. 285 to Hwy 9 north of Breckenridge. Allow at least 2 hours one way.

To Get There: Take 285 southwest from Denver to Jefferson. Jefferson is about an hour from Denver depending on where you start. Turn right at Jefferson on Michigan Creek Road. If you are starting from the Breckenridge end, Tiger Road is about 3 miles north of Breckenridge off Route 9. Follow signs to the Breckenridge Golf Course.

Trail Description: Reset your odometer as you turn off 285 at Jefferson (01). Michigan Creek Road is paved at the start but quickly becomes a smooth dirt road. At 2.2 miles continue straight past Rd. 37, which goes right to Jefferson Lake. At 3.1 miles (02) bear to the right on County Road 54, a slightly rougher road. There should be a sign here for Georgia Pass 9 miles. At 5.3 miles you enter the Pike National Forest and about a mile farther you go by the Michigan Creek F.S. Campground on the left. At 11 miles the road narrows as you complete the last mile to the pass. At about 12 miles (03), you reach a wide flat area with roads going in several directions. There is a large sign to your left indicating that you have reached Georgia Pass and the Continental Divide. The short side road behind you heads west in the direction of Mt. Guyot, a distinctive cone-shaped peak. Directly ahead leads to a more difficult alternate route across the west face of Glacier Peak. The main trail is to your left and is almost indistinguishable as it heads down the north side after the flat area.

Reset your odometer at the pass (03). As you head down the north side, do your best to stay on the main road. The next few miles are the roughest part of the trip as you drop down quickly over some fairly bumpy terrain and pass through a meadow that can be muddy in the spring. There is also some brush here that may lightly touch your vehicle. Bear to the right at 0.9 miles. At 1.1 there is a unused seasonal gate that is scheduled for removal. At 1.3 miles the road splits and then comes back together again. Keep to the right. You pass a small stream and a road that goes to the right at 1.5 miles. Follow the main road at 1.7 miles. At 3.7 miles (04), cross a bridge and turn right. At 4.5 turn right and cross the Swan River through an area of dredge tailings. When you reach the other side of the river at 4.6 miles (05), turn left and follow Tiger Road to Hwy. 9 at 10.9 miles (06). If you have time, stop at the dredge exhibit on the north side of Tiger Road.

Return Trip: At Hwy. 9, turn right for I-70 or left to Breckenridge.

Reverse Directions: Reset odometer (06) and head east on well-marked Tiger Road about 3 miles north of Breckenridge. Continue after pavement ends and go by camping/staging area on right at 4.8 miles. Stay right past North Fork of Swan River at 5.8. Cross bridge and continue to a fork at 6.3 miles (05). Straight goes to Middle Fork of Swan River. Turn right, cross river, then follow road south along river. At 7.2 miles (04), turn left and cross another bridge. Continue straight at white house at 8.6 miles. Bear left at 9.1 and right at 9.3 and 9.4. Bear left at 9.9 following sign to Georgia Pass. Road climbs steeply to pass reached at 10.9 miles (03).

Reset odometer at pass (03) and continue straight across wide, flat area. Follow larger County Road 54 downhill to the right. Stay on the main road as it winds downhill past Michigan Creek Campground. At about 8.9 miles (02), turn left on Michigan Creek Road, C.R. 35. Follow it east then south to Hwy. 285 at Jefferson at approximately 12 miles (01).

Services: Full services in Breckenridge.

Historical Highlights: Georgia Pass was the most popular way to reach Breckenridge from the south in the early 1860s as thousands of crazed miners brought their wagons over the pass and down through the Swan River Valley. Eventually Hoosier Pass and Boreas Pass became the more popular routes, and Georgia Pass was abandoned.

Maps: Pike and White River National Forests. DeLorme Atlas & Gazetteer.

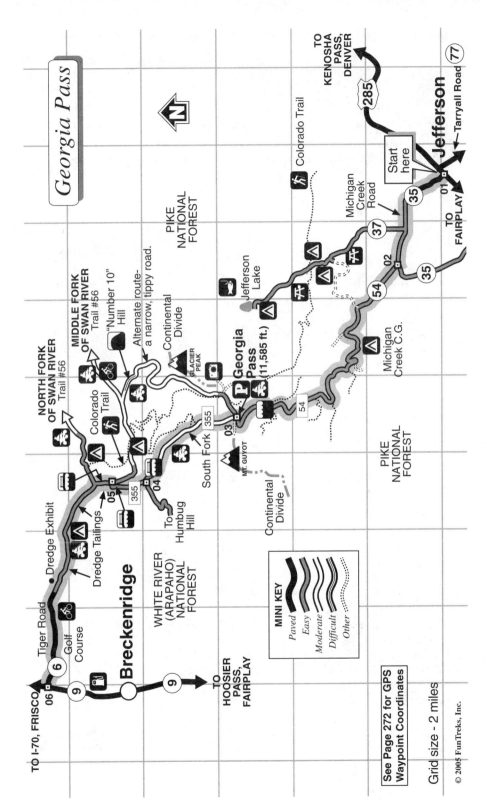

Georgia Pass

N

TO I-70, FRISCO

TO KENOSHA PASS, DENVER

77

Tarryall Road

Jefferson

285

TO FAIRPLAY

Start here

35

37

35

01

02

54

Michigan Creek Road

Michigan Creek C.G.

PIKE NATIONAL FOREST

Jefferson Lake

Colorado Trail

PIKE NATIONAL FOREST

Continental Divide

MT. GUYOT

South Fork

54

03

355

Georgia Pass (11,585 ft.)

GLACIER PEAK

Continental Divide

Alternate route– a narrow, tippy road.

"Number 10" Hill

MIDDLE FORK OF SWAN RIVER
Trail #56

NORTH FORK OF SWAN RIVER
Trail #56

Colorado Trail

04

355

05

To Humbug Hill

WHITE RIVER (ARAPAHO) NATIONAL FOREST

Dredge Tailings

Dredge Exhibit

Breckenridge

Tiger Road

Golf Course

06

6

9

9

TO HOOSIER PASS, FAIRPLAY

MINI KEY
Paved
Easy
Moderate
Difficult
Other

See Page 272 for GPS Waypoint Coordinates

Grid size - 2 miles

© 2005 FunTreks, Inc.

221

Road is easy but very bumpy in places.

Signs at pass explain railroad history

Bakers Tank along route.

Restored buildings at Boreas Pass.

Looking south to Como.

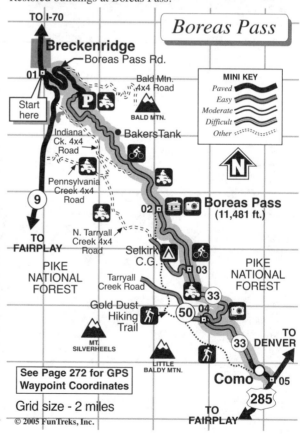

TO I-70

Breckenridge
← Boreas Pass Rd.

01

Start here

Bald Mtn.
4x4 Road

BALD MTN.

Boreas Pass

MINI KEY
Paved
Easy
Moderate
Difficult
Other

N

Indiana
Ck. 4x4
Road

BakersTank

Pennsylvania
Creek 4x4
Road

9

02

Boreas Pass
(11,481 ft.)

TO
FAIRPLAY

N. Tarryall
Creek 4x4
Road

Selkirk
C.G.

PIKE
NATIONAL
FOREST

Tarryall
Creek Road

03

PIKE
NATIONAL
FOREST

33

Gold Dust
Hiking
Trail

50   04

33

TO
DENVER

MT.
SILVERHEELS

LITTLE
BALDY MTN.

Como   05

**See Page 272 for GPS
Waypoint Coordinates**

285

Grid size - 2 miles

© 2005 FunTreks, Inc.

TO
FAIRPLAY

Location: Between Breckenridge and Como.

Difficulty: Easy. Bumpy in places but suitable for passenger cars when dry. Side roads, including Pennsylvania Creek, Indiana Creek, North Tarryall Creek and Bald Mountain, are narrow and rough but mostly moderate.

Features: Scenic drive with historic stops, seasonal wildflowers and fall color. Once a railroad, converted to auto traffic in 1952. See railroad exhibits at start, Boreas Pass and Como. ATVs allowed on forest portion of road. Fun 4x4 side roads to explore (see map).

Time & Distance: Allow about an hour to drive this 21.2-mile trip.

To Get There: Turn east on paved Boreas Pass Road just south of downtown Breckenridge. Look for normal street sign.

Trail Description: Reset your odometer at start (01). Stay on paved Boreas Pass Road as it climbs above city. Forest gate at 3.7 miles starts dirt road (ATVs start here). Overlook at 4.6 miles; Bakers Tank at 6.7. Boreas Pass, at 10.1 miles (02) has several restored buildings and a railcar. Continue straight at 14.0 miles (03) where road goes right to North Tarryall Creek and Selkirk Campground. Davis Overlook on left at 15.9. Stay left at 17.4 miles (04) where C.R. 50 goes right (no ATVs south of this point). Pass through town of Como before reaching Hwy. 285 at 21.2 miles

Return Trip: Denver is 75 miles to left; Fairplay is 10 miles to right.

Reverse Directions: Reset odometer at Hwy. 285 (05) as you turn north on C.R. 33 towards Como. Turn right uphill at 3.8 miles (04) where C.R. 50 goes left. Continue straight at 7.2 miles (03) where road goes left to North Tarryall Creek and Selkirk Campground. Boreas Pass is reached at 11.1 miles (02). Go past Bakers Tank at 14.5 miles before reaching F.S. gate at 17.5. Follow paved Boreas Pass Road downhill to Hwy. 9 at 21.2 miles (01). Turn right for downtown Breckenridge.

Services: Full services at Breckenridge. Gas is available at Jefferson and Fairplay on Hwy. 285. Toilets at pass and Selkirk Campground.

Maps: Pike National Forest. Trails Illustrated Breckenridge, Tennesee Pass #109. DeLorme Atlas & Gazetteer. (For flyer of numbered wagon-wheel posts along route, contact Fairplay N.F. Ranger Station.)

Equestrian trail crosses Crow Creek Road. Be careful.

Tippy spot next to trees.

Rock obstacle along southeast portion of trail.

Muddy in spots, at times.

Several camp spots along route.

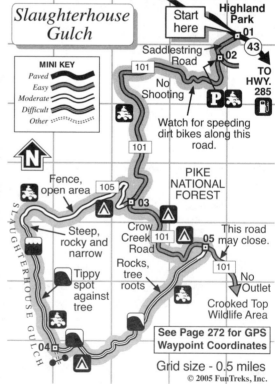

Slaughterhouse Gulch

MINI KEY
Paved
Easy
Moderate
Difficult
Other

Start here

Highland Park

01

43

Saddlestring Road

02

TO HWY. 285

101

No Shooting

P

Watch for speeding dirt bikes along this road.

101

N

PIKE NATIONAL FOREST

Fence, open area

105

03

Steep, rocky and narrow

Crow Creek Road 101

05

This road may close.

101

No Outlet

Tippy spot against tree

Rocks, tree roots

Crooked Top Wildlife Area

S L A U G H T E R H O U S E   G U L C H

04

See Page 272 for GPS Waypoint Coordinates

Grid size - 0.5 miles

Slaughterhouse Gulch ◆62◆

Location: Southwest of Denver. Northwest of Bailey.

Difficulty: Difficult. Narrow, tippy and rutted with washouts, rock obstacles, tree roots and steep sections. One tippy spot slides vehicle against tree when trail is wet and slippery. Not overwhelmingly difficult for a well-equipped, hard-core vehicle, but enough challenge to make it interesting. Not suitable for stock SUVs, unless you don't mind roof and body damage.

Features: A fun hard-core trail close to Denver. Most of trail is entirely in the trees and not very scenic. Great area for ATVs and dirt bikes. Slow down for blind curves but be cautious of those who don't. Watch for horseback riders and hikers. Shooting is no longer allowed in area.

Time & Distance: The entire loop returning to start is 11.5 miles. Add another 6.5 miles from Hwy. 285 to start. I drove everything in about 3 hours, not counting travel time from Denver.

To Get There: Take Hwy. 285 southwest from Denver. At a point 25.0 miles from C470, turn right on C.R. 43A at traffic light by large gas station. (C.R. 43A is a shortcut to C.R. 43.) At 6.5 miles from 285, turn left on Saddlestring Road.

Trail Description: Reset odometer at start of Saddlestring Road (01). Parking and staging at 0.3 miles (02). Bear right after parking area at yellow sign. Follow rough, twisting road west then south. *Reset odometer* at 2.9 miles (03) and bear right on Slaughterhouse Gulch Road 105. (Loop can be driven in either direction.) Uneventful road climbs gradually over varied terrain to high point at 0.9 miles, marked by a fence and open area. Steep road drops downhill and swings left into Slaughterhouse Gulch. Difficult terrain begins at 1.5 as narrow road drops through gulch. Driver's choice at 1.6 followed by small stream crossing. Tippy spot against trees at 2.2. Be very careful if road is wet. Turn left out of gulch at 2.6 miles (04) up steep, washed-out hill. Difficult road climbs over ridge and back to F.S. 101 at 4.6 miles (05). Turn left to get back to Slaughterhouse Gulch Road 105 at 5.7 miles (03).

Return Trip: Bear right and return the way you came.

Services: Gas at Hwy. 285. Dispersed camping on trail but no toilets.

Maps: Pike National Forest. DeLorme Atlas & Gazetteer.

225

AREA 6

Colorado Springs, Pueblo, Pikes Peak Region

63. Dakan Road/ Long Hollow Rd.
64. Phantom Creek, Signal Butte
65. Balanced Rock Road
66. Mt. Herman, Rampart Range
67. Schubarth Road
68. Eagle Rock
69. Mt. Baldy
70. Shelf Road, Phantom Canyon
71. Independence Trail

Bonus Trails: "The Gulches"

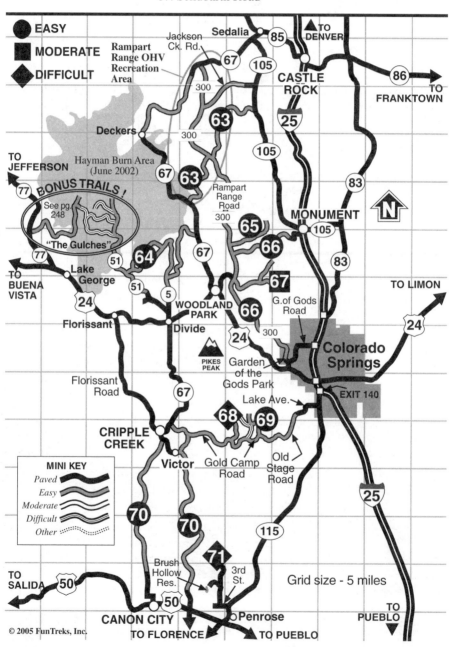

● EASY
■ MODERATE
◆ DIFFICULT

Rampart Range OHV Recreation Area

Jackson Ck. Rd.

Sedalia

TO DENVER

85

67   105

CASTLE ROCK

86

TO FRANKTOWN

300

63

25

Deckers

300

105

TO JEFFERSON

Hayman Burn Area (June 2002)

67   63

Rampart Range Road
300

83

BONUS TRAILS!

See pg. 248

65

MONUMENT

66

105

"The Gulches"

77

TO BUENA VISTA

51

64

67

66

67

83

TO LIMON

Lake George

51

5

WOODLAND PARK

G. of Gods Road

24

Florissant

Divide

PIKES PEAK

66

24

300

Garden of the Gods Park

Colorado Springs

24

Florissant Road

67

Lake Ave.

EXIT 140

68   69

CRIPPLE CREEK

Victor

Gold Camp Road

Old Stage Road

MINI KEY
Paved
Easy
Moderate
Difficult
Other

70

70

115

25

71

Brush Hollow Res.

3rd St.

Grid size - 5 miles

TO SALIDA   50

50

© 2005 FunTreks, Inc.

CANON CITY

TO FLORENCE

Penrose

TO PUEBLO

TO PUEBLO

N

Colorado Springs, Pueblo, Pikes Peak Region

A great thing about the trails in Area 6 is that most are a short drive from the front range. In addition, many are rated easy and suitable for novice drivers. Five trails are close enough to leave late and still get home in time for dinner. They include Dakan Road, Balanced Rock Road, Mt. Herman Road, Schubarth Road and Mt. Baldy. Phantom Creek/Signal Butte requires a slightly longer drive to Divide, Colorado, and Shelf Road/ Phantom Canyon is a full-day trip leaving and returning to Cripple Creek. Difficult Eagle Rock departs from a point just 16 miles west of the Broadmoor Hotel, while extremely difficult Independence Trail is located close to Penrose, Colorado, just 3 miles off Highway 115 about 30 miles west of Pueblo.

A special situation involves three trails that, at the time of this writing, are closed due to damage from the massive Hayman Fire that occurred in 2002. These great trails are included in the event they open after this book is printed. Should this happen, they become a bonus beyond the 75 trails mentioned on the cover.

Mt. Baldy, Trail #69, easy. Rock slides can make trail more difficult.

Great camp spot on Dakan Road.

Typical road condition.

Many OHV trails off Rampart Range Road.

Start of Long Hollow Road 348.

Dakan road climbs to forest.

TO HWY. 67
To Jackson Creek Rd.
Rampart Range Road (No ATVs, except on north end in winter.)
300
Devils Head C.G.
503
Jackson Creek Road
300
Jackson Creek C.G.
563

TO HWY. 105
02
563

TO SEDALIA
Dakan Rd.
22
01
105

Start here

Seasonal gate (Closed to full-sized vehicles 12/1-4/1 or until area dries out.)
03

TO PALMER LAKE

Designated camp spot with large rock overhang

N

PIKE NATIONAL FOREST
300
05
348
Long Hollow Road
Seasonal Gate
650
06
348F
634
348E
351
Rainbow Falls Road
347
67
08
07

04
Rampart Range Road (No ATVs)
300

TO CO. SPGS.

MINI KEY
Paved
Easy
Moderate
Difficult
Other

See Page 272 for GPS Waypoint Coordinates

Grid size - 2 miles

Dakan Road, Long Hollow Road

© 2005 FunTreks, Inc.

TO WOODLAND PARK

Dakan Rd., Long Hollow Rd. 🆖

Location: Southwest of Sedalia, north of Woodland Park.

Difficulty: Easy. Fun dirt roads with many twists, turns and undulations.

Features: Unique east/west OHV route across Rampart Range. Connects to many ATV and dirt bike trails in the Rampart Range Recreation Area. Camping, parking and fires in designated sites only. Day use only unless camping. Closed to full-sized vehicles Dec.1 to about Apr.1 but open to unlicensed vehicles in winter. Contact South Platte R.D. for exact dates. No unlicensed vehicles allowed on Rampart Range Road, F.S. 300, except on north end during the winter. New OHV trail will connect Wpt. 04 to 05.

Time & Distance: Dakan Road is 13.3 miles. Long Hollow Road is 9.9 miles. Allow 3 to 4 hours for entire trip.

To Get There: Head west 0.5 miles on Hwy. 67 from Sedalia and turn left on Hwy. 105. Go south 9.1 miles to Dakan Road (C.R. 22) on right.

Trail Description: Reset odometer at start of Dakan Road (01). Follow wide, graded road west. Road goes right through ranch gate at 2.4. Stay right at 4.3. At 4.9 miles (02), bear left at T, then stay right when road forks. Stay right at 5.4 and enter forest at seasonal gate. Park and unload at 6.6 miles. Camp and park in designated spots only along Dakan Road. Great camp spot with rock overhang at 9.4. Stay left at 9.5 miles (03) where 503 goes right. Rampart Road 300 is reached at 13.3 miles (04). Left goes to Colorado Springs. Right goes to Hwy. 67 and Sedalia. Turn right and go 0.2 miles to start of Long Hollow Road on left (05).

Reset odometer at start of Long Hollow Road 348 (05). Head south on rough dirt road. Stay left at 0.6, 0.9, 1.1, 1.5, and 2.0. Stay right at 2.2, 2.3 and 2.9. Stay left at 4.1 miles (06) where F.S. 650 goes right. Pass through seasonal gate at 5.2. Continue straight on 348 through "S" curve at 5.7 miles where 348F goes right and 351 joins on left. Go straight again at 6.3 where 348E goes right. Ignore many other side roads. Stay right at 7.0 miles (07) where 347 joins on left. F.S. 348 continues and is fenced on both sides starting at 8.6 miles. Road winds downhill to large parking/staging area at 9.6 miles. Pass through parking area and turn left on Rainbow Falls Road to reach Hwy. 67 at 9.9 miles (08). Turn left on 67 for Woodland Park.

Services: In Sedalia and Woodland Park. F.S. campgrounds have toilets.

Maps: Pike National Forest. Rampart Range Motorcycle Trail Map.

Phantom Creek Road 363.

Backside of Pikes Peak.

ATV and dirt bike Trail #717.

Hopefully, F.S. 364 will open soon.

Phantom Creek, Signal Butte

Closed in 2004, may open later. 364

366

MANCHESTER CR.

Closed after 2.5 miles in 2004, may open later.

04

364

364

03

Hayman Burn Area

Hayman Burn Area

363A

N

SIGNAL BUTTE

PIKE NATIONAL FOREST

End of burn area

Signal Butte Road

Phantom Creek Road

MINI KEY

Paved
Easy
Moderate
Difficult
Other

362

363

PIKE NATIONAL FOREST

Start here

02

See Page 272 for GPS Waypoint Coordinates

TO GULCHES

51

01

P

OHV Trail #717

TO DIVIDE

Grid size - 0.5 miles

© 2005 FunTreks, Inc.

230

Phantom Creek, Signal Butte

Location: Northwest of Divide.

Difficulty: Easy. Rutted and bumpy forest road. Fairly wide except on the north end where switchbacks wind tightly downhill. Suitable for all 4-wheel-drive SUVs. Side trip towards Manchester Creek on 364 is very narrow and washed out in spots. This road is closed after 2.5 miles at private property. Dispute with property owner could be resolved soon.

Features: Convenient loop wanders through forest with views of Pikes Peak to the east. Northern portion of Signal Butte Road 362 passes directly through Hayman Burn Area, providing a close-up look at the destruction and remarkable recovery. Springtime should bring beautiful wildflowers. Popular ATV and dirt bike Trail #717 leaves from the initial parking area and connects to other OHV trails in the area.

Time & Distance: Allow 1 to 1-1/2 hours for this 13.8-mile loop.

To Get There: Take Hwy. 24 west from Colorado Springs about 20 miles to Divide. Turn right at the light in the center of town on County Road 5. Bear left at 0.5 miles onto C.R. 51. Go another 2.9 miles and bear right, still on C.R. 51. After another 5.9 miles, turn right on Phantom Creek Road 363.

Trail Description: Reset odometer at start of Phantom Creek Road (01). Head north on wide dirt road. Reach parking/staging area at 0.6 miles (02). (Note OHV Trail #717 departs from right of parking area.) Bear right through parking area following sign for F.S. 363. Stay left at 1.5. Trees open up with views of Pikes Peak to the east at 2.8 miles. Stay left at 4.7 miles where 363B goes right. Stay left again at 5.9 where 363A goes right. Road narrows and winds steeply downhill. You intersect with 364 after a creek crossing at 6.7 miles (03). (Turn right for more difficult side trip to Manchester Creek. At time of this writing, road is gated closed at 2.5 miles).
   To continue to Signal Butte, *reset odometer and turn left* (03). Within 100 feet, turn right uphill then bear left at 0.2. Bear right uphill at 0.3. Continue straight at 1.2 and 1.3, then bear left at 1.4 miles (04) where 364 goes right. Follow 362 through burn area back to parking area at 6.5 miles (02). Turn right back to C.R. 51, then turn left for Divide.

Services: Gas and food in Divide. Full services in Woodland Park.

Maps: Pike National Forest. DeLorme Atlas & Gazetteer.

231

View of Pikes Peak from high point along route.

The other "Balanced Rock."

Great spot to relax and soak up some sun.

Road is deeply rutted.

Take short side trip to this wind-protected picnic spot.

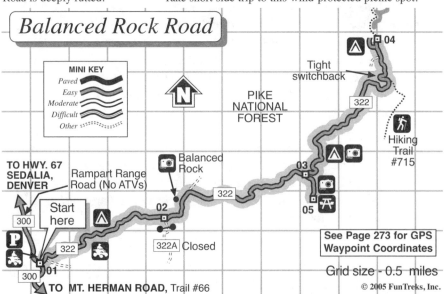

Balanced Rock Road

MINI KEY

Paved
Easy
Moderate
Difficult
Other

N

PIKE
NATIONAL
FOREST

Tight
switchback

▲ 🔲 04

322

🏃 Hiking
Trail
#715

Balanced
Rock

TO HWY. 67
SEDALIA,
DENVER

Rampart Range
Road (No ATVs)

322

03

📷

🅿️

Start
here

300

322

02

322A Closed

05

🍽️

300 01

TO MT. HERMAN ROAD, Trail #66

See Page 273 for GPS
Waypoint Coordinates

Grid size - 0.5 miles

© 2005 FunTreks, Inc.

232

Balanced Rock Road ⑥⑤

Location: West of Monument and Palmer Lake. North of Woodland Park.

Difficulty: Easy. Natural granite gravel road over roller-coaster terrain. East end narrows and drops steeply down to gate at reservoir for town of Palmer Lake. Suitable for stock, high-clearance SUVs with 4-wheel drive.

Features: Fun road descends to remote camp spot above Palmer Lake. Side road ends at wind-protected picnic spot at base of large rock outcrop. Views of front range from top of rock. Good ATV trail. Staging at start.

Time & Distance: Balanced Rock Road dead ends at 7.6 miles. Side trip is 0.4 miles. Allow 2-1/2 to 3 hours for entire round trip.

To Get There: Follow directions for Mt. Herman Road, Trail #66. When you reach Rampart Range Road 300 at the end of Mt. Herman Road, turn right. Go 1.0 miles north to start of Balanced Rock Road 322 on right. You can also reach Balanced Rock Road by coming north on Rampart Range Road from Colorado Springs or Woodland Park. (See map for Area 6)

Trail Description: Reset odometer at start of 322 (01). Head east and immediately bear left where lesser road goes right. Stay left at 0.7 and right at 1.1. Stay left at 2.1 miles (02) where 322A goes right. (Road is indefinitely closed.) Trail begins to descend more steeply with deeper road cuts and narrow drop-offs. Balanced Rock on left at 2.5 miles. (Not to be confused with the better-known Balanced Rock in Garden of the Gods Park.) Stay right at 2.7 where lesser road goes left. Stay left at 4.6 miles (03) to continue on trail. Right is side trip to overlook which ends at picnic table and rock outcrop in another 0.4 miles (05). (Mileage for side trip not included on main route.)

Stay right at 5.1 miles where small road goes left uphill to secluded camp spot with views. Stay right at 6.6. Go past Hiking Trail #715 at 6.9 miles. Narrow road drops steeply downhill and winds around a tight switchback. Trail ends at gate at 7.6 miles (04). More camp spots on road to left.

Return Trip: Return the way you came back to Rampart Range Road 300. From there, turn north for Sedalia and Denver, south for Colorado Springs.

Services: Full services in Monument and Woodland Park. Dispersed camping along trail but no toilet facilities.

Maps: Pike N.F. Trails Illustrated #137. DeLorme Atlas & Gazetteer.

Mt. Herman Road above Monument.

Upper part of Mt. Herman Road is smoother.

Pikes Peak as seen from Rampart Range Rd.

Garden of the Gods Park.

Marked side roads for ATVs.

Rampart Range Road.

Mt. Herman, Rampart Range

Monument

2nd St.

Red Rock Drive

TO DENVER

Mt. Herman Road

Rampart Range Road

Baldwin Road

McD. Rest.

Loy Ck. Rd.

SCHUBARTH RD.
Trail #67

Rampart Reservoir

PIKE NATIONAL FOREST

Woodland Park

Rampart Range Road

Colorado Springs

Garden of the Gods Park

Garden of the Gods Rd.

ATVs on side roads only.

R.V. Park

Mitchell Ave.

EXIT 161

EXIT 146

Vis. Ctr.

30th St.

Start here

MINI KEY
Paved
Easy
Moderate
Difficult
Other

See Page 273 for GPS Waypoint Coordinates

Grid size - 3 miles

© 2005 FunTreks, Inc.

Balanced Rock

234

Mt. Herman, Rampart Range 66

Location: Northwest of Colorado Springs, southwest of Monument and east of Woodland Park.

Difficulty: Easy. Maintained gravel road with occasional rocky spots and small washouts. Rampart Range Road, in the area around Rampart Reservoir, is suitable for 2WD cars, but as you descend towards Colorado Springs, the road gets very rough. Mt. Herman Road is rocky, steep and narrow in a few places but suitable for stock, 4x4 SUVs in good weather.

Features: A convenient introduction to the backcountry around Colorado Springs. Great views of the front range, Air Force Academy, Pikes Peak and Garden of the Gods Park. Unlicensed vehicles are not allowed on Rampart Range Road or Mt. Herman Road. Just a few marked side roads are long enough to enjoy. (Exception: Rampart Range Recreation Area on north end of Rampart Range Road near Sedalia. See Trail #63 for details.)

Time & Distance: Allow 3 to 5 hours driving time for this 36-mile trip.

To Get There: Get off I-25 at Monument exit 161. From light on west side of overpass, head west on what becomes 2nd Avenue through town. Cross R.R. tracks and turn left on Mitchell Ave. Go 0.6 miles and turn right on Mt. Herman Road. Head west 2.4 miles and turn left on well-marked F.S. 320.

Trail Description: Reset odometer at start of 320 (01). Wide, rocky road heads south, then turns into the mountains and becomes narrow shelf road with views of Air Force Academy. Pass Mt. Herman Hiking Trail at 2.6. After 5.4 miles, lesser roads for ATVs begin to branch off. Turn left at 10.6 miles (02) when you reach wider Rampart Range Road 300. Stay left at 13.2 where paved road goes right to Woodland Park. Go straight again at 14.8 miles (03) where Loy Creek Road goes right to Woodland Park. Stay right at 18.7 miles (04) where paved road goes left to Rampart Reservoir. Follow rocky, winding road downhill to Garden of the Gods Park at 35.9 miles (05).

Return Trip: Right goes to Hwy. 24. Left goes through park to visitor center on 30th St. Go north on 30th, then east on G.of.G. Road to I-25, exit 146.

Services: Full services in Colorado Springs, Monument and Woodland Park. Toilets at Rampart Reservoir and Springdale F.S. Campground.

Maps: Pike N.F. Trails Illustrated #137. DeLorme Atlas & Gazetteer.

Views of Pikes Peak from first part of trail.

Road is narrow and rough in places.

Tight squeeze between large boulders.

View of front range from end of F.S. 311.

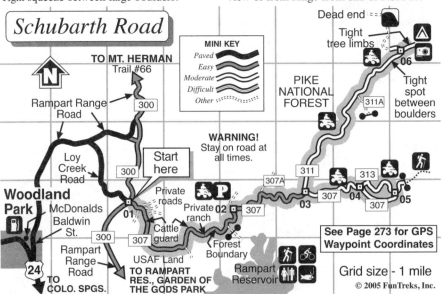

Schubarth Road

MINI KEY
Paved
Easy
Moderate
Difficult
Other

Dead end
Tight tree limbs
06
Tight spot between boulders

TO MT. HERMAN
Trail #66

Rampart Range Road

300

PIKE NATIONAL FOREST

311A

Loy Creek Road

300

Start here

WARNING!
Stay on road at all times.

311

313

307A

307

04

05

Woodland Park

McDonalds
Baldwin St.

01

Private roads

P

02

Private ranch

307

03

307

307

Rampart Range Road

300

307

Cattle guard

Forest Boundary

USAF Land

TO RAMPART
RES., GARDEN OF
THE GODS PARK

Rampart Reservoir

See Page 273 for GPS
Waypoint Coordinates

24

TO
COLO. SPGS.

Grid size - 1 mile

© 2005 FunTreks, Inc.

Schubarth Road 67

Location: East of Woodland Park, northwest of Colorado Springs.

Difficulty: Moderate. Narrow and washed out in places with tight brush and tree branches in the way as you near the end of 307 and 311. Suitable for smaller stock, high clearance 4x4s. Possible paint scratches.

Features: A fun backcountry getaway close to Woodland Park. F.S. 311 ends at overlook of front range. First part of road crosses private land including a U.S. Air Force installation. Warning signs apply to land on each side of road, not the road itself. Travel only on marked Forest Service roads. Keep moving until you cross Pike National Forest boundary at 2.4 miles. Trail not recommended for oversize vehicles. ATVs on forest roads only.

Time & Distance: If you drive everything, you'll cover about 23 miles by the time you get back to Rampart Range Road. Allow 3 to 4 hours.

To Get There: Take Hwy. 24 west from Colorado Springs. As you come into Woodland Park, turn right at light onto Baldwin Street just before the McDonald's Restaurant. Baldwin becomes Rampart Range Road as you head uphill past the school. After 2.9 miles, bear right on paved Loy Creek Road. Go another 1.4 miles to top of hill. Continue straight across Rampart Range Road to Schubarth Road.

Trail Description: Reset odometer at start of Schubarth Road (01). Drop downhill to turnaround area and continue straight on open road. (No trespassing signs apply to private roads only.) Stay right around knoll and cross cattle guard. Pass through trees and then back out into the open. Continue straight at 1.7 miles and cross another cattle guard into private ranchland. Don't stop until you cross forest boundary. Stay left at 2.9 then follow 307 right past parking area at 3.3 miles (02). Stay right at 5.2 miles (03) on 307. Bear right again at 6.4 miles (04) on 307. At 7.3 miles (05), road to right dead ends at fence and hiking trail to overlook. Turn left and follow brushy road 313 through trees back to 307. Turn right and go back to 311 at Waypoint 03. *Reset odometer and turn right (03).* Road passes through tight boulders before switchback at 3.6 miles (06). Turn right on narrow road through tight trees to overlook at 3.7. (Or hike last tenth of mile, if you prefer.)

Services: Full services in Woodland Park. Nothing along trail.

Maps: Pike N.F. Trails Illustrated #137. DeLorme Atlas & Gazetteer.

First obstacle is steep and loose.

Tight squeeze between trees along route.

Great route for ATVs.

F.S. 379 is flat and easy in a few places.

SUV on easier part of trail.

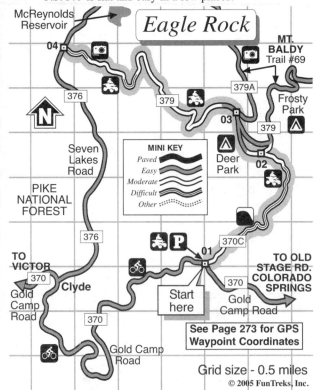

Eagle Rock

McReynolds Reservoir

04

MT. BALDY Trail #69

379A

379

Frosty Park

03

379

376

N

Seven Lakes Road

Deer Park

02

MINI KEY
Paved
Easy
Moderate
Difficult
Other

PIKE NATIONAL FOREST

376

370C

01

TO VICTOR

370

Clyde

Gold Camp Road

Start here

370

TO OLD STAGE RD. COLORADO SPRINGS

Gold Camp Road

370

Gold Camp Road

See Page 273 for GPS Waypoint Coordinates

Grid size - 0.5 miles

© 2005 FunTreks, Inc.

Location: Southwest of Colorado Springs; east of Cripple Creek.

Difficulty: Difficult. Narrow, steep and rocky. Muddy and slippery in places, especially early in the year. Not suitable for stock vehicles.

Features: Eagle Rock refers to the first half of the trail that climbs and merges with Mt. Baldy, Trail #69, at Deer Park. The route described here adds F.S. 379 as an exit route. This route passes through a remote area down the back side of Almagre Mountain. Dispersed camping at Deer Park. Good trail for ATVs. Stay on routes marked with white arrow signs.

Time & Distance: Eagle Rock is just 2.1 miles long. Allow 1 to 2 hours depending upon the capability of your vehicle. Add another hour to descend the additional 4 miles down F.S. 379. Takes about a half day for entire loop.

To Get There: From Nevada Ave., south of Colorado Springs, head west on Lake Ave. towards the Broadmoor Hotel. Bear right and circle around the backside of hotel until you get on El Pomar Road, heading south. When you reach Penrose Blvd., bear left and continue south. Turn right and head uphill on Old Stage Road and merge with Gold Camp Road in 7 miles. Continue west on Gold Camp Road another 8.1 miles to start of 370C on right. *(Note: Discussions are underway to open the east end of Gold Camp Rd., which has been closed for years. This would be a great alternative to Old Stage Rd.)*

Trail Description: Reset odometer at start of 370C (01). Head uphill staying right at 0.2. Stay right across open area at 0.3 on marked 370C. Stay right after creek until you reach first difficult spot at 0.8 miles. Narrow road climbs steeply through tight trees. Stay left at clearing at 2.1 miles (02). (Right shortcuts to Mt. Baldy, Trail #69.) Follow easy road through Deer Park as it merges with 379 going north. Stay left on 379 at 2.9 miles (03) where 379A goes right. (For description of 379A, see Trail #69.) Stay on main road as it meanders west across a variety of terrain. Climb rocky hill at 5.1 and follow 379 as it descends steeply to 376 at 6.3 miles (04).

Return Trip: Turn left on 376. After 3.2 miles, turn left on Gold Camp Road and go east 5 miles back to start of 370C. Return the way you came.

Services: Full services in Colorado Springs. Nothing along route.

Maps: Pike N.F. Trails Illustrated #137. DeLorme Atlas & Gazetteer.

239

Gold Camp Road follows old R.R. grade.

Fallen rock often collects at this point,

Narrow shelf road near end of trail.

ATV rider arrives at end of road.

Plenty of room to camp and unload equipment at Frosty Park.

Start of trail passes through private land.

Camping at Deer Park.

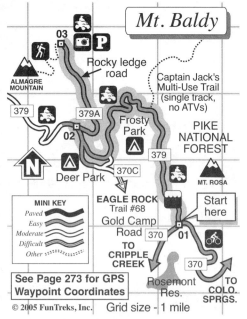

Mt. Baldy

03

Rocky ledge road

Captain Jack's Multi-Use Trail (single track, no ATVs)

ALMAGRE MOUNTAIN

379

379A

Frosty Park

PIKE NATIONAL FOREST

02

379

MT. ROSA

N

370C

Deer Park

EAGLE ROCK
Trail #68

Start here

MINI KEY
Paved
Easy
Moderate
Difficult
Other

Gold Camp Road

370

01

TO CRIPPLE CREEK

See Page 273 for GPS Waypoint Coordinates

© 2005 FunTreks, Inc.

Rosemont Res.

370

TO COLO. SPRGS.

Grid size - 1 mile

240

Location: Southwest of Colorado Springs. (Official name: Almagre Mtn.)

Difficulty: Easy. Service road to towers at top 12,349-ft. Almagre Mountain is usually in good condition, but rock falls on the upper portion of road can increase difficulty. Gate stops vehicles near top. Suitable for stock, high-clearance, 4WD SUVs if trail is clear of rocks and snow.

Features: Short, convenient drive to high point above Colorado Springs. An exhilarating backcountry experience with great views of the front range. Unlicensed vehicles are permitted on F.S. 379 but not on Gold Camp Road.

Time & Distance: Gate is 6.3 miles from start. Allow an hour one way.

To Get There: From Nevada Ave., south of Colorado Springs, head west on Lake Ave. toward Broadmoor Hotel. Bear right and circle around backside of hotel until you get on El Pomar Road, heading south. When you reach Penrose Blvd., bear left and continue south. Turn right and head uphill on Old Stage Road and merge with Gold Camp Road in 7 miles. Continue west on Gold Camp Road another 5.6 miles to start of F.S. 379 on right. *(Note: Discussions are underway to open the east end of Gold Camp Rd., which has been closed for years. This would be a great alternative to Old Stage Rd.)*

Trail Description: Reset odometer at start of 379 (01). Beginning of road passes through private property where it is fenced on both sides. Rocky road climbs gradually and winds through Frosty Park at 1.4 miles. Stay left through this area, avoiding all roads to the right. After Captain Jack's Multi-use Trail (single track, no ATVs), road begins series of switchbacks at 2.4 miles. Stay right at 4.0 where short road to left cuts over to Eagle Rock, Trail #68. At 5.0 miles (02), make a sharp right turn at tight switchback on F.S. 379A. Road winds around to front side of mountain and begins scenic climb up narrow shelf road. Loose rock may be scattered across road at any point. Gate is reached at 6.3 miles (03). You'll find plenty of room to park and turn around. Great hiking around the corner after the gate.

Return Trip: Return the way you came or continue west on rougher 379.

Services: Full services in Colorado Springs. Nothing along trail.

Maps: Pike National Forest. Pikes Peak Atlas by Robert Ormes and Robert Houdek. DeLorme Atlas & Gazetteer.

241

Bennett Avenue in Cripple Creek.

Northern end of Shelf Road.

Approaching Window Rock.

Shelf Road is narrow where it winds above Helena Canyon.

New bridge along Phantom Canyon Road.

Drive through old train tunnels.

Beautiful rolling hills near Victor.

242

Shelf Road, Phantom Canyon

Location: Between Cripple Creek and Canon City.

Difficulty: Easy. Shelf Road is rough and steep in places. High clearance is helpful, but the road, when dry, can be driven in 2-wheel drive. You'll feel more secure with 4-wheel drive when the road is wet. Phantom Canyon Road can be driven in any passenger car but is restricted to vehicles shorter than 25 feet. Both roads are susceptible to overnight washouts from major storms and may be closed without notice.

Features: The route starts just south of historic Cripple Creek, a major tourist attraction and gambling town. Many historic mining attractions can be seen from paved Highways 67 and 81 which circle through Victor and Goldfield. The loop described here is a longer and more rugged backcountry route and part of the Gold Belt Tour. Shelf Road offers many miles of rugged side roads that depart west of Sand Gulch Campground and Red Canyon Park and north of "The Bank" Campground. Unlicensed vehicles are allowed on side roads but not on Shelf Road and Phantom Canyon Road. Rock climbers can enjoy "The Bank," a popular climbing area. Red Canyon Park is a great family area with picnic tables tucked between dramatic red rock formations. Phantom Canyon Road follows an old railroad grade and has a rich mining history.

Time & Distance: The entire loop is about 66 miles. Allow 4 to 5 hours total driving time. Both roads have many blind curves which are dangerous at high speeds. Don't get in a hurry.

To Get There: To get to Cripple Creek, take Route 24 west from Colorado Springs to Divide. Turn left at Divide and follow Hwy. 67 on a beautiful winding drive to Cripple Creek. Pass through the center of town on Bennett Avenue to the bottom of the hill and turn left on Second Street. Drive 0.2 miles south and turn right on County Road 88. If you prefer to drive Phantom Canyon Road only, continue following paved Hwy. 67 (2nd St.) though Victor, then follow signs south for Phantom Canyon.

Trail Description: **Shelf Road:** *Reset odometer at start of C.R. 88* (01). Follow washboard road as it winds south through a scenic valley. Small stream on right is Cripple Creek. Scenic pullover at 4.5 miles is followed by gated tunnel on the left at 5.1. After the mine, "Window Rock" comes into view. The road gradually comes out of the canyon, and by 10 miles you find yourself on a winding shelf road high above Helena Canyon. At 13.1 miles (02),

243

the road curves left. Right goes to "The Bank" Campground and climbing area.

At 13.2 miles, Sand Gulch Campground is to the right. The road into the campground has a lesser road that branches to the left after a cattle guard. This 4x4 road winds through the forest and comes out at "The Bank" Campground. Unlicensed vehicles must return the way they came because they are not allowed on the county road. In wet weather, a gate closes off the area. Lesser roads that crisscross the area are scheduled for closure.

To proceed on the main route, continue south. The road becomes paved before reaching F24 on the right at 15.9 miles (03). F24 goes into Red Canyon Park and continues beyond the park many miles into the backcountry. You can spend many hours exploring the area in a 4x4 vehicle.

Stay on the main paved road south, which is now C.R. Road 9. At approximately 22.9 miles (04), bear left on Field Avenue. It heads directly south into Canon City. At 25.2 miles, turn left on Pear St., then immediately jog right onto Raynolds Avenue which runs into Hwy. 50 at 26.0 miles (05). To reach Phantom Canyon Road, turn left and go 5.2 miles to a major intersection with traffic light at Hwy. 67 (06), then turn left.

Phantom Canyon Road: *Reset odometer as you turn off Hwy. 50* (06). Continue north after pavement ends in about 5 miles. Sign for Gold Belt Tour is located at mile marker 6. Pass through tunnel to first rest stop and picnic area at 7.9 miles. "McCourt" sign at 9.6 miles marks road to camping spot next to Eightmile Creek. Pass through another tunnel, then over a new steel bridge at 13.5 miles. An historic wooden bridge of years past finally had to be replaced. Signs along the route mark other historic points of interest. Another rest stop and picnic area is located at 18.6 miles. At 23.0 miles, a Gold Belt Tour Sign marks route for southbound traffic.

The road comes out of the canyon and crosses a beautiful area of rolling hillsides. Continue straight at 28.8 miles where C.R. 861 joins on right. Paved C.R. 81 is reached at 29.6 miles (07). Left goes through Victor on Hwy. 67 back to Cripple Creek. Right circles around on paved C.R. 81 and joins Hwy. 67 northeast of Cripple Creek. Both roads are part of a tour of the world's largest gold camp (different from Gold Belt Tour) that is explained on signs along the route. There are many old mines and mine buildings along the route, including a giant, active, modern-day strip mine.

Services: Full services in Cripple Creek and Canon City. Toilets at campgrounds along Shelf Road and rest stops along Phantom Canyon Road. If you have time, visit the wonderful museum in Cripple Creek. It will help you understand the extensive mining history of the area.

Maps: Trails Illustrated Map #137. DeLorme Atlas & Gazetteer.

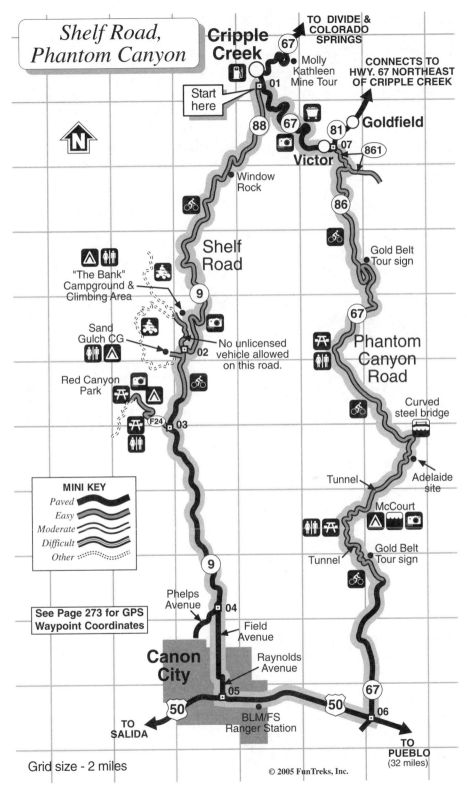

Shelf Road, Phantom Canyon

Cripple Creek

TO DIVIDE &
COLORADO SPRINGS

67

Molly Kathleen Mine Tour

CONNECTS TO
HWY. 67 NORTHEAST
OF CRIPPLE CREEK

01

Start here

N

88

67

Goldfield

81

07

Victor

861

Window Rock

86

Shelf Road

Gold Belt Tour sign

"The Bank" Campground & Climbing Area

9

Sand Gulch CG

No unlicensed vehicle allowed on this road.

02

Red Canyon Park

67

Phantom Canyon Road

Curved steel bridge

F24

03

Tunnel

Adelaide site

MINI KEY

Paved
Easy
Moderate
Difficult
Other

McCourt

Gold Belt Tour sign

Tunnel

See Page 273 for GPS Waypoint Coordinates

9

Phelps Avenue

04

Field Avenue

Canon City

Raynolds Avenue

67

05

50

50

06

TO SALIDA

BLM/FS Ranger Station

TO PUEBLO (32 miles)

Grid size - 2 miles

© 2005 FunTreks, Inc.

245

Review information on main sign at start of trail.

Exiting Freedom Trail.

First ledge coming down Bunker Hill.

Spotter assists on lower part of Bunker Hill.

Start of Liberty Trail. Easiest entry point.

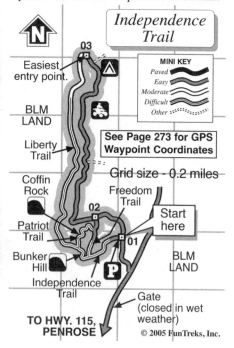

Independence Trail

MINI KEY

Paved
Easy
Moderate
Difficult
Other

Easiest entry point.

BLM LAND

Liberty Trail

Coffin Rock

Patriot Trail

Bunker Hill

Independence Trail

Freedom Trail

See Page 273 for GPS Waypoint Coordinates

Grid size - 0.2 miles

Start here

BLM LAND

Gate (closed in wet weather)

TO HWY. 115, PENROSE

© 2005 FunTreks, Inc.

Exiting Patriot Trail usually requires winch.

Independence Trail ◆71◆

Location: Northwest of Penrose and Pueblo. Northeast of Canon City.

Difficulty: Extremely difficult. When you see this trail, it is hard to believe that any kind of vehicle can get through it. Tall rock walls and giant boulders are the norm. Expect rollovers and vehicle damage. Heavy-duty roll cage and giant tires a must. Scout trail first. Winch anchor points are provided. Trail is dangerous. (Note: Author did not drive this trail.)

Features: Trail has been carved out of a narrow, rocky canyon for the specific purpose of challenging ultimate 4x4 rigs. Difficult enough for competitive rock-crawling events. Hot in summer. Watch for rattlesnakes. Camp at existing fire rings. Pack out all trash. Bring own firewood. If you stack rocks, remove them afterwards. ATVs and dirt bikes can ride on designated roads above the canyon, but canyon itself is too difficult.

Time & Distance: Liberty, the longest trail, is less than a mile. The other trails measure only a few hundred feet. Expect to spend between 2 and 8 hours in the canyon. If you have a lengthy breakdown, try to move your vehicle to one side so others can get around.

To Get There: Just north of Penrose, between mile markers 16 and 17 on Hwy. 115, turn west on 3rd Street following signs to Brush Hollow Reservoir. At 0.2 miles, turn right on "E" Street (C.R. 127). Continue north about 3 miles. Don't turn for boat ramp or anywhere else. After weaving through trees, cross cattle guard at BLM gate. (Area closed when wet.) Turn left 0.1 miles after gate and proceed to large sign and parking area (01).

Trail Description: An easy road heads north along rim of canyon providing access to trail at various points. A short walk from road is needed so see down into canyon. Head west from **Wpt. 01** to enter Independence Trail. Patriot Trail ends near **Wpt. 02**. Liberty Trail starts at **Wpt. 03**. Drop down giant ledge into canyon at start of Independence Trail. First trail on the right is Freedom Trail. It's your only chance to exit before difficult Bunker Hill. Stay right after Bunker Hill. At next fork, Liberty Trail goes left, Patriot Trail goes right. The easiest way to enter canyon is to drive Liberty Trail from north to south starting at **Wpt. 03**.

Services: Gas, food and basic services in Penrose. No toilets at trail.

Maps: DeLorme Atlas & Gazetteer shows roads into area.

Despite the fire, the area remains strikingly beautiful. Photo taken from Hackett Gulch.

Hackett Rock is tougher than it looks.

Longwater Rock cannot be bypassed.

A few spots along trail are washed out.

Sand bar has formed at Longwater crossing.

"The Gulches" BONUS

Author's Note: In June of 2002, the massive Hayman Fire ripped through Wildcat Canyon northwest of Divide, Colorado. The area, known locally as "The Gulches," was one of the most popular four-wheeling destinations in the state. **At the time of this writing, the trails are closed.** The U.S. Forest Service has announced the trails will not reopen unless another public entity assumes responsibility. Local county governments have expressed a strong interest in doing so and there is a good chance the trails will open in the near future. Therefore, the trails are included in this book as a bonus, but are not counted in the total of 75. To leave them out of the book, if they open later, would be unfortunate. The author was encouraged by local county governments to include this area in the book. He was given a special tour of the area, approved by the U.S.F.S., on September 28, 2004, two years after the fire. All photos were taken at that time. The area is rapidly recovering from the fire, and, in many ways, is more beautiful than ever. **As soon as trails open, details will be posted on our Web site at www.funtreks.com**.

Location: Northwest of Colorado Springs, Woodland Park and Divide.

Difficulty: Difficult. Trails are steep, narrow and tippy, with tight brush, rock obstacles and deep water crossings. Modified vehicles with high clearance and lockers are recommended.

Features: Long, winding roads descend steeply into remote, scenic valley. Area previously offered great camping, hiking and fishing. Trails closed to unlicensed vehilces, but may open later. They were allowed before the fire.

Time & Distance: The loop down Hackett and back up Longwater is 11.2 miles not counting side trips. Metberry is 4.4 miles one way. In a properly equipped vehicle, allow one day to drive all trails.

To Get There: **East-side approach.** Take Hwy. 24 west from Colorado Springs about 20 miles to Divide. Turn right at the light in the center of town on County Road 5. Bear left at 0.5 miles onto C.R. 51. Go another 2.9 miles and bear right, still on C.R. 51. After another 6.7 miles, you reach parking/staging area on the right. Just after the parking area, make a soft left turn on F.S. 360 towards Cedar Mountain. Turn left for Hackett at 5.4 miles, Longwater 7.3 miles and Metberry 7.7 miles. **West-side approach.** Before the fire, you could enter Wildcat Canyon via Corral Creek Road, F.S. 540. This road will likely never open again. The only way to get down to the river from this side is to hike down Corral Creek Road. To reach Corral Creek Road, drive north 6.9 miles on C.R. 77 from Hwy. 24 west of Lake George. Turn right on Matukat Road, C.R. 211, and drive 9.4 miles to gated Corral Creek Road on right (08). Hike 2.9 miles to Platte River.

Trail Description: Reset odometer at start of Hackett Gulch 220 (01). Head west downhill. Road gradually gets steeper and rougher as you descend. Steep, rocky section precedes difficult Hackett Rock at 1.9 miles. Stay right at 2.3 miles past scenic overlook. Bear right on what used to be 220A at 3.7 miles (02). (Left goes steeply downhill through a badly damaged area to a camp spot along the river. This was a popular hard-core area before the fire. It will be the last place to open, if it opens at all.) Follow 220A down a steep rock slab and through an area of tight brush. At 4.0 miles, stay right and go around a steep, dirt hill that was once a popular mogul challenge. Descend steeply to river crossing at 4.7 miles (03). (Note: A sand bar has filled in much of the crossing and it is significantly different.)

After crossing river, bear right and follow road north. Cross Tarryall Creek as road winds along the Platte River. (This portion of road was badly washed out in places. Repairs will be needed.) At 6.4 miles (04), the old Corral Creek Road 540 is on left. *Reset odometer and bear right.* Cross Platte River again. (Changes to this crossing are similar to Hackett Crossing.) Stay left at 0.3 miles where roads crisscross. The road climbs steeply to challenging Longwater Rock at 1.7 miles. (A bypass has been washed away. You must go up the rock.) The road remains steep then begins to level off. (Portions of the road are washed out and repairs will be needed.) Longwater connects to Cedar Mountain Road 360 at 4.6 miles (05). Turn left for Metberry Gulch, F.S. 205, reached in another 0.4 miles (06).

Reset odometer at top of Metberry Gulch (06). The road is relatively level before it begins a long, steep descent. (Washed-out sections will need repair.) Stay left at 2.7 and 3.0. Chicken Scratch Hill is reached at 3.8 miles. Stay left to bypass the hill. The trail ends at 4.4 miles (07) at a flat area next to the river. Custer's Log Cabin was once located here. It was completely destroyed by the fire. Under no circumstances are any kind of vehicles allowed to cross or enter the river at this point. You must stop here.

Return Trip: Turn around and retrace the route back to Cedar Mountain Road 360. Bear right to return to C.R. 51, reached in 7.7 miles.

Services: Gas, food and basic services in Divide. Full services in Woodland Park. Nothing along trails.

Maps: Pike National Forest. Trails Illustrated Map # 137. DeLorme Atlas & Gazetteer.

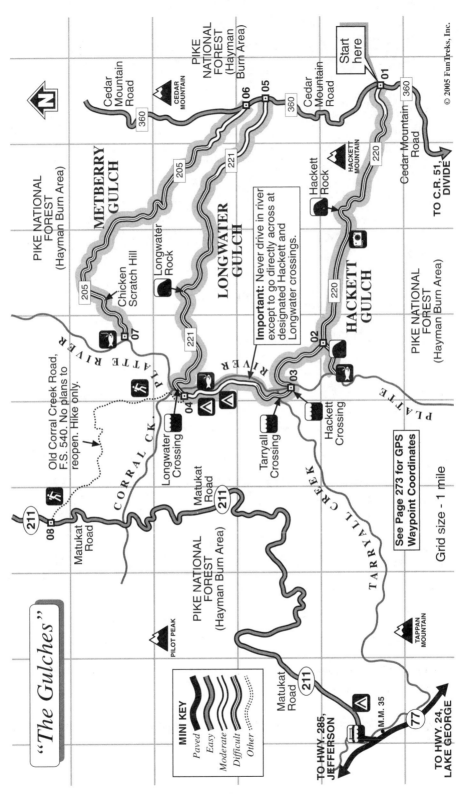

"*The Gulches*"

Start here

PIKE NATIONAL FOREST (Hayman Burn Area)

Cedar Mountain Road 360
CEDAR MOUNTAIN

06
05

360

Cedar Mountain Road

Hackett Rock
HACKETT MOUNTAIN

220

Cedar Mountain Road 360

TO C.R. 51, DIVIDE

METBERRY GULCH

PIKE NATIONAL FOREST (Hayman Burn Area)

205

221

Chicken Scratch Hill

Longwater Rock

205

LONGWATER GULCH

Important: Never drive in river except to go directly across at designated Hackett and Longwater crossings.

07

221

221

PLATTE RIVER

02

220

HACKETT GULCH

PIKE NATIONAL FOREST (Hayman Burn Area)

PLATTE

Old Corral Creek Road, F.S. 540. No plans to reopen. Hike only.

CORRAL CK.

04

Longwater Crossing

03

Tarryall Crossing

Hackett Crossing

TARRYALL CREEK

211

08

Matukat Road

211

Matukat Road

PIKE NATIONAL FOREST (Hayman Burn Area)

PILOT PEAK

See Page 273 for GPS Waypoint Coordinates

Grid size - 1 mile

TAPPAN MOUNTAIN

MINI KEY
Paved
Easy
Moderate
Difficult
Other

Matukat Road
211

M.M. 35

77

TO HWY. 285, JEFFERSON

TO HWY. 24, LAKE GEORGE

AREA 7

Sangre De Cristo
Mountains,
Great Sand Dunes
National Park

72. Hayden Pass
73. Hermit Pass
74. Medano Pass
75. Blanca Peak

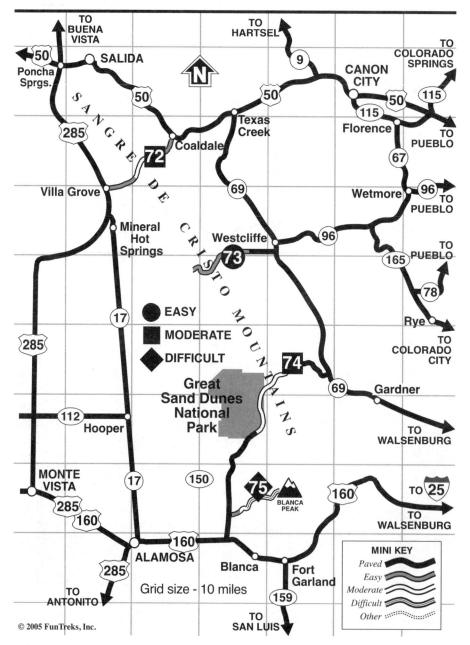

TO
BUENA
VISTA

TO
HARTSEL

TO
COLORADO
SPRINGS

50

Poncha
Sprgs.

SALIDA

9

CANON
CITY

TO

50

50

115

115

285

Texas
Creek

Florence

TO
PUEBLO

72

Coaldale

67

Villa Grove

69

Wetmore

96

TO
PUEBLO

Mineral
Hot
Springs

Westcliffe

96

TO
PUEBLO

73

165

78

17

EASY

Rye

285

MODERATE

TO
COLORADO
CITY

DIFFICULT

74

Great
Sand Dunes
National
Park

69

Gardner

112

Hooper

TO
WALSENBURG

MONTE
VISTA

17

150

75

160

TO 25

285

BLANCA
PEAK

TO
WALSENBURG

160

160

ALAMOSA

Blanca

Fort
Garland

MINI KEY

285

Paved

TO
ANTONITO

Grid size - 10 miles

159

Easy
Moderate
Difficult
Other

TO
SAN LUIS

© 2005 FunTreks, Inc.

252

Sangre De Cristo Mtns., Great Sand Dunes N. Park

The majestic Sangre De Cristo Mountains form an 80-mile long barrier between the front range and the San Luis Valley. There are no major roads that cross this barrier and very few 4-wheel-drive roads. To further complicate the situation, much of the mountain range is wilderness closed to motorized vehicles. Two of the trails, Hayden Pass and Medano Pass, completely cross the mountains, leaving you with a choice of a long paved drive or returning the way you came. The other two trails, Hermit Pass and Blanca Peak, dead end, so you must return over the same route. If you are coming from the front range, you should plan for a long day. Many people drive these trails over a weekend and camp overnight.

For the hard-core 4-wheeler, a popular weekend trip combines two trails. If you leave early, you can cross Medano Pass in the morning and ascend Blanca Peak in the afternoon. That leaves the next day to get down Blanca Peak and return home. Remember, Medano Pass comes through the Great Sand Dunes National Park. A fee will be charged to pass through. Save your receipt if you plan to return via Medano Pass.

Blanca Peak, Trail #75, difficult. Early morning at Lake Como.

253

Tight brush and rocky in places.

Narrow ledge is dangerous if icy.

ATVs approach pass from south side.

Convenient rest stop at Villa Grove.

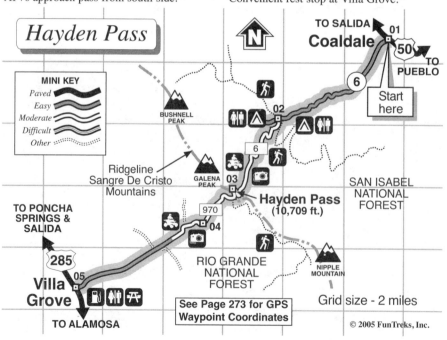

Hayden Pass

N

TO SALIDA
01
Coaldale
50
TO PUEBLO

6

MINI KEY
Paved
Easy
Moderate
Difficult
Other

BUSHNELL PEAK

02

6

Start here

Ridgeline Sangre De Cristo Mountains

GALENA PEAK

03

Hayden Pass (10,709 ft.)

SAN ISABEL NATIONAL FOREST

TO PONCHA SPRINGS & SALIDA

970

04

285

Villa Grove
05

RIO GRANDE NATIONAL FOREST

NIPPLE MOUNTAIN

TO ALAMOSA

See Page 273 for GPS Waypoint Coordinates

Grid size - 2 miles

© 2005 FunTreks, Inc.

254

Location: West of Pueblo and Canon City between Coaldale and Villa Grove. Southeast of Salida.

Difficulty: Moderate. Rating applies to upper portion of trail, only. Lower portions are easy. Travel only when dry and in the summer. During the spring and fall underground springs flow across the road, creating dangerous patches of ice on the narrowest part of the trail.

Features: A gorgeous drive with just enough challenge to make it fun. Two Forest Service campgrounds with hiking trails on the north side. ATVs okay.

Time & Distance: About 16.5 miles from Coaldale to Villa Grove. Allow about two hours driving time one way.

To Get There: Take Route 50 west from Pueblo or south from Salida. Turn south at Coaldale 0.7 miles west of mile marker 242.

Trail Description: Reset odometer as you turn off Route 50 (01). An easy road takes you to the Coaldale Campground at 3.7 miles, followed by the Hayden Campground at 5.0 miles (02). The four-wheel drive part of the trail goes up the hill to the left of the Hayden Campground. The trail is marked as F.S. 6. The trail is rocky and steep in spots so shift into low range at the start. Careful tire placement may be necessary in a few places. As you climb, beautiful vistas appear to the north. At 8.7 miles the road becomes a narrow ledge. Underground springs keep this part of the trail wet, and in the fall and spring it may be icy. This section is very dangerous if icy so turn around if any ice is present. *(Note: In late November of 1995, a Jeep slid off this portion of the trail and the driver was killed.)* You reach the top of the pass at 9.3 miles (03) and the trail number changes to 970. The descent down the other side is easier with only an occasional stretch of loose shale. You come out of the trees at a wide spot at 11.3 miles (04), where the road swings to the right then drops to the valley below. Follow the main road to Villa Grove on Hwy. 285 at 16.5 miles (05).

Return Trip: Return the way you came or go right to Hwy. 50 at Salida.

Services: Gas and rest stop with picnic tables and toilet at Villa Grove. Full services in Canon City and Salida.

Maps: San Isabel and Rio Grande Nat. Forests. DeLorme Atlas & Gazetteer.

Cross scenic ranch land on way to trailhead.

Road is rocky but fairly wide most of the way.

Hike short distance to see this waterfall.

F.S. Road 160 climbs past Horseshoe Lake above timberline to near 13,000 feet.

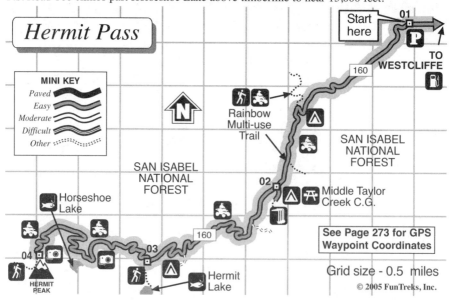

Hermit Pass

Start here

01

P

TO WESTCLIFFE

160

MINI KEY
Paved
Easy
Moderate
Difficult
Other

N

Rainbow Multi-use Trail

SAN ISABEL NATIONAL FOREST

SAN ISABEL NATIONAL FOREST

Horseshoe Lake

02

Middle Taylor Creek C.G.

160

03

See Page 273 for GPS Waypoint Coordinates

04

HERMIT PEAK

Hermit Lake

Grid size - 0.5 miles

© 2005 FunTreks, Inc.

Hermit Pass 73

Location: Southwest of Westcliffe.

Difficulty: Easy. Rocky and rough but no major obstacles. Road is fairly wide all the way. Suitable for any high-clearance, 4-wheel-drive SUV.

Features: In-and-out trail climbs to remote Hermit Pass near 13,000 feet. Great hiking, camping and fishing along the route. Popular ATV area with access to Rainbow Multi-use Trail. Take short hike to interesting waterfall from Middle Taylor Creek Campground. Make sure to see rustic downtown Westcliffe. Many people miss the main part of town because it is located west of Hwy. 69.

Time & Distance: Allow about 2 hours for the one-way, 9-mile trip.

To Get There: From the intersection of Hwys. 69 and 96 in Westcliffe, head south on 69 just 0.3 miles. Across from gas station, turn right on paved road following signs to Hermit Lake. Continue straight at 3.1 miles when paved road goes left. Go another 3.3 miles on dirt road to start of F.S. 160 on left. You can park here, along roadside, to unload ATVs and dirt bikes.

Trail Description: Reset odometer at start (01). Rocky road winds uphill with views of the old Conquistador Ski Area before entering San Isabel National Forest. Stay right past camp spots before passing Rainbow Multi-use Trail at 2.0 miles. Enter state wildlife area at 2.7 miles. Note special regulations. At 3.0 miles (02), stay right past picnic/camping area. (Later, you might want to visit the dramatic waterfall that is a short hike from south end of campground.) Stay right at 3.5 and 5.1 miles. The road curves sharply to the right at 5.8 miles (03) where Hermit Lake Hiking Trail goes left. Climb above timberline past Horseshoe Lake at 7.3 miles. The road ends at 9.0 miles (04).

Return Trip: Return the way you came.

Services: Dispersed camping along trail. Picnic tables at Middle Taylor Creek Campground. Most services in Westcliffe.

Historical Highlights: Hermit Pass Road was built to reach a uranium mine part way down the west side of the pass. The road never went all the way down the other side. Hike beyond road into Sangre De Cristo Wilderness.

Maps: San Isabel National Forest. DeLorme Atlas & Gazetteer.

Rocky in places on east side of Medano Pass.

Many water crossings. Can be deep.

Sandy part of trail in park is very soft.

POINT OF NO RETURN
4-WHEEL DRIVE ONLY
SOFT SAND AHEAD
TIRE PRESSURE 15 LBS. ADVISED
AIR NEAR CAMPGROUND ENTRANCE
CAMPING BY PERMIT ONLY
MINIMUM WRECKER FEE $100.00

Note towing fee if you get stuck.

Fun spot for kids in park at Waypoint 04.

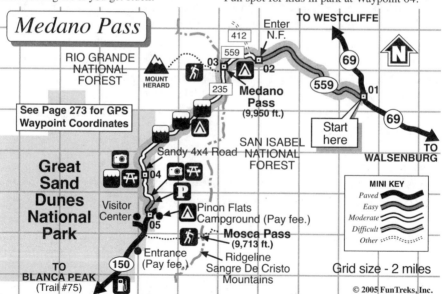

Medano Pass

TO WESTCLIFFE

Enter N.F.

412
559

RIO GRANDE NATIONAL FOREST

MOUNT HERARD

03
02
235

Medano Pass (9,950 ft.)

69
559
01

See Page 273 for GPS Waypoint Coordinates

Start here

69

TO WALSENBURG

Great Sand Dunes National Park

Sandy 4x4 Road

SAN ISABEL NATIONAL FOREST

04

Visitor Center

05

P

Pinon Flats Campground (Pay fee.)

Mosca Pass (9,713 ft.)

Ridgeline Sangre De Cristo Mountains

150

Entrance (Pay fee.)

TO BLANCA PEAK (Trail #75)

MINI KEY
Paved
Easy
Moderate
Difficult
Other

Grid size - 2 miles

© 2005 FunTreks, Inc.

258

Medano Pass 74

Location: South of Westcliffe between Hwy. 69 and Great Sand Dunes N.P.

Difficulty: Moderate. Mostly easy with a few steep, rocky spots. Soft sand in park. Numerous water crossings can be deep in the spring.

Features: Back way to Great Sand Dunes National Park. Camp in numbered designated sites only along route inside park or at Pinon Flats C.G. Picnic next to stream at base of giant sand dunes. Fall color. Fee required entering or leaving park at main gate on south side. Unlicensed vehicles are allowed on marked roads in national forest but not inside national park.

Time & Distance: 20.4 miles. Allow 1-1/2 hours driving time.

To Get There: At a point 23.7 miles south of Westcliffe on Hwy. 69, turn west on well-marked County Road 559. **To find trail from south side**, take Hwy. 160 from I-25 at Walsenburg. Go west past town of Blanca and turn right on Hwy. 150. Go north 19 miles to main gate at national park.

Trail Description: Reset odometer at start (01). Head west on C.R. 559. Dirt road is muddy at times. Bear left at 0.9 miles where private road goes right. Enter San Isabel National Forest at 6.9 miles (02). Stay left at 7.4 miles where F.S. 412 goes right. Rocky road climbs to gate at Medano Pass at 9.3 miles (03). (Call park in advance to make sure gate is open. See appendix.) Road drops down other side of pass. Stay left at 9.9 at Medano Lake Trailhead. First of many creek crossings at 10.8. Picnic area next to stream and dunes at 18.0 miles (04). Soft sand follows. Air down tires and keep moving. Parking on left at 19.3 miles. Bear right at pavement at 20.4 miles (05). Follow paved road south past visitor center to main gate at 22.0 miles.

Reverse Directions: From main gate on south side of park, follow paved road north 1.6 miles. *Reset odometer and turn left on dirt road at campground* (05). Continue past parking area onto sandy 4WD road. Pass picnic area at 2.4 miles (04). Climb to Medano Pass at 11.1 miles (03). Stay right at 13.0 miles where 412 goes left. Leave forest at 13.5 miles (02). Continue east to Hwy. 69 at 20.4 miles (01). Turn left for Westcliffe, right for I-25.

Services: Gas and restaurant 2.8 miles south of main park entrance on Hwy. 150. Campground, picnic areas and visitor center in park. No toilets on trail.

Maps: San Isabel National Forest. Park Map. DeLorme Atlas & Gazetteer.

Correct line going up dangerous Jaws 2.

Talus ledge between Jaws 3 and Lake Como.

Camping on south side of Lake Como.

Tires are usually wet going up steep Jaws 4.

Near end of trail above 12,000 ft.

Bighorn sheep seen near Blue Lakes.

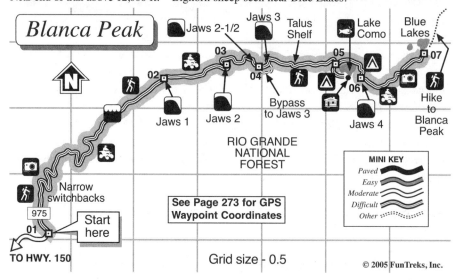

Blanca Peak

Jaws 2-1/2

Jaws 3

Talus Shelf

Lake Como

Blue Lakes

N

03

02

05

07

04

Bypass to Jaws 3

06

Jaws 1

Jaws 2

Jaws 4

Hike to Blanca Peak

Narrow switchbacks

975

RIO GRANDE NATIONAL FOREST

See Page 273 for GPS Waypoint Coordinates

MINI KEY
Paved
Easy
Moderate
Difficult
Other

01

Start here

TO HWY. 150

Grid size - 0.5

© 2005 FunTreks, Inc.

Blanca Peak

Location: West of Walsenburg, northeast of Alamosa, north of Blanca.

Difficulty: Difficult. One of the most popular hard-core trails in Colorado with many difficult rock obstacles. Be very careful on dangerous Jaws 2, where several vehicles have rolled over the edge. Trail is very narrow and passing is tricky. Recommend 33-inch tires, at least one locker and a winch.

Features: Memorable climb to beautiful Lake Como where you can camp and fish. Please be extra courteous to hikers. Pack out trash. Very difficult and dangerous for ATVs. Trail subject to closure, if abused.

Time & Distance: Difficult portion, shown here, is just 4.3 miles to Lake Como. Trail ends another mile past lake. Add 3.5 miles of rough road from Hwy. 150 to start. Allow 4 to 6 hours one way. Much of time is spent waiting for other vehicles to get over obstacles, so start early.

To Get There: Take Interstate 25 to Walsenburg and Hwy. 160 west. Just after small town of Blanca, turn north on Hwy. 150 and go 3.2 miles to Road 975 on right. Head west on flat road past several open areas to camp, park, and unload. Road goes from sand to jarring rocks as you begin to climb. Tight switchback and sign at 3.5 miles marks start of trail (01). Alternate way to reach trail is via Medano Pass, Trail #74.

Trail Description: Reset odometer at start (01). Road climbs steeply up series of tight switchbacks. Engine overheating is common through this stretch. Dip in road at 1.8 can be deep with standing water. Cross Jaws 1 at 2.3 miles (02). When you reach Jaws 2 at 3.0 miles (03), stay far right. Use winch quickly if you start sliding left. Large rocks at 3.4 unofficially called Jaws 2-1/2. Stay right at 3.5 miles (04) to bypass axle-hungry Jaws 3. Cross narrow talus ledge before arriving at fork by Lake Como at 4.3 miles (05). Right dead ends at log cabin and camp spots after mud bog. Left goes around lake to more camping where trail continues uphill over extremely difficult Jaws 4 at 4.6 miles (06). Most people stop at Lake Como or hike. Trail ends above timberline at Blue Lakes at 5.3 miles (07). If lucky, you might see bighorn sheep. Return the way you came.

Services: Gas and food in Blanca, Fort Garland, Walsenburg and on Hwy. 150, 2.8 miles south of entrance to Great Sand Dunes National Park.

Maps: Rio Grande National Forest. DeLorme Atlas & Gazetteer.

You'll pass Animas Forks Ghost Town on Trails #12, #13, #14.

These ATVers came all the way from Texas to ride up Mt. Antero. Note fresh snow on July 29.

The "Waterfall" on Chinaman Gulch, Trail #28, difficult.

APPENDIX

Lead King Basin, Trail #18, difficult.

GPS Basics

Frequently asked Questions:

What is GPS? GPS stands for Global Positioning System. Satellites circle the earth and broadcast signals to receiving units below. These signals allow you to determine your position on the earth. Five to 12 satellites can be picked up at any one time. A GPS unit with 12-satellite capability has the best chance of determining your position quickly.

Is GPS necessary to use this book? No. Some people prefer to rely on instinct, orienteering and map-reading skills. In many areas, roads are well defined and easy to follow. You may travel with people who are familiar with the trail or you may prefer hiring a guide. Most of the trails in this book can be driven without the use of GPS.

Then why should I buy a GPS unit? It's the fastest, easiest and surest way to determine your location. Like any new device, you'll wonder how you got along without it.

What kind of GPS unit do I need? There are many brands and models in all price ranges. It depends on your needs. Don't get one with less than 12 parallel satellite channels. It's handy to be able to download and upload data to a computer, but this is not required. Some GPS units allow you to upload maps into the unit. The amount of space available for the maps is usually a function of price.

How complicated is it to use a GPS unit? My GPS unit came with a small 100-page user's manual. It took a little time to read but it was simple and easy to understand. After a little practice, using the unit becomes second nature. Basic units are much simpler.

What are waypoints and trackpoints? Waypoints are important locations you choose to mark along your route, like where you start, key intersections along the way, and your final destination. Waypoints are recorded when you consciously hit a button. Trackpoints are automatically recorded as you move along. They're often referred to as a breadcrumb trail.

How accurate is GPS? It's gotten much better since the government reduced the *Selective Availability* error in May of 2000. Prior to that, they scrambled the signal, allowing a worst-case error of about 300-ft. The error was reduced to a worst-case scenario of about 60 ft. In practice, I've found the error to be much less. There's been talk of rescrambling the signals since the 9-11 disaster, but so far that hasn't happened.

264

Do I need a computer to use a GPS unit? No, but if you have a computer, you'll be able to do a lot more. You can download waypoints and trackpoints to your home computer onto digital maps and see exactly where you went. You can print maps showing your exact route. You can save a large number of routes to upload to your GPS unit anytime you want. You can exchange routes and maps with friends. You can store many detailed maps in the computer at a very low cost per map. You can see a much bigger picture of a map than what you see on your tiny GPS screen. You can use maps with more detail. If you use a laptop, you can take it with you and follow your progress on the screen. You can upload waypoints into your GPS unit and avoid the tedious task of entering them by hand. Most GPS units don't have a keypad, so entering numerical data takes a long time without a computer. Garmin has a patented system that allows you to upload both waypoints and trackpoints back into the GPS unit exactly as the original information was collected.

Is a laptop handy to use in the field? No. It's hard to find a good place to set it up. The screen is hard to see in the sun. It's exposed to damage from dust and vibration. I keep mine in its case much of the time and pull it out when I need it. Despite these drawbacks, it has been indispensable at times and saved me many hours of wandering around aimlessly. I'm less likely to get lost when I have it with me.

I already have paper maps. Will a GPS unit help me? Yes. You can plot your GPS location on any map that has tick marks along the edge for latitude/longitude coordinates. You can get a general idea where you are by sighting across the map. To determine a more exact position, you'll need to draw lines. Large fold-out maps can be awkward in the car. I like the handy booklet-style format of an atlas like *DeLorme's Colorado Atlas & Gazetteer*.

What maps do I need? Again it depends on your needs. The greatest amount of detail is shown on USGS 7.5 minute maps, but many maps are needed to cover a large area. Forest Service maps are practical when you're on forest land but don't help in other areas. The BLM also has maps but they vary in quality. Your best buy is an atlas-style map that covers an entire state. If you're using a computer, several companies now offer statewide map packages with the same detail as 7.5 minute maps. A state the size of Colorado requires 6 or 7 CDs for these rasterized maps. The packages also include the software to manipulate the data. Vector quality maps have less detail but cover more area.

What's the difference between rasterized and vector maps? A rasterized image looks like a photograph of the original map. It takes a lot of computer space. When you zoom out you lose detail. Up close, however, it has the best detail. A vector map is a line conversion and looks more like a drawing in flat color. It lacks detail, but looks the same as you zoom in and out. It doesn't require as much computer space and maps can be uploaded directly into some GPS units.

What's mapping software do? Among other things, it allows you to manipulate maps on the screen, download and upload your waypoints and trackpoints, save map images and print them out. For non-seamless maps, it finds the next map as you run off the page and switches automatically when you're moving with your GPS on.

What specific equipment do you use, Mr. Wells? (Please note: I am not paid to recommend any specific brand. This just happens to be what I use.) I recently upgraded to a Garmin GPS V unit. It stores 3,000 track-points which is enough for a long day of driving. It also allows me to upload maps. The black and white screen is small but batteries last a long time. If I need a big color screen, I hook the GPS unit up to my computer. The unit is very durable and waterproof. I bought two additional accessories—a dash mount and a computer cord. The computer cord is split with one part that goes to my cigarette lighter which powers the GPS unit. I've never needed an outside antenna but many people find them helpful.

I have a Dell Inspiron 600m laptop with a 14″ screen, 40-gig HD, 512 MB ram and 1400 MHz. I upgraded to this computer so I could permanently install all my mapping software. I no longer have to insert individual CDs and DVDs.

I've been using this equipment for about a year, so it is probably already out of date; however, for my needs it works perfectly. Make sure you compare brands and check out the latest equipment before you buy.

What mapping software do you use? I use several different software packages, but most people can get along with just one. Each has advantages and disadvantages.

For backcountry detail, I'm using *National Geographic TOPO, version 2.7.7*. The state of Colorado has 7 CDs, all of which I installed into my computer. The 7.5-minute maps are seamless and I can scroll from border to border without interruption. The maps are very detailed with shaded relief.

For street detail, the Garmin GPS V unit came preinstalled with a simplified nationwide street program. In addition, the package included Garmin's MapSource software, *North American City Select v5*. You install this software in your computer and it functions compatibly with the GPS unit. Again the entire U.S. is included, but there is much more detail. A great feature of MapSource software is that waypoints and trackpoints can be uploaded back into the Garmin unit exactly as they were first collected.

I've also been using DeLorme's Topo USA, Version 5.0. Vector maps have excellent street and backcountry detail. Although the detail is not as good as a 7.5-minute map, it is an excellent compromise. The maps have shaded relief and the entire U.S. comes on one handy DVD.

I also use a professional map package called *All Topo Maps by iGage*. The maps are exact 7.5-minute USGS maps that can be printed to exact sizes specified in tenth of 1% increments. This map package has an astounding search engine that allows me to find just about anything printed on a map. Because so much information is available, the Colorado package requires 12 CDs.

How much did you spend on your GPS equipment? I spent about $400 on my Garmin GPS V unit plus a little more for the accessories. My Dell laptop was about $2,000. Mapping software runs from $50 to $150. I also carry many folding maps that would be expensive to replace.

I don't want to spend that much but would still like to have a GPS unit. What can I do? The most important thing a GPS unit does is provide coordinates of your location. A simple unit will do that. You can buy a quality GPS unit with basic features for about $100. Once you know your coordinates, you can determine your location on a map. The cheapest way to buy maps is in atlas form. *DeLorme's Colorado Atlas & Gazetteer* covers the entire state for about $20.

If you have a home PC, I'd definitely spend a little more for a GPS unit that can download and upload data to your computer. The first time you try to key waypoints into your GPS unit, you'll know why a computer is important.

How can I learn more about GPS?

A great deal of free information is available online. I like Garmin's Web site (www.garmin.com). They have an excellent 24-page *GPS Guide for Beginners* (www.garmin.com/aboutGPS/manual.html) that you can download as a PDF file. Also, check out www.GPSNOW.com, which sells GPS equipment and mapping products. They show and compare most GPS products and have the latest information on new products. You can also contact the manufacturers directly. (See addresses and phone number section that follows.)

If you don't have access to the Web, go to your local bookstore or library. I bought a copy of *GPS Made Easy* by Lawrence Letham (see references and reading section). It explains GPS in easy-to-understand terms.

GPS Coordinates

The following table lists waypoints for each trail. Waypoints are shown in latitude/longitude displayed in format of degrees/minutes.thousandths of minutes. (Note: This format is a change from my previous books which were in degrees/minutes/seconds.) No coordinate should be in error more than 20 meters or approximately 60 feet. All coordinates were compiled using National Geographic TOPO software, Datum WGS84.

Wpt.	Latitude North		Longitude West	
1. Last Dollar Road				
01	38	05.994	107	54.748
02	38	03.041	107	57.436
03	37	59.008	107	56.997
04	37	58.414	107	54.380
05	37	57.188	107	53.684
06	37	57.057	107	52.115
2. Yankee Boy Basin				
01	38	01.057	107	40.481
02	37	58.523	107	44.707
03	37	58.756	107	45.533
04	37	59.344	107	46.630
05	37	59.696	107	47.080
3. Governor Basin				
01	37	58.756	107	45.533
02	37	58.490	107	45.927
03	37	58.268	107	46.338
04	37	58.207	107	46.618
4. Imogene Pass				
01	37	56.406	107	48.665
02	37	55.890	107	44.100
03	37	57.226	107	43.503
04	37	57.974	107	43.740
05	37	58.516	107	44.720
5. Black Bear Pass				
01	37	53.808	107	42.802
02	37	53.927	107	44.379
03	37	53.970	107	44.597
04	37	55.324	107	45.569
05	37	55.849	107	46.701

Wpt.	Latitude North		Longitude West	
6. Ophir Pass, Alta Lakes				
01	37	50.856	107	43.494
02	37	51.050	107	46.767
03	37	51.719	107	52.194
04	37	53.038	107	53.311
05	37	53.077	107	50.801
7. Clear Lake				
01	37	49.091	107	42.148
02	37	48.330	107	45.776
03	37	49.570	107	46.923
8. Mineral Creek				
01	37	59.321	107	38.961
02	37	58.022	107	37.637
03	37	57.716	107	35.736
04	37	57.443	107	34.528
9. Poughkeepsie Gulch				
01	37	58.031	107	37.629
02	37	56.003	107	37.322
03	37	55.917	107	37.552
04	37	55.223	107	37.193
10. Corkscrew Gulch				
01	37	54.624	107	38.728
02	37	54.394	107	39.653
03	37	55.380	107	40.519
04	37	56.338	107	40.293
11. Red Mountain Mining Area				
01	37	55.312	107	41.915
02	37	54.236	107	42.192
03	37	53.834	107	42.777
04	37	53.744	107	42.742
05	37	53.453	107	42.442
06	37	51.727	107	42.961
07	37	51.492	107	43.442

Wpt.	Latitude North		Longitude West	

12. California Gulch

01	37	55.619	107	33.825
02	37	55.908	107	35.406
03	37	55.058	107	37.050

13. Engineer Pass

01	37	57.443	107	34.528
02	37	58.453	107	35.123
03	38	00.451	107	27.992
04	38	01.231	107	24.034
05	38	01.641	107	19.007

14. Cinnamon Pass, Wager Gulch

01	38	00.022	107	17.938
02	37	56.949	107	18.126
03	37	54.351	107	21.649
04	37	52.129	107	21.739
05	37	54.227	107	24.719
06	37	55.881	107	30.873
07	37	56.035	107	34.114

15. Picayne & Placer Gulches

01	37	54.988	107	33.481
02	37	54.715	107	34.455
03	37	54.408	107	36.231
04	37	55.897	107	35.394

16. Eureka Gulch

01	37	53.121	107	33.854
02	37	52.977	107	34.855
03	37	54.049	107	36.872

17. Stony Pass

01	37	50.136	107	35.704
02	37	48.921	107	34.699
03	37	49.009	107	34.174
04	37	47.752	107	32.967
05	37	45.734	107	28.016
06	37	43.233	107	30.397
07	37	42.717	107	31.511
08	37	48.570	107	33.308

18. Lead King Basin

01	39	04.486	107	09.545
02	39	04.680	107	07.495
03	39	04.403	107	05.286
04	39	03.555	107	05.780

Wpt.	Latitude North		Longitude West	

19. Devil's Punchbowl

01	39	04.357	107	10.901
02	39	04.486	107	09.545
03	39	03.555	107	05.780
04	39	02.994	107	04.663
05	39	00.958	107	02.844

20. Paradise Divide

01	38	52.808	106	58.584
02	38	58.462	107	03.462
03	38	59.306	107	03.854
04	39	00.965	107	02.841
05	38	59.347	107	00.661
06	38	57.479	106	59.344

21. Aspen Mtn., Richmond Hill

01	39	11.112	106	49.057
02	39	09.068	106	49.122
03	39	01.217	106	45.358
04	39	03.614	106	48.052
05	39	09.632	106	50.888
06	39	08.166	106	49.643

22. Lincoln Creek Road

01	39	07.253	106	41.153
02	39	05.690	106	39.600
03	39	04.780	106	36.823
04	39	01.071	106	36.481
05	39	01.120	106	36.142

23. Montezuma Basin

01	39	01.755	106	48.466
02	39	00.322	106	50.287
03	39	01.154	106	51.293

24. Pearl Pass

01	38	51.078	106	57.118
02	38	53.766	106	53.356
03	38	54.950	106	51.031
04	38	56.293	106	51.387
05	38	58.767	106	49.433
06	39	00.328	106	50.282
07	39	01.750	106	48.470

25. Taylor Pass

01	39	03.607	106	48.050
02	39	01.215	106	45.345
03	38	59.754	106	42.209

Wpt.	Latitude North		Longitude West	

26. Italian Creek, Reno Divide

Wpt.	Latitude North		Longitude West	
01	38	57.246	106	37.287
02	38	57.355	106	43.472
03	38	56.851	106	43.428
04	38	55.961	106	44.391
05	38	54.453	106	45.790
06	38	53.052	106	47.463
07	38	48.279	106	53.408

27. Fourmile Area

01	38	50.093	106	01.376
02	38	51.487	106	03.271
03	38	52.276	106	01.424
04	38	52.898	105	59.846
05	38	54.843	106	01.283
06	38	54.101	106	05.375
07	38	54.800	106	06.562
08	38	53.980	106	07.823
09	38	53.059	106	08.454
10	38	52.468	106	08.674
11	38	54.599	105	58.538

28. Chinaman Gulch, Carnage Canyon

01	38	47.520	106	05.167
02	38	47.735	106	05.129
03	38	47.686	106	04.494
04	38	48.207	106	04.720
05	38	47.885	106	03.980
06	38	48.053	106	03.255
07	38	48.296	106	04.687

29. Mt. Princeton

01	38	44.395	106	10.509
02	38	44.710	106	12.595
03	38	44.189	106	12.824

30. Mt. Antero, Browns Lake

01	38	42.600	106	17.498
02	38	40.949	106	16.375
03	38	39.706	106	15.477
04	38	40.600	106	14.977
05	38	38.630	106	14.738

31. Baldwin Lakes, Boulder Mtn.

01	38	42.599	106	17.534
02	38	42.220	106	16.522
03	38	40.954	106	16.407
04	38	40.142	106	17.531
05	38	39.923	106	18.712
06	38	41.234	106	17.388

32. Grizzly Lake

01	38	42.230	106	20.613
02	38	42.165	106	20.468
03	38	40.227	106	20.050

33. Iron Chest Mine

01	38	42.135	106	20.787
02	38	40.714	106	20.950
03	38	40.294	106	20.939

34. Pomeroy Lakes

01	38	40.390	106	22.004
02	38	39.942	106	21.377
03	38	39.588	106	21.130
04	38	39.311	106	20.714
05	38	38.906	106	20.381
06	38	40.100	106	21.101

35. Tincup Pass, St. Elmo

01	38	42.237	106	20.920
02	38	42.544	106	26.068
03	38	43.006	106	26.165
04	38	43.276	106	26.278
05	38	44.780	106	25.861
06	38	45.287	106	28.829

36. Hancock Pass, Alpine Tunnel

01	38	42.353	106	20.410
02	38	38.416	106	21.669
03	38	38.292	106	21.679
04	38	37.252	106	22.485
05	38	36.685	106	22.711
06	38	36.823	106	23.397
07	38	38.303	106	24.487

37. Tomichi Pass

01	38	36.685	106	22.711
02	38	36.200	106	23.005
03	38	34.227	106	22.240
04	38	34.084	106	22.457
05	38	30.109	106	25.293
06	38	29.165	106	24.611

38. Marshall Pass, Poncha Creek

01	38	26.894	106	06.414
02	38	24.934	106	08.300
03	38	23.899	106	10.404
04	38	23.496	106	14.890
05	38	22.204	106	20.612
06	38	24.432	106	24.921

Wpt.	Latitude North		Longitude West	

39. Mill Creek Road
01	39	38.328	106	22.438
02	39	37.576	106	21.282
03	39	37.365	106	19.200
04	39	36.273	106	18.123
05	39	36.088	106	18.122

40. Shrine Pass
01	39	31.774	106	13.082
02	39	32.770	106	14.477
03	39	33.606	106	15.352
04	39	32.430	106	18.301
05	39	31.422	106	19.534
06	39	31.390	106	20.187
07	39	30.804	106	22.085

41. Lime Creek, Benson Cabin
01	39	31.390	106	20.187
02	39	33.829	106	18.430
03	39	33.639	106	15.507
04	39	32.430	106	18.301
05	39	31.833	106	17.931

42. McCallister Gulch
01	39	27.272	106	19.986
02	39	26.880	106	19.147
03	39	27.744	106	19.797
04	39	29.256	106	17.861
05	39	31.217	106	18.896
06	39	31.405	106	19.541

43. Wearyman Creek
01	39	31.405	106	19.541
02	39	31.217	106	18.896
03	39	29.590	106	15.202
04	39	26.882	106	19.147
05	39	27.272	106	19.986

44. Holy Cross
01	39	24.195	106	26.626
02	39	24.593	106	27.315
03	39	25.241	106	28.497
04	39	24.877	106	28.740
05	39	24.895	106	28.800
06	39	25.056	106	29.029
07	39	23.433	106	28.229
08	39	23.896	106	26.641

45. Hagerman Pass
01	39	16.113	106	25.044
02	39	14.886	106	28.212
03	39	15.790	106	28.874
04	39	17.530	106	31.668

46. Wheeler Lake
01	39	21.441	106	04.868
02	39	21.874	106	07.588
03	39	22.104	106	07.687

47. Mt. Bross, Kite Lake
01	39	17.030	106	03.762
02	39	17.803	106	06.483
03	39	19.103	106	05.104
04	39	19.282	106	04.859
05	39	19.661	106	07.750

48. Mosquito Pass
01	39	15.575	106	13.110
02	39	16.151	106	11.791
03	39	16.863	106	11.161
04	39	17.979	106	09.210
05	39	17.576	106	08.920
06	39	16.706	106	07.332
07	39	16.716	106	05.226

49. Weston Pass
01	39	09.215	105	59.963
02	39	05.888	106	05.322
03	39	07.885	106	10.931
04	39	10.594	106	19.323

50. Spring Creek
01	39	45.780	105	38.009
02	39	45.753	105	37.786
03	39	45.426	105	37.880
04	39	44.350	105	38.468
05	39	43.922	105	38.726
06	39	43.664	105	39.410

51. Saxon Mountain
01	39	43.167	105	41.490
02	39	43.791	105	40.365
03	39	43.664	105	39.410
04	39	43.358	105	40.318

Wpt.	Latitude North		Longitude West	

52. Argentine Pass, McClellan Mountain

Wpt.	Latitude North		Longitude West	
01	39	40.991	105	42.170
02	39	39.988	105	44.377
03	39	38.270	105	45.900
04	39	37.528	105	46.933
05	39	38.826	105	45.722
06	39	39.062	105	46.649
07	39	38.593	105	46.297

53. Peru Creek

01	39	35.530	105	52.259
02	39	36.026	105	50.291
03	39	36.160	105	48.795
04	39	36.558	105	47.955
05	39	37.589	105	47.943
06	39	35.855	105	48.815

54. Santa Fe Peak

01	39	34.918	105	52.113
02	39	34.667	105	50.365
03	39	34.084	105	50.111

55. Deer Creek, Saints John

01	39	34.801	105	52.052
02	39	34.078	105	51.619
03	39	31.597	105	51.922
04	39	31.255	105	52.136
05	39	31.381	105	52.911
06	39	32.858	105	53.119
07	39	33.413	105	52.932
08	39	34.275	105	52.886

56. North/Middle Fork of Swan River

01	39	30.787	105	56.823
02	39	30.982	105	56.254
03	39	31.622	105	54.818
04	39	30.798	105	54.168
05	39	31.376	105	52.925
06	39	31.251	105	52.142
07	39	30.806	105	51.748
08	39	30.166	105	54.072
09	39	30.383	105	56.789

57. Radical Hill

01	39	34.821	105	52.057
02	39	34.083	105	51.619
03	39	32.294	105	50.504
04	39	32.170	105	51.384
05	39	31.667	105	51.801

58. Webster Pass, Handcart Gulch

01	39	34.821	105	52.057
02	39	34.083	105	51.619
03	39	32.294	105	50.504
04	39	31.881	105	49.966
05	39	29.040	105	48.298

59. Red Cone

01	39	27.407	105	43.294
02	39	29.040	105	48.298
03	39	31.613	105	49.326
04	39	31.881	105	49.966

60. Georgia Pass

01	39	22.642	105	48.012
02	39	23.727	105	50.578
03	39	27.488	105	55.003
04	39	29.949	105	56.930
05	39	30.383	105	56.794
06	39	31.942	106	02.605

61. Boreas Pass

01	39	28.466	106	02.519
02	39	24.618	105	58.103
03	39	22.082	105	56.380
04	39	20.781	105	55.851
05	39	18.639	105	53.184

62. Slaughterhouse Gulch

01	39	29.862	105	31.737
02	39	29.741	105	31.937
03	39	28.635	105	32.822
04	39	27.573	105	33.528
05	39	28.302	105	32.060

63. Dakan Road, Long Hollow Rd.

01	39	18.248	104	58.122
02	39	18.545	105	01.872
03	39	15.757	105	03.473
04	39	13.191	105	03.712
05	39	13.159	105	03.878
06	39	10.850	105	04.683
07	39	09.196	105	05.138
08	39	08.040	105	06.579

64. Phantom Creek, Signal Butte

01	39	01.274	105	15.177
02	39	01.576	105	14.719
03	39	04.001	105	10.932
04	39	04.386	105	11.960

Wpt.	Latitude North	Longitude West

65. Balanced Rock Road

01	39 04.009	105 01.312
02	39 04.483	104 59.506
03	39 04.971	104 57.503
04	39 06.424	104 56.475
05	39 04.711	104 57.378

66. Mt. Herman, Rampart Range

01	39 05.306	104 54.666
02	39 03.357	105 01.098
03	39 00.274	105 00.937
04	38 57.689	104 59.731
05	38 51.952	104 53.787

67. Schubarth Road

01	39 00.262	105 00.939
02	39 00.099	104 58.841
03	39 00.429	104 57.358
04	39 00.474	104 56.330
05	39 00.388	104 55.597
06	39 02.531	104 55.514

68. Eagle Rock

01	38 44.123	104 59.289
02	38 45.251	104 58.471
03	38 45.667	104 58.987
04	38 46.225	105 01.107

69. Mt. Baldy

01	38 44.439	104 57.375
02	38 45.664	104 58.981
03	38 46.607	104 59.110

70. Shelf Road, Phantom Canyon

01	38 44.563	105 10.582
02	38 36.882	105 13.498
03	38 34.748	105 14.127
04	38 29.510	105 12.544
05	38 26.905	105 12.413
06	38 26.239	105 06.837
07	38 42.630	105 07.990

71. Independence Trail

01	38 29.625	105 01.904
02	38 29.680	105 02.008
03	38 30.160	105 02.034

Wpt.	Latitude North	Longitude West

Bonus Trails "The Gulches"

01	39 04.705	105 16.321
02	39 05.302	105 19.647
03	39 05.649	105 20.312
04	39 06.793	105 20.409
05	39 05.884	105 16.510
06	39 06.145	105 16.625
07	39 07.396	105 19.602
08	39 08.189	105 22.072

72. Hayden Pass

01	38 22.067	105 45.132
02	38 19.786	105 49.399
03	38 17.580	105 50.991
04	38 16.748	105 52.148
05	38 14.949	105 56.954

73. Hermit Pass

01	38 07.993	105 34.498
02	38 06.327	105 36.235
03	38 05.598	105 37.905
04	38 05.667	105 39.293

74. Medano Pass

01	37 50.191	105 18.457
02	37 51.646	105 24.141
03	37 51.356	105 25.935
04	37 46.299	105 30.433
05	37 44.658	105 30.431

75. Blanca Peak

01	37 33.088	105 33.398
02	37 34.104	105 32.393
03	37 34.195	105 31.873
04	37 34.179	105 31.560
05	37 34.197	105 30.943
06	37 34.106	105 30.723
07	37 34.271	105 30.178

Glossary

Airing down - Letting air out of your tires to improve traction.

ARB lockers - A brand of differential locker that can be quickly activated when needed but turned off when not in use. (See differential locker.)

Articulation - Suspension system flexibility. Greater articulation means wheels travel up and down farther to better accommodate ground undulation.

Clevis - A U-shaped device with a pin at one end that is used to connect tow straps.

Come-along - A hand-operated ratchet that functions as a crude winch.

Corduroy road - Roadbed formed with split logs lying flat-side up.

Differential locker - Gearing installed inside your differential that equalizes power to wheels on both sides of an axle. Eliminates loss of power when climbing steep undulating hills. Not the same as locking-in your hubs.

High centered - When your undercarriage gets stuck on a rock, mound, log, or ridge. Usually requires you to jack up your vehicle to get free.

High clearance - This book suggests that lowest point of vehicle (usually the differential) be at least 7 to 8 inches off the ground. Rocker-panel clearance should be about a foot. This is just the minimum starting point. Careful maneuvering may still be required since obstacles are often higher than this, even on easy and moderate trails. Difficult trails require much greater clearance. Shorter vehicles need less ground clearance and longer vehicles more.

High lift jack - Optional tool that lifts vehicle much higher than a normal jack, which is often necessary in the backcountry, especially on difficult trails. A high lift jack can also function as a crude winch.

Lift - A vehicle modification that raises the suspension or body of a vehicle to provide greater ground clearance.

Low-range gearing - A second range of lower gears that increases the power of your vehicle. Used for climbing very steep grades, especially at higher altitude.

Moguls - Large bumps which form on steep hills.

Paved trail (slang)- A trail made easier by stacking rocks in front of obstacles so that lesser-equipped vehicles can pass. Helper rocks should be removed by anyone placing them.

Shelf road - A narrow road cut into a mountainside.

Skid plates - Heavy metal sheets that protect vulnerable parts of undercarriage.

Snatch block - A pulley that opens so it can be slipped over your winch cable.

Switchback - A tight turn on a zig-zag road that climbs a steep grade.

Talus - Loose, fragmented rock formed by freezing and thawing above timberline.

Timberline - The point on a mountainside where trees stop growing. In Colorado about 11,000 ft.

Tow point, tow hook - A point on your vehicle that enables you to quickly and safely attach a tow strap. Considered a basic necessity for four wheeling.

Tow strap - A heavy-duty nylon strap used to pull vehicles when stuck.

Tree strap - A short tow strap that is used to wrap around trees and large rocks.

References & Reading

Adventures of the Pass Patrol, by Larry E. Heck. Guidebooks with maps, photos and lighthearted stories of 4-wheel-drive adventures. Several volumes cover Colorado. Available only at www.outbackusa.com. (1987-1999)

ATV Riding, by Tread Lightly!, Inc. Ogden, UT. Illustrated 20-page guide featuring minimum impact ATV riding techniques and safety tips. (2003)

Backcountry Travelers Maps, Durango, CO. Handy pocket-sized guides of the Ouray/Silverton/Telluride area covering routes in great detail. Three versions cover the Alpine Loop, Ophir/Imogene Loop and San Juan Skyway (paved route).

Central Colorado 4-Wheeling, by Wayne W. Griffin, Who Press, Basalt, CO. Guidebook with maps and photos covering Aspen, Vail, Leadville, and Crested Butte. (ISBN 1-882426-01-0, 1994)

Colorado Atlas and Gazetteer, DeLorme Mapping Company, Yarmouth, ME. Oversize 104-page map atlas of entire state of Colorado. (ISBN 0-89933288-9, 2004)

Colorado Byways, by Tony Huegel, Wilderness Press, Berkeley, CA. Guidebook with maps and photos covering 80 sport-utility adventures across Colorado, 254 pages. (ISBN 0899973256, 2003)

Colorado Campgrounds, The 100 Best and All the Rest, by Gil Folsom and Bill Bonebrake, Westcliffe Publishers, Inc., Englewood, CO. Detailed, 294-page guide to 434 campgrounds in Colorado. 129 color photos. (ISBN 1-56579-334-X, 2000)

Colorado Ghost Towns, by Robert L. Brown, Caxton Printers, Ltd. Caldwell, ID. Historical descriptions of Colorado ghost towns accessible by 4-wheel drive in 1972. Photos compare yesteryear to 1972. (ISBN 0-87004-218-1)

(The) Colorado Pass Book, by Don Koch, Pruett Publishing Company, Boulder, CO. Illustrated guide to Colorado passroads with in-depth historical analysis. (ISBN 0871088797, 1980, revised 2000)

Exploring the Historic San Juan Triangle (Formerly: Mountain Mysteries - The Ouray Odyssey), by P. David Smith, Wayfinder Press, Ridgway, CO. A detailed history of the Ouray/Silverton/Telluride area with photos and illustrations. (ISBN 0-943727-26-X, 2004)

Ghost Towns of the Colorado Rockies, by Robert L. Brown, Caxton Printers, Ltd. Caldwell, ID. Historical descriptions of Colorado ghost towns accessible by 4-wheel drive in 1968. Photos compare yesteryear to 1968. (ISBN 0-87004-342-0)

GPS Made Easy, by Lawrence Latham, Mountaineers Books, Seattle, WA. Handbook covers basics of GPS. (ISBN 0898868238, 2003)

Jeep Trails to Colorado Ghost Towns, by Robert L. Brown, Caxton Printers, Ltd. Caldwell, ID. Historical descriptions of Colorado ghost towns accessible by 4-wheel drive in 1963. Photos compare yesteryear to 1963. (ISBN 0-87004-021-9)

(The) Mining Camps Speak, by Beth and Bill Sagstetter, BenchMark Publishing of Colorado, Denver, CO. Instructional guide explains how to examine and understand ghost town remains. Photos and illustrations, 284 pages. (ISBN 0-9645824-1-4, 1998)

Scenic Driving Colorado, by Stewart Green, Falcon Press Publishing Co., Inc., Helena & Billings, MT. Scenic drives for passenger cars with maps and photos. (ISBN 1-56044-451-7, revised 1998)

Southern Colorado 4-Wheeling the San Juans, by Wayne W. Griffin, Who Press, Basalt, CO. Guidebook with maps and photos covering Telluride, Ouray, Silverton and Lake City. (ISBN 1-882426-07-X, 1998)

Tomboy Bride, by Harriet Fish Backus, Pruett Publishing Company, Boulder, CO. A woman's personal account of life in mining camps of the west, including town of Tomboy near Imogene Pass. (ISBN 0-87108-512-7, 1969)

Tread Lightly! Guide to Responsible Four Wheeling, Published by Tread Lightly!, Inc. Ogden, UT. Illustrated guide featuring minimum impact four-wheel-drive techniques and safety tips. (2004)

4WD Adventures Colorado, by Peter Massey and Jeanne Wilson, Swagman Publishing, Castle Rock, CO. Guidebook with color photos and maps covering 71 sport-utility adventures across Colorado, 228 pages. (ISBN 0-9665675-5-2, 1999)

4WD Trails Southwest Colorado, by Peter Massey and Jeanne Wilson, Swagman Publishing, Castle Rock, CO. Guidebook with maps and photos covering 31 sport-utility adventures in southwest Colorado, 130 pages. (ISBN 0-9665675-4-4, 1999)

4-Wheeler's Bible, by Jim Allen, MBI Publishing Company, St. Paul, MN. "How-to" guide covers all aspects of 4-wheeling from beginner to advanced. High-quality color photos and illustrations, 224 pages. (ISBN 0-7603-1056-4, 2002)

Adresses & Phone Numbers

(Note: All information correct as of Mar. 1, 2005.)

Bureau of Land Management
Web site: www.blm.gov

Colorado State Office
2850 Youngfield Street
Lakewood, CO 80215
(303) 239-3600

Arkansas Headwaters
Recreation Area (State Parks/BLM)
307 West Sackett Ave.
Salida CO 81201
(719) 539-7289

Columbine East Field Office (BLM/USFS)
367 South Pearl Street
Bayfield, CO 81122
(970) 884-2512

Glenwood Springs Field Office
50629 Highways 6 & 24
Glenwood Springs, CO 81601
(970) 947-2800

Gunnison Field Office
216 N. Colorado Street
Gunnison, CO 81230
(970) 641-0471

Royal Gorge Field Office (BLM/USFS)
3170 East Main Street
Canon City, CO 81212
(719) 269-8500

Saguache Field Office (BLM/USFS)
(San Luis Valley North)
46525 Hwy. 114
Saguache, CO 81149
(719) 655-2547

San Juan Public Lands Center
15 Burnett Court
Durango, CO 81301
(970) 247-4874

Uncompahgre Field Office
2505 S. Townsend Avenue
Montrose, CO 81401
(970) 240-5300

Chambers of Commerce/ Visitor Information

Alamosa	(719) 589-3681
Aspen	(970) 925-1940
Basalt	(970) 927-4031
Breckenridge	(970) 453-2913
Buena Vista	(719) 395-6612
Canon City	(719) 275-2331
Castle Rock	(303) 688-4597
Colorado Springs	(719) 635-1551
Crested Butte	(970) 349-6438
Cripple Creek	(719) 689-2169
Denver	(303) 534-8500
Dillon (Summit County)	(800) 530-3099
Divide	(719) 686-7587
Durango	(800) 525-8855
Frisco	(970) 668-5547
Georgetown	(303) 569-2405
Glenwood Springs	(970) 945-6589
Golden	(303) 279-3113
Gunnison County	(970) 641-1501
Idaho Springs	(303) 567-4660
Johnson Village (Bue.Vista)	(719) 395-6612
Lake City	(800) 569-1874
Leadville	(800) 933-3901
Manitou Springs	(800) 642-2567
Montezuma (Summit Cnty.)	(800) 530-3099
Montrose	(970) 249-5000
Monument (Tri Lakes)	(719) 481-3282
Ouray	(970) 325-4746
Paonia	(970) 527-3886
Penrose	(719) 372-3994
Pueblo	(719) 542-1704
Ridgway	(970) 626-5181
Salida	(719) 539-2068
Silverton	(800) 752-4494
Summit County	(800) 530-3099
Telluride	(888) 605-2578
Vail	(970) 476-1000
Woodland Park	(719) 687-9885

Maps, Books & GPS Sources

4X4*BOOKS*.com
(308) 381-4410
Fax: (877) 787-2993

All Topo Maps (iGage Map Corp.)
1545 South 1100 East #3
Salt Lake City, UT 84105
(888) 450-4922, www.igage.com

DeLorme Mapping
P. O. Box 298
Yarmouth, ME 04096
(207) 846-7000, www.delorme.com

Garmin International
1200 E. 151st Street
Olathe, KS 66062
(800) 800-1020, www.garmin.com

Lowrance Electronics, Inc.
12000 E. Skelly Drive
Tulsa, OK 74128-1703
(800) 324-1356, www.lowrance.com

Magellan Corporation
960 Overland Court
San Dimas, CA 91773
(909) 394-5000, www.magellangps.com

National Geographic Maps
P.O. Box 4357
Evergreen, CO 80437 1-800-962-1643
www.nationalgeographic.com/maps

National Parks/Monuments
Web site: www.nps.gov

**Black Canyon of the Gunnison
National Park**
102 Elk Creek
Gunnison, CO 81230
(970) 641-2337

**Curecanti National
Recreation Area**
102 Elk Creek
Gunnison, CO 81230
(970) 641-2337

**Florissant Fossil Beds
National Monument**
P.O. Box 185
15807 Teller County 1
Florissant, CO 80816-0185
(719) 748-3253

**Great Sand Dunes
National Park**
11500 Highway 150
Mosca, CO 81146-9798
(719) 378-6300

Mesa Verde National Park
P.O. Box 8
Mesa Verde, CO 81330-0008
(970) 529-4465

State Parks
Web site: www.parks.state.co.us

Arkansas Headwaters Recreation Area
307 W. Sackett
Salida, CO 81201
(719) 539-7289

Chatfield State Park
11500 N. Roxborough Park Road
Littleton, CO 80125
(303) 791-7275

Eleven Mile State Park
4229 County Road 92
Lake George, CO 80827
(719) 748-3401

Lake Pueblo State Park
640 Pueblo Reservoir Road
Pueblo, CO 81005
(719) 561-9320

Lathrop State Park
70 County Road 502
Walsenburg, CO 81089
(719) 738-2376

Mueller State Park
P.O. Box 39
Divide, CO 80814
(719) 687-2366

Paonia/Crawford State Park
P.O. Box 147
Crawford, CO 81415
(970) 921-5721

Ridgway State Park
28555 Highway 550
Ridgway, CO 81432
(970) 626-5822

Roxborough State Park
4751 Roxborough Drive
Littleton, CO 80125
(303) 973-3959

278

Spinney Mountain State Park
4229 County Road 92
Lake George, CO 80827
(719) 748-3401

U.S. Forest Service
Web site: www.fs.fed.us

Arapaho National Forest Supervisors Office
2150 Centre Avenue
Building E
Fort Collins, CO 80526-8119
(970) 295-6600

> **Clear Creek Ranger District**
> 101 Chicago Creek Road
> P.O. Box 3307
> Idaho Springs, CO 80452
> (303) 567-3000

Pike National Forest and
San Isabel National Forest Supervisors Office
2840 Kachina Drive
Pueblo, CO 81008
(719) 553-1400

> **Leadville Ranger District**
> 2015 North Poplar Street
> Leadville, CO 80461
> (719) 486-0749

> **Pikes Peak Ranger District**
> 601 South Weber
> Colorado Springs, CO 80903
> (719) 636-1602

> **Salida Ranger District**
> 325 West Rainbow Blvd.
> Salida, CO 81201
> (719) 539-3591

> **San Carlos Ranger District**
> 3170 East Main Street
> Canon City, CO 81212
> (719) 269-8500

> **South Park Ranger District**
> P.O. Box 219, 320 Hwy. 285
> Fairplay, CO 80440
> (719) 836-2031

> **South Platte Ranger District** (SW Denver)
> 19316 Goddard Ranch Court
> Morrison, CO 80465
> (303) 275-5610

San Juan National Forest Supervisors Office
15 Burnett Court
Durango, CO 81301
(970) 247-4874

> San Juan Mountains Center
> (Joint FS/BLM office, closed in winter)
> P.O. Box 709
> 1246 Blair Street
> Silverton, CO 81433
> (970) 387-5530

Uncompahgre National Forest and
Gunnison National Forest Supervisors Office
2250 Highway 50
Delta, CO 81416
(970) 874-6600

> **Gunnison Ranger District**
> 216 North Colorado
> Gunnison, CO 81230
> (970) 641-0471

> **Norwood Ranger District** (Telluride area)
> P.O. Box 388
> 1150 Forest
> Norwood, CO 81423
> (970) 327-4261

> **Ouray Ranger District**
> 2505 S. Townsend
> Montrose, CO 81401
> (970) 240-5300

> **Paonia Ranger District**
> P.O. Box 1030
> North Rio Grande Avenue
> Paonia, CO 81428
> (970) 527-4131

White River National Forest Supervisors Office
P.O. Box 948
900 Grand Avenue
Glenwood Springs, CO 81602
(970) 945-2521

> **Aspen Ranger District**
> 806 West Hallam
> Aspen, CO 81611
> (970) 925-3445

> **Dillon Ranger District**
> P.O. Box 620
> 680 Blue River Parkway
> Silverthorne, CO 80498
> (970) 468-5400

Holy Cross Ranger District (Vail area)
P.O. Box 190
24747 US Highway 24
Minturn, CO 81645
(970) 827-5715

4-Wheel-Drive Associations

Blue Ribbon Coalition
4555 Burley Drive Ste. A
Pocatello, ID 83202-1921
(800) 258-3742
www.sharetrails.org
`

**Colorado Association of
4-Wheel Drive Clubs, Inc.**
P.O. Box 1413
Wheat Ridge, CO 80034
(303) 857-7992
www.cohvco.org/ca4wdci

Colorado Off Highway Vehicle Coalition
(COHVCO)
P.O. Box 620523
Littleton, CO 80162
www.cohvco.org

Tread Lightly!, Inc.
298 24th Street, Suite 325
Ogden, UT 84401
(800) 966-9900
www.treadlightly.org

United Four Wheel Drive Associations
7135 S. PR Royal Springs Drive
Shelbyville, IN 46176
(800) 448-3932
www.ufwda.org

4-Wheel-Drive Guide Service

Bill Burke's 4-Wheeling America
307 N. Ash Street
Fruita, CO 81521-2316
(970) 858-3468
www.bb4wa.com

Other

Durango & Silverton Railroad
Gateway Reservations
2615 Main Avenue, Suite A
Durango, CO 81301
(800) 409-7295
www.durangosilvertonrailroad.com

Garden of the Gods Park
1805 N. 30th Street
Colorado Springs, CO 80904
(719) 634-6666
www.gardenofgods.com

National Forest Camping Reservations
Web site: www.ReserveUSA.com
1-877-444-6777

National Mining Hall of Fame & Museum
120 W. 9th
Leadville, CO 80461
(719) 486-1229
www.mininghalloffame.org

Old Hundred Gold Mine Tour
P.O. Box 430
Silverton, CO 81433
(800) 872-3009
www.minetour.com

Rampart Range Recreation Area
Pike National Forest
South Platte Ranger District
(303) 275-5610
or see Rampart Range Motorcycle
Committee Web site at www.rampartrange.org

Red Canyon Park
Red Canyon Road, 7 miles north of Canon City
For information contact:
Canon City Administration
128 Main Street
Canon City, CO 81212
(719) 269-9011

Yankee Boy Regional Conservation Association
YBRCA
P.O. Box 1448
Ouray, CO 81427
www.yankeeboy.org

Index

283

The Author & His Vehicles

Charles A. Wells graduated from Ohio State University in 1969 with a degree in graphic design. After practicing design in Ohio, he moved to Colorado Springs in 1980 and worked 18 years in the printing business. Over the years, he and his family enjoyed a wide array of recreational activities including hiking, biking, rafting, and skiing. He bought his first SUV in 1994 and immediately got hooked exploring Colorado's remote backcountry. He later joined a four-wheel-drive club and learned about hard-core four-wheeling. Since writing his original Colorado guide in 1998, he has written five other guidebooks—one on Moab, UT and Arizona, two on California and a second volume on Colorado.

The author drives all the trails himself, writes the directions from detailed notes, shoots the photos and creates the maps using computer software and GPS track logs. As a result, his guidebooks include meaningful detail and are extraordinarily accurate. The vehicles he used to drive the trails, over the years, are shown below.

Author with 1994 Jeep Grand Cherokee, Engineer's Pass, CO. Factory equipped with automatic transmission, skid plates and tow points. Author added CB radio and all-terrain tires.

1995 Jeep Cherokee on the Rubicon Trail in California. Equipped with Tomken rocker skids, bumpers, tire carrier, brush guard and 5″ lift; 8,000 lb. Warn winch; Dana 44 rear axle; 410 gears; ARBs front & rear; Tera Low 4/1 transfer case; skid plates; stock 4-liter engine; K&N air filter; interior roll cage; 33 x 10.50 BFG A/T tires; tow points; fold-in mirrors; and CB radio.

2001 Jeep Wrangler at top of Yankee Boy Basin. Equipped with TeraFlex 3″ lift with long-arm kit, 9,000 lb. Warn winch, Dana 44 rear axle; 410 gears, Tera Low 4/1 transfer case, ARB lockers front and rear, York on-board air system, Predator transmission skid plate, High-Country rocker panel guards, Curry bumpers, Alumiflex tie rod, Xenon extended flairs, stock 4-liter engine, 33 x 12.50 BFG A/T tires and CB radio.